Bowing to the Emperor

We Were Captives in WWII

Robine Andrau

Klara Sima Andrau

Robine Andrau

ARP

Apple Rock Publishing

Scituate, Massachusetts

Klara's sections of this book first appeared in somewhat different form in *Bowing to Fate*, Copyright © 1988 by Klara Sima Andrau, published by Miga Publishers, Myrtle Beach, SC 29572 and are used here by permission of Klara Sima Andrau's living heirs, Maya Andrau and Robine Andrau.

Special thanks to Donald Versaw for allowing me to quote from his self-published memoir, *Mikado no Kyaku (Guest of the Emperor): The Recollections of Marine Corporal Donald L. Versaw as a Japanese Prisoner of War During World War II*, and to J.F. (Frits) Wilkens's daughter, Louisette Hartmann, who kindly gave me permission to use material from her father's unpublished manuscript, *The Missing Years: 1940 to 1947*, which formed the backbone of Wim's story.

ISBN: 978-0-9964119-0-5
Cover and Interior Design by Julia Gecha Designs

Published by Apple Rock Publishing, 160 Mann Lot Rd., Scituate, MA 02066
www.robineandrau.com

Publisher's Cataloging-In-Publication Data
(Prepared by The Donohue Group, Inc.)

Andrau, Robine.
    Bowing to the emperor : we were captives in WWII / Robine
Andrau, Klara Sima Andrau.

        pages : illustrations, map ;   cm

        Issued also as an ebook.
        Includes bibliographical references.
        ISBN: 978-0-9964119-0-5

    1. Andrau, Klara Sima. 2. Andrau, Willem Hendrik. 3.
World War, 1939-1945--Personal narratives, Dutch. 4. World
War, 1939-1945--Japan--Prisoners and prisons. 5. World War,
1939-1945--Indonesia--Prisoners and prisons. 6. Concentra-
tion camps--Indonesia--Java. I. Andrau, Klara Sima. II.
Title.

D811.5.A54 A3 2015
940.53492092

In honor of and gratitude to my parents
Klara and Wim

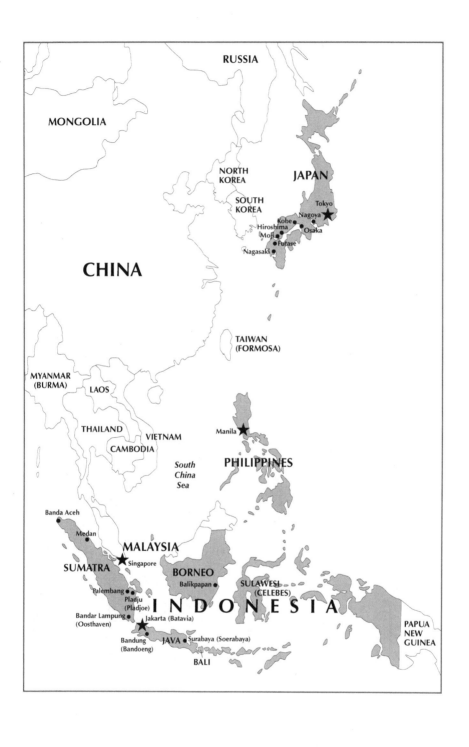

Contents

Prologue

"Sit down," my sister Yvonne said. "Are you sitting down? Now listen to this." And so began the bizarre tale of the mysterious reappearance of an old suitcase belonging to my father, dating from the year 1945.

At the start of World War II, my Dutch father, Wim, an engineer working for an American oil refinery construction company, was called up for Dutch military service. War runs on oil, and Indonesia, a Dutch colony at the start of the war, was rich in that liquid black gold. Because of his engineering expertise, Wim was temporarily released from service on the European front and sent in 1940, along with my Hungarian mother, two sisters, and me, to the then-Dutch East Indies. He was to be the construction manager for an aviation fuel plant located in Pladjoe, near Palembang, on the island of Sumatra.

With the attack on the American fleet at Pearl Harbor in 1941, the Japanese military had inflicted great damage on the major force capable of resisting its advance. And advance it did, spreading down the Malayan peninsula and engulfing countries in its path like a swollen river swallows the countryside during a flood.

Trapped in Indonesia, we, along with thousands of others, were placed in an internment camp. The men, Wim among them, were first imprisoned in Java, then taken to Singapore, and subsequently crammed into one of the notorious "hell ships," unmarked freighters/troop ships, and sent to forced POW labor camps in Japan. Wim was sent to Fukuoka #7, a POW camp in the coal-mining town of Futase on the Japanese island of Kyushu.

Meanwhile, the women and children were imprisoned in numerous internment camps in Java and on the other islands of Indonesia. My mother, Klara, my two sisters, and I were interned in two different camps in Java,

1

first Karees and later Tjideng. Tjideng camp, into which more than ten thousand women and children were crammed and which was run by the sadistic Japanese commander Lieutenant Kenichi Sonei, was reputed to be the worst civilian internment camp in the Dutch East Indies.

Until our liberation in 1945, we didn't know where Wim was or whether he was alive. And he didn't know anything about our whereabouts or well-being.

Miraculously, we were reunited after the war and, having lost everything, including our home in Hungary, we came to America, the land of opportunity and hope. Although Klara had kept a diary during the war years, chronicling our experience in the Japanese camps in Java, what Wim had endured in Japan was a subject we never discussed and we as children knew little about. We put the war years behind us and built our lives anew, hardly ever speaking about those dark times.

Until, that is, April 2005, when my sister Yvonne received a strange letter from the Dutch Red Cross.

"The Red Cross found Daddy's suitcase from the war," my sister said. I was dumbfounded. "With photographs and documents," she added. My eyes widened with a daughter's as well as a writer's greed. What an opportunity to touch our father again. And what a potential treasure trove of original source documents. "How? What?" I asked my sister. She read me the letter.

While cleaning up a storage room in their headquarters in The Hague, Red Cross employees found a mysterious suitcase whose tag indicated that it had been sent by the Dutch Department of War to the Red Cross in 1950. That's all the information they had. Enthralled and intrigued, we made plans to fly to Holland to pick up the suitcase in person.

The old suitcase, girdled by three strips of curved wood attached to its body with brass rivets, contained three albums of family photographs (one of an unnamed turn-of-the-century Indonesian family and two others of trips taken by unnamed others), a towel and knapsack stenciled with the name W.H. Andrau, and some twenty photos of the POW camp and of Wim and other POWs.

In addition it contained several dozen documents, some of them written in pencil by Wim, some typed on scraps of paper and signed by him as the senior Dutch officer in charge of the four hundred Dutch military men in this camp and later of the additional two hundred Americans and two British who joined them in 1944. The typed documents recount serious injuries prisoners received as the result of dangerous conditions in the coal mine where they were forced to work. Other handwritten documents are Wim's records of the men and their mental and physical condition. Still others appear to be a first partial draft of a report Wim was writing on the conditions of the camp and the health, nutrition, treatment, and so on of the POWs.

Since most of the reports are in English, we conjecture Wim might have written them as a report for the Allied liberation forces or as a preliminary draft of reports written for the postwar trials documenting brutal treatment of POWs by various members of the Japanese military. Sonei, the commander of Tjideng, our women's internment camp in Java, for example, was tried as a war criminal and executed in 1946 for his treatment of the women prisoners while he was in charge of this camp.

The Red Cross tracked us down by doing the most obvious—checking Dutch phonebooks for the name "Andrau"—and found a 98-year-old cousin of Wim's. The old woman's son, Henry, identified the suitcase as Wim's and gave the Red Cross my sister Yvonne's address.

And so Yvonne and I flew to Holland to retrieve this artifact of our father's past. On the way the airline lost *my* suitcase for a day. I wonder if Wim had anything to do with that. He loved a good joke when he was alive, and how could this not be a cosmic joke: a lost suitcase in exchange for a found one.

We hoped for answers to questions about the suitcase: How could it have resided in the Red Cross storage room unnoticed for fifty-five years? Why had Wim never mentioned the suitcase? Was it really Wim's suitcase at all? To whom do the photo albums belong? We also hoped for answers about what life had been like in the camp: What did Wim do, feel, experience in the three and a half years he was a prisoner of the Japanese?

But instead what we found after traveling to Holland, reading the documents, and studying the photos was that the suitcase and its contents were a teaser. We hungered for more. The information provided was not enough and it was incomplete. Wim is gone, most of the men in that camp are probably also gone, and their stories and experiences have vanished with them. What a pity, we lamented, that we hadn't talked to our father about this life-altering experience while we'd had the chance.

Gripped by the wish, the need, to recover these lost years, I pieced together my father's story from various sources. Then I interwove Wim's and Klara's stories to create a cohesive account of our family's wartime experience.

The alternating his and her stories, in a point-counterpoint structure, reveal how each faced and dealt with incredible adversities in his and her respective camps as captives of the Japanese in WWII. It is both a universal story of survival and a personal story of the fierce determination, love, and ingenuity of a mother and the strength, leadership, and optimism of a father when faced with starvation, cruelty, and beastly living conditions.

Other than wanting to introduce my remarkably resilient and resourceful parents, Klara and Wim, to a larger audience, my broader objective for writing this book is to shine a light on a lesser-known reality of WWII. Although the attack on Pearl Harbor and the horrors of the Bataan Death March are familiar to most, not as many know about the atrocities the Japanese inflicted on the European population of the Dutch East Indies during WWII. Many thousands of mostly Dutch women and children and some men were packed into Japanese internment camps on the islands of the Dutch East Indies. Additional thousands of military men were crammed into the holds of the infamous hell ships and transported to Japan or elsewhere to work as slave laborers for the Japanese in coal mines, in shipyards, on railways, and in manufacturing plants.

To recount this story I have gathered together information from various sources. They include family letters, Wim's camp documents, and Klara's diary, which she had self-published for family and friends earlier. Government sources include U.S. Department of Defense reports and documents from the National Archives and Records Administration (NARA). Two other original sources include *Mikado no Kyaku (Guest of the Emperor)*, a self-published account by Don Versaw, an American marine who was a POW in the same camp as Wim and whom I also interviewed; and an unpublished account, entitled *The Missing Years: 1940 to 1947*, by Frits Wilkens, a Dutch lieutenant who was at Wim's side every step of the way and who chronicled the events they experienced during the years 1941 to 1945. Frits's daughter, Louisette, kindly gave me permission to use material from her father's manuscript.

Alternating between what is happening to Klara and us children, as Klara recounts in her own words, and what is happening to Wim, as I have pieced

4

together from the above-mentioned sources, *Bowing to the Emperor* is a chronological account of my family's experience during World War II. The two principal players in this drama are Willem Hendrik (called Wim) Andrau and Klara Sima Andrau.

Wim, a five-foot-seven, well-built Dutchman with dark hair and laughing green eyes, was an affable dreamer. He was well liked and well regarded by his friends and by his fellow engineers at work, had a delicious sense of humor, and was effortlessly multilingual. Wim was comfortably at home wherever he lived, and he had lived in many different countries.

Klara, a barely five-foot-one, small-boned, wiry Hungarian with deep-set brown eyes and an indomitable will, could adapt herself to whatever situation she found herself in. She had a strong work ethic and, although very independent from a young age on, freely accompanied Wim wherever his work took him, from the cold of snowy Sweden to the steamy jungles of Sumatra. She too was multilingual and corresponded in several different languages with her many friends around the world.

We three children are Yvonne, the eldest, who was born in Germany and was eleven at the end of the war; Maya, the middle daughter, who was born in India and was nine at the time of liberation; and I, Robine, the youngest. I was born in Sumatra and turned eight in October 1945, shortly after we were liberated.

Other family members include Klara's brothers, Laci and Gabor, and her mother, Mami (pronounced "mummy"); and Wim's brother, Evert, and his parents, Vader and Moeder (father and mother). Although not a person, another important player is Aracs, the name Klara and Wim gave to their paradise home near Lake Balaton in Hungary. The thirty-five acres of land contained orchards, a vineyard, and forests.

So come and join us as we travel back to 1926 and the first meeting of Wim and Klara in London and then as they travel to various countries in the world until the war sends them to Indonesia in 1940 to meet their fate, bowing to the emperor as captives of the Japanese.

1
Klara
1926

*The Indies would now come into the picture. We would be in the
middle of it. Java was the heart of the Dutch East Indies. If Java fell,
the Indies would be lost. And so would we.*

The Romance

The boat at Hoek van Holland, bound for England, was ready to leave. Another twenty minutes and her horn would blow three times, the deep, throaty
sound that accelerates the heartbeat of anyone bitten by the travel bug.

Two sailors stood by the ladder, helping the latecomers up the wobbly
steps. When an elderly woman dropped her handbag into the water, shouts
for help came from all sides. In no time the floating bag was fished out.

A road-weary Sunbeam covered with dust stood on the quay, tilted on
its third leg. A lanky, blue-eyed young man leaned against the motorbike,
lit a cigarette, and watched the last minute commotion with apparent wist-
fulness. He made no move to board the boat.

His gaze wandered over the water. On this late summer afternoon in
1926, the gray-blue sea smoothed out its last silvery ripples and settled
down as if preparing to go to bed. The setting sun cut a golden path on the
water. Peace descended.

Another young man, green-eyed, muscular, somewhat shorter and young-
er than the Sunbeam-man, scrutinized the other's bike. A student at Delft University in Holland, he had just been on a visit to Hungary and was heading to
London. When he discovered the Budapest license plate on the Sunbeam, he
approached the owner and in German asked, "Are you Hungarian?"

7

"Yes," replied the lanky man.

"Are you boarding?"

"I had hoped to," the Hungarian answered.

"You'd better get moving, then," the Dutchman said in a commanding, yet friendly, voice. "The boat's about to leave and you've still got to check your bike in. I'll help you with customs. I know the men here."

Without waiting to be asked, the Dutchman started to push the Sunbeam toward the boat. The Hungarian stood still for a moment, reluctant to follow. Then he stepped forward, pulled out his business card, and showed it to the Dutchman.

"I'm in the Hungarian diplomatic service in London," he said. "I've just come from Budapest where I spent my vacation. Unfortunately, a number of unexpected and costly repairs to my bike en route have left me without enough money to pay for my ticket."

Before he could continue, the Dutchman replied, "That's not a problem. I'll pay your fare."

Together they pushed the bike toward the boat. The Dutchman bought a ticket for the Hungarian and both men went aboard. Later they dined together, paid for by the Dutchman naturally, and they became well acquainted during the meal. They found they liked each other's company.

Next morning in London they parted ways: the Dutchman to his hotel and the Hungarian to his apartment, where I, Klara, was waiting for him. The Hungarian was my older brother Laci, short for Laszlo. Laci and I shared an apartment in London. He worked at the Hungarian Legation and I worked as a translator of five languages at the Canadian Immigration Service in Canada House.

As I listened to Laci's suprising story, I couldn't help but think what a nice young man the Dutchman was. As soon as Laci had finished his account of their meeting, I suggested he go immediately to repay the loan and invite the Dutchman out for dinner that evening.

The three of us had a lively and convivial evening in Chelsea. Willem, Wim for short, had an easy laugh and a pleasing manner. We meshed perfectly. We felt we had known him, and he us, for years.

Wim left for Birmingham the following day to work in a factory as a mechanical engineer. It was the final stint of his year of practical training before getting his degree from Delft University. He promised to come see us before returning to Holland after he had completed his month of training.

In September Wim was back, knocking on our door. Again the three of us spent a pleasant day together. Before parting, Wim asked me out for lunch the following day. I was already aware of his special interest in me. Those sparkling eyes couldn't hide it.

Knowing he didn't have much money, I suggested an Italian restaurant in Soho and ordered spaghetti. To my chagrin I learned you should never eat spaghetti in the company of a man who is falling in love with you. Our conversation was choppy, interrupted each time by my attempt to consume the dangling strands of pasta reaching almost to my chin. I must have looked ridiculous. I almost choked on an especially long strand when Wim, looking into my eyes, said he loved me and wanted me to marry him.

I was taken aback by his sudden outburst of emotion, but also touched and pleased. I wasn't interested, however, in getting married. I had been on my own for years. I had spent the years of World War I in a convent school in Switzerland. After the war I taught French in Budapest and then, working for the Red Cross, helped to organize and supervise the placement of starving Hungarian children in foster homes in Holland.

Yet there was something so wonderful about him. I didn't want to lose him as a friend. In the past men had fallen in love with me and had proposed marriage. They, however, were freight trains compared to this express—a man of decision, courage, and action.

"You're still a student," I said. "First go back to Delft and finish your last year of school, then we'll see."

He didn't argue or protest. We returned to the apartment where Laci was waiting for us. The three of us made plans for a cathedral trip through southern England at Easter time. We saw Wim off with a warm handshake. No hug, no embrace.

Easter came, and Wim with it—on his bike, a Harley-Davidson. The fourth in our foursome was Maria Ugron, a Hungarian friend of ours who was studying in London.

It was a fun-filled trip, full of beauty, youth, and laughter. Three of the cathedrals still stand out in my mind: Winchester, scientific, mental, with its beautiful old clock where the Apostles march around in a circle as the clock chimes the hours; Salisbury in its pure, austere, Gothic splendor, which reminded me of a prayer speeding unrestrained straight to heaven; and Exeter, with her warm colors and liberal proportions, inviting her children to her generous bosom.

Wim made no overtures of love or marriage. And my feelings were those of pure friendship, except for the one time when I was sitting behind him on his bike and had a sudden urge to kiss his neck. I resisted the impulse, however.

The two-week period of wonderful, diverse situations allowed us to get to know one another. I grew ever more fond of Wim. He had a smiling, optimistic nature and was generous, patient, and always ready to help. Both Laci and I felt we had found a real friend in Wim. No doubt, too, my friendly feelings were speckled with stronger emotions.

At the end of the year, Wim cabled that he had finished school and was coming over. At the first opportunity to be alone with me, Wim repeated his marriage proposal. He was serious. He wanted a serious answer. If I agreed to marry him, he said, he would accept a job offered to him in Holland. If not, he would go to America and "face the world alone," as he jokingly put it.

What could I say? My heart was so happy. He had come back. Back to me. Back for me. But how could I tie down a man who was yearning to embrace the world? I felt so much more grown-up, having gone through the war with all its suffering and having earned my own living for eight years. Besides, I was twenty-eight, four years his senior. I couldn't put fetters on his bursting energy. I knew he would feel he had missed something in life if I tied him down. No, now was not the right time. He would come back if he loved me more than his freedom. I was sure of that.

He left for the United States. Alone.

Wim's letters were full of the rich life of Americans. Not knowing America at all, I imagined it to be a land of honey, cakes, and juicy steaks. Wim got a job with Universal Oil Products Company and stayed in America for two years until he was transferred to their European headquarters in London. On his first day back in London, he went straight to Laci and was chagrined to learn I had left London for Hungary.

I was working for Countess Francisca Karolyi, the wife of Count Laszlo Karolyi. As her assistant, I helped to expand the countess's creation of a village for war veterans in Fot, not far from Budapest.

So Wim was in London and I was in Hungary and there didn't seem much chance of us meeting. I hadn't counted on fate, however.

A few weeks after arriving in London, Wim was reassigned to a refinery reconstruction project in Romania. He was to take the Orient Express from Paris, which stopped in Budapest for a few hours. He phoned me and asked me to meet him at the railway station.

We had lunch on Margit Sziget, an island in the middle of the Danube. Two years had to be condensed into one hour and how short that hour was. Before we knew it we were standing at the train station, still searching each other's faces. Neither one of us mentioned marriage. Too shy? Too proud? Too unprepared? All we said to each other was goodbye, then we embraced lightly and Wim was off.

We knew we were friends for life. Was that all?

Our letter writing became more frequent. Through our words we peeked into the most hidden corners of each other's character. We liked what we saw. Our friendship deepened.

Letters came and went. Months passed, perhaps a full year, when a note arrived from Venice, Italy. Wim was there, rebuilding an oil refinery.

He wrote that he would come to see me in Budapest as soon as the job in Venice was finished, sometime in the fall. I waited, but he never came. Instead I received a long explanatory letter. The day he intended to leave Venice, he had received an urgent telephone call from the Italian police asking him to postpone his departure because one of his colleagues had been shot on the Lido and was dying. Wim was needed as a translator of the dying man's whispered information, which might lead to finding the murderer.

The man died after giving Wim the details. The Lido was sealed off and after a two-day search the killer was found.

Wim had had practically no sleep for forty-eight hours. Despite his fatigue, he got into his car and drove off. He had to be at his new job in Dortmund, Germany, but was hoping to slip into Budapest, even if only for a few hours.

He crossed into Austria, stopped at a country inn—so the letter ran—got into bed, and started to write a report for the company. For a moment, or so he thought, he put his pillow up against the bedside lamp and closed his eyes for a catnap. He awoke to find the pillow in flames and the bed starting to burn. More delays, of course, ensued. His hope for a Budapest visit evaporated.

When I let my mother read the letter, she tactfully remarked, "Your Dutch friend may be a nice man, but I wouldn't believe everything he tells you." As fantastic as it sounded, I believed it all.

As Christmas drew near, Wim cabled that he would come to Budapest on New Year's Eve for just two days.

Wim and Klara, 1930s

This time he actually came.

We hadn't seen each other for three years. Meeting again was true happiness. We talked nonstop for hours, catching up on each other's lives.

Finally Wim stood up, took both of my hands in his, and, with those electrically charged eyes on me, said, "Won't you marry me now?" This time I said yes with a singing heart.

We spent New Year's Eve with Mami and friends. The next morning, the first day of 1933, we took a long walk in the nearby woods, which the freshly fallen snow had transformed into a fairy-tale garden. We talked and talked about our own fairy-tale future.

Three months later Wim came back to Budapest and we were married. What I had thought six years earlier proved to be true. He loved me more than he loved his freedom.

Return to the Indies

Wim loved his job of building refineries. His American firm, Universal Oil Products Company, sent him abroad because, besides being a more-than-capable engineer, he was multilingual and adapted himself exceptionally well to changing circumstances and people. During our first years of marriage, we wandered around the world. Our first daughter, Yvonne, was born in Dortmund, in Hitler's Germany. The second, Maya, was born in Digboi, Assam, India. And the third, Robine, was born in Pladjoe, Sumatra, the Dutch East Indies.

Klara, 1938

September 1939 found us in Ploiesti, Romania. Wim was working on the construction of an oil refinery for Dutch Shell. At the first official news of the outbreak of World War II, Wim reported to the Dutch consul in Bucharest to find out whether, as a captain in the Royal Dutch Air Force, he had to return to Holland for military service. The consul had no information or specific instructions, but Wim assumed he would be called up. We took the first train back to Hungary and left the three children in care of my mother at our country place.

In Budapest Wim tried to catch a train, any train, to Holland. Only three days had elapsed since the official outbreak of war and the trains were already not running on schedule. It took Wim six days to reach Holland instead of the usual twelve hours. War had

(from left) Robine, Yvonne, Maya, at Aracs in Hungary, January 1939

not yet been declared between Holland and Germany, but everyone knew it was inevitable. An almost vibrating fear of a German invasion pervaded the small nation. Wim was sent to Soesterberg, a Dutch military air base.

Wim (right), in Hilversum, Holland, November 1939

After I saw Wim off at the railway station in Budapest, I returned to Mami and the children. We had thirty-five acres of land with orchards, a vineyard, and forests near Lake Balaton, forty miles south of Budapest.

On it we had built a big house and a small summer cottage, the latter for Wim's parents. We called our place Aracs (pronounced "ARE-aah-tch"). The vintner and his family also lived on the property. He looked after the land and handled the growing of grapes and the making of wine.

Vintage had just started, a happy time for all. The gatherers were busy, carrying their *puttonys*, wooden baskets, on their backs, filling them with freshly picked grapes, and dumping the grapes into the wooden vat. Two men operated the wooden handpress and put the must into wooden barrels. The children, glass in hand, circulated among the men, the press, the grapes, the must, and the heaps of almonds and walnuts, drinking all the time, or so it seemed, and not wanting to miss out on anything going on. Regular meals were not compulsory during the heavenly topsy-turvy vintage time.

The first day of work drew to a close. As the sky darkened and the chill set in, a big bonfire was lit. We gathered around it, barbecuing bacon on the tips of long sticks and catching the dripping fat on pieces of handheld bread. This was the snack preceding the spicy *gulyás* bubbling away in the copper caldron, so tasty and welcome after a day's hard work. Glasses were filled and refilled with last year's wine.

The women started singing. In no time gypsies with violins appeared. The gypsies had an uncanny way of materializing out of thin air at any happy gathering. They were always welcomed. Who could resist Hungarian gypsy music? The crying violins, the whispering oboes, the deep, comforting big bass, the sweet sad songs that make you want to laugh and cry at the same time and to embrace the whole world. We sang and danced while at the same time shedding tears as we remembered that a war had started and young men would soon be killing other young men.

After a few weeks of this happy country life, I felt guilty and restless. Wim phoned and asked me to join him in Holland. What was I to do? Should I stay with the children or join my husband? Wim won. I packed my bags, comforting myself with the knowledge that the children could never be in better hands than with Mami. Although my mother was seventy-five, she was in excellent health, was very active, and loved the children.

I had only a hazy recollection of the following three months. A confused, blurred picture of planes, car rides in the night, long walks in the forest, dancing in nightclubs, true comradeship, and uniforms, always uniforms. When I recalled this time, I could still picture their young faces in their planes, although they had long ago left for the other world. Against all hope, brave little Holland prepared to defend herself in the air and on land. The land defense plan consisted principally of flooding a strip of land on the German border where the invasion was expected. How unrealistic and naive.

Around this time Dutch Shell had plans to build an aviation gasoline plant in Pladjoe, Sumatra, in the Dutch East Indies. They were going to use the patented process belonging to Universal Oil Products, Wim's American company, and Wim was offered the position of construction manager. Shell had a lot of influence in Holland and managed to have Wim released from military service. We booked passage on the Dutch ship *Slamat*, leaving from Genoa, Italy, and heading to Medan, in Sumatra.

Wim's goodbye party from the air force was fantastic. Wim rented the bar of the posh Gooi Hotel, band and all. Young men in uniform packed the place. Spirits were high. The men carried me around on their shoulders after I had performed a solo Hungarian *czárdás* for them. When the time came for us to leave, the officers lined up on both sides of the spiral staircase leading down to the main exit, holding swords above our heads. The colonel took my arm and led me to the waiting limousine.

On the fourth of January, we arrived back in Aracs to pick up the children. We had only thirty-six hours to unpack and repack for the tropics. Mami saw us off at the edge of the property, tearful but smiling. Why was she so sad? We promised to return as soon as the building of the refinery was completed. She continued to stand there after the goodbyes, her figure becoming smaller and smaller as the distance between us lengthened. Then she disappeared from view. I am sure she knew she would never see us again.

We took a train to Genoa and caught our ship just in time. Three pleasant, carefree weeks at sea followed. By the end of January, we were back in Pladjoe, Sumatra. Back in the place where we had spent two years on a previous Shell assignment, where Robine had been born in 1937, and where Wim himself had been born thirty-eight years earlier.

Mention the Dutch East Indies, now Indonesia, to someone and they might say, "Oh, yes, I know what you mean . . . the island of Java, with some islands around it."

Well, there is more to this country than that. Besides Java, you have Borneo, Celebes (now Sulawesi), Sumatra, Bali, and several thousand lesser islands*.

In 1595 the Dutch made their appearance on the islands and started trading with the native population, as the Portuguese had done before them. Apparently the Dutch were more successful in their trading and formed the Dutch East India Company to regulate their export-import business. With a firm footing on the land, they were soon running the administration of the island of Java, which they considered their colony.

They committed all the usual follies of the early colonial exploitation; but in the course of time they turned out to be among the more humane colonizers. Unlike the English, the Dutch learned the language of the natives and did not consider intermarriage between Indonesians and Dutch to be taboo. The resulting biracial offspring were called Indo-Blandas, or Indo-Europeans.

The native population ran most of the local institutions, except at the highest level. The Dutch governor general was the head of this rich colonial empire, which produced rice, tea, coffee, tobacco, sugar, rubber, black oil, and the thousand spices.

The educated natives went to Holland for higher education, consequently the ties between the two nations became close and friendly, but, as was natural after hundreds of years of foreign rule, an underground national independence movement developed. Sukarno, who had a Japanese wife, headed this movement. During the war, when the Japanese overran the Dutch East Indies, the invaders backed Sukarno. Sukarno's followers steadily increased in numbers as the nationalist movement spread. After the war and after the Dutch recolonialization effort failed, the Dutch finally relinquished control and Sukarno became the head of the independent Republic of Indonesia.

We found the landscape of the islands to be as varied as its inhabitants. Rocks, volcanoes, jungles, beaches, rice paddies, tea plantations, and

---

*According to *The World Factbook*, Indonesia comprises 17,508 islands in all, 6,000 of which are inhabited. As the fourth most populated country in the world, it has an estimated population of 253,609,643 (July 2014 est).

cultivated gardens, which the eyes never tired of. The same was true of its people: the women in their long colorful batik *sarongs* and *kabayas*, the men in white pants and long-sleeved jackets closed at the neck, called *tutup jasjes*, and batik head covering or a black cap. Originally the people belonged to the Hindu religion, but later they converted to Islam. Their religious beliefs were of a mixed nature. They kept their favorite nature spirits and prayed to Allah at the same time. They were keen fishermen and hunters, with rice playing an important role in their lives.

It was good to be back in the palm-bordered avenues of tropical Pladjoe. The village was located on the Moesi River. The Dutch Shell oilfields and refineries, as well as housing for the Dutch employees, were a distance away from the native village. The latter consisted of neat homes with big gardens, palm trees, and tropical fruit trees.

Newcomers on arrival and those about to depart stayed at the *passangrahan*, the company hotel. The clubhouse, the Soos, was the social center, especially on Saturday evenings when films were shown and drinks flowed freely. The prime spot to sit and have a drink at sundown or to give a dinner party was on the clubhouse terrace, which floated on the river. Pladjoe prided itself on having a hospital that offered private rooms, each with a bathroom and a terrace, and a permanent Dutch Shell doctor on its staff.

Because the refinery was nearby, the men biked to work and came home for lunch. Work started at 7 a.m. and ended at 5 p.m., with a long lunch hour at noon. At five there was just enough time for a swim before sunset. Punctually and rapidly the huge orange disk disappeared below the horizon at six. We tried to be near the river for the gorgeous sight. At night, despite the hot and humid climate, we played tennis on the well-lit courts.

Each European family had at least four servants. In a short time the Europeans learned enough Malay to communicate with their servants and with other natives with whom they had contact.

The nearest town was Palembang, on the other side of the river. Because no bridges spanned the river, we would hire a sampan for a few pennies to row us to the other side. The children found such a trip exciting. Something was "happening."

A few hours after our arrival, our old *baboe*, children's nanny, who was called Willem and who had been in our service on Wim's previous assignment here, came to see us and asked to work for us again. We never found out why she had a masculine name or how she found out about our arrival.

Enjoying a real *rijsttafel** once again was wonderful. As was bartering with the *toekang sajoer*, vegetable vendor, or any other *toekang* who came to the door, balancing his wares at both ends of a long bamboo pole resting on his shoulders. We found it delightful to once again taste the deliciously stinky tropical fruits and spices, to play tennis by artificial light, and, when bathed in perspiration, to take showers by simply throwing buckets of water over ourselves.

But this idyllic life was bound to change. On May 10, 1940, as on any other day, the men went to work and we women were busy with the children and the servants. At nine o'clock in the morning the news that the Germans had invaded Holland was like a kick in an anthill. Pedestrians and bicycles tore down the main road, telephones rang, women ran in and out of the houses, and newspaper vendors dashed past the houses with a special edition of the paper.

The general excitement swept me to our neighbor, the Velders. Nel was expecting her first baby any day, and I feared the consequences of a sudden emotional shock. I found her in tears. "What will happen to my parents and my brother in Holland?" she cried. Many were asking the same question.

I calmed her down as best I could and stayed with her until the midday whistle blew. The men poured out of the offices and refinery. Of course, they didn't know any more about the invasion than we did. Would Hitler now take one country after another? Western Europe wasn't united and the statesmen and politicians had hidden their heads in the sand.

Tennis courts and swimming pools were deserted. Friends gathered at other friends' houses and speculated on the future. Which country would fall next? What would happen to the Indies?

---

*An Indonesian meal consisting of rice and different meat, seafood, and vegetable dishes, many of them spicy.

On the following day Wim was the first in Pladjoe to be called up by cable for military service in Java. We spent the afternoon packing.

A separation might mean anything. It would be only a week's absence, I told myself, fooling myself into thinking that Wim was needed at the refinery construction. Or would it be a year? Longer? My heart was heavy. Even though I knew worrying would not help, I worried. The next morning Wim left by plane for the military headquarters in Bandoeng (now Bandung), Java.

A few days later Yvonne started coughing. Soon the other two girls joined in. They had whooping cough. Braying in concert, they sounded like a bunch of donkeys. Listening to them was awful. It hurt to see them suffering. For days at a time, no food would stay in their tummies. *Baboe* Willem and I would feed them after each attack of coughing and throwing up, just to get some food into them for at least ten or twenty minutes. Before the start of each coughing fit, they would gasp for air, their faces turning blue.

At night I ran from one to the other, somehow always arriving too late with the bowl. The bed was already full. While changing one girl's sheets, another would start, and before I could attend to her, the third would spit up. I had a child in one hand, a bowl in the other, and a clean sheet in the third. It really did seem as though I had three hands and half a dozen children.

By morning I was exhausted. To have less distance to cover, I moved my bed into their room. I got up forty-eight times during one night. In the end it was easier not to lie down at all. I would stay up until five in the morning when their coughing, strangely, would subside. Then I slept two hours and stole the rest of my sleep during the day, when *baboe* Willem took over. At least I had no time to worry about the future. Three months passed as in a trance.

In the meantime the Germans had overrun Holland and had bombed Rotterdam flat. Thirty thousand civilians had lost their lives in about half an hour. To avoid other cities' having to endure a similar fate, Holland gave up the struggle. Belgium and France were invaded. The Maginot Line proved to be a grand illusion.

News reached me that Wim would be returning to Pladjoe. I dressed the children in cheerful summer dresses and tied ribbons in their short hair. All dolled-up, we went to meet Wim at the airfield in Palembang. The children were excited. Something was "happening" again.

As we watched the plane make a last circle in the air, we made bets on who would see Daddy first. The passengers poured out, but hard as we looked, we failed to spot him. Suddenly there he was, standing before us. None of us had recognized him in his uniform.

Wim had been temporarily released from his military duties in order to complete the construction of the refinery. We stayed in Pladjoe another four months, while in Europe one country after another succumbed to the Nazis.

Once the refinery construction was completed, Wim had to resume his military duties in Bandoeng. His American firm dismissed him on the grounds that he was unable to return to the United States. This was hard to take in light of the way Dutch Shell treated our neighbors and friends, paying their full salaries while they were in military service.

In mid-January 1941 we packed our trunks once again. Whenever I have to move from a place where I have lived for some time, I am overcome by a foreshadowed homesickness for that very place. Curious. While still in Pladjoe, I was already homesick for it. The present and the future intermingled.

The boat from Palembang, Sumatra, to the Port of Priok, Batavia (now Jakarta), on the island of Java, took two nights and a day. The boring trip took place in stifling heat, with an enforced blackout from sunset on. Only the children were happy. Something was "happening." They couldn't imagine anything more exciting than moving, the farther the better. Wim's friends met us on our arrival in Batavia. A couple of cool drinks, a friendly chat, and we were off by car.

The road from Batavia to Bandoeng led through the lovely Puncak mountain pass. Unfortunately it started to rain. We hoped it would stop. Instead it developed into a tropical deluge.

When we were at the farthest point from civilization, we got a flat tire. For half an hour we sat in the car, waiting in vain for the rain to stop. Finally Wim undressed down to the last fig leaf and crept out of the car to change the tire. I wanted to help him, but from long experience with a motoring husband I had learned that in such situations I should remain invisible and mute.

The children were delighted. Something was really "happening" now. They giggled seeing their almost naked daddy wrestling with the spare tire in that curtain of rain.

Just before the tropical nightfall overtook us, we arrived at our new home, a rented, furnished house. If homes have souls, this one had none. We were disheartened.

The next day I explained to the servants, who had been hired along with the house, that I expected decent work in return for good treatment and excellent wages. As a sign of my trust in them I told them I would not lock up anything in the house and hoped never to miss anything. How could I have made such a foolish mistake?

Bandoeng

Bandoeng was the second largest city in Java. At the outbreak of the war, it had about two hundred thousand inhabitants. At an elevation of about 2,500 feet, it had a cool, malaria-free climate. Paradoxically, it also had the largest quinine factory in the Indies. A modern, pleasant town, Bandoeng had schools, universities, clubs, hospitals, a Pasteur Institute, a racecourse, and a powerful radio station.

As soon as we arrived, Wim reported to the air force headquarters. From then on we saw little of him. He was often away for two or three weeks at a stretch. His job consisted of finding new sites for airfields. Aided by an air force crew, he identified the sites and then planned and installed the airfields. The sites ranged from New Guinea in the east, Sabang at the northwest tip of Sumatra, Tarakan in North Borneo, to Menado in North Celebes.

When on occasion he was home for a few days, most of his time was spent at the Bandoeng airfield. He would leave the house early in the morning and return just before sunset. After the evening meal he would work on his plans far into the night, even on Sundays. I helped him as much as I could, but more often than not my assistance boiled down to sitting quietly next to him, emptying his ashtray, sharpening his many colored pencils, and bringing him fresh cups of coffee to keep him awake. I sometimes added a gentle kiss, which always revived him.

Once or twice a month, we managed to go to a movie, but every time we came back more depressed than before. The newsreels were too graphic and showed too much of the war, exactly the thing from which we wanted to escape.

I often went swimming with the children, and once or twice a week we went to the zoo. The kids were enthusiastic about these excursions, although Robi never forgave the black puma that turned his behind on her and gave her a salvo full in the face. The little bull elephant was cunning too. If a woman passed in the company of a man, the elephant would fill his trunk with water, sneak up to the railing, and blow a muddy shower all over the man. Only the man. We were amazed at how he could tell the difference in gender.

(from left) Robine, Maya, Yvonne in Bandoeng, Java, 1941

A few months after our arrival in Bandoeng, our hopes for leaving the Indies were raised. Because oil engineers were desperately needed on the so-called industrial home front, Dutch Shell in London offered Wim a position on their staff. The request came by cable through Shell. Dutch Shell in Batavia was taking care of our passports and visas because they took it for granted that Wim would be released from his military duties.

At the time London was being heavily blitzed. Since we would be traveling through Canada, we discussed the possibility of my staying in

Canada with the children for a while and then joining Wim later in London when the blitz, we hoped, would be over. So ran our dreams.

Wim saw General van Ooien about the matter. I stayed home and crossed my fingers. I so much wanted him to join Shell in London and for us to move back there. I would see my brother Laci in London and might even get a chance to see Mami and my other brother, Gabor, in Hungary.

Van Ooien read the cables from Shell. Then he shook his head. "We need engineers too," the general said. "I can't let you go. But I'll ask for a confirmation from the commander in chief of the armed forces." The commander in chief's verdict was the same. The matter went all the way up to the governor general of the Indies, whose decision was that Wim stay in the Indies where he was needed.

So we stayed. A decision that sealed our fate.

Wim hardly ever came home for lunch, even when he was working at the Bandoeng airfield. One day, however, I heard his car honking at noon. The children rushed out to meet him, and I right behind them. "Letter from Laci," Wim shouted. Laci was still in the Hungarian diplomatic service in London.

The news, although not good, could have been much worse. Laci had been bombed out of his Chelsea apartment, the same one we had shared when I was working in London. He had lost his worldly possessions but had escaped with his life thanks to, of all things, a duck.

One of Laci's hobbies was cooking. On a Sunday during the heaviest blitz days, he had invited three friends over for lunch and was preparing his famous *canard à la Reine Pédauque*. The duck had been in the oven for some time when the first guest arrived. After a little aperitif in the living room, the two of them went to the kitchen, which was separated from the main building by a short corridor. While they were inspecting the duck and turning it over, a German bomb fell through the roof and exploded in the living room. The whole house collapsed, except for the separately built kitchen. My brother and his friend were thrown against the wall by the force of the explosion, and the duck flew out of the oven.

At that point the other two guests arrived. They helped Laci and his friend out of the kitchen, which the debris had blocked. The four of them rescued the duck, a luxury in those years, got into their cars, and finished roasting and eating the duck at the home of one of the guests.

A few months after we received this bitter-sweet letter, Laci cabled from Glasgow that diplomatic relations between England and Hungary had been suspended and he was being sent to Lisbon, Portugal, as secretary and acting chargé d'affaires of the Hungarian legation there. He was to travel via Canada and New York. He would be safe because Portugal had remained neutral and wouldn't be bombed. We also thought that since he was going to a neutral country, he might be able to serve as a link between Hungary and the Indies and we might be able to get some news from Mami.

Shortly after that we decided to move out of town and found a bungalow with a large garden in the hills, some five miles outside Bandoeng. The property was surrounded by rice fields and looked out onto the high mountain range of the Malabar. Its setting was perfect. The bungalow was small and primitive, but we made plans to enlarge it. To our surprise the owner, Mrs. Merz, the widow of a Bandoeng doctor, readily agreed to our plans once she heard that we would pay for half the rebuilding costs.

Wim designed a big dining room table, cupboards, a sideboard, and chairs. He found a man who promised to have them ready in two weeks. Meanwhile we gathered together the rest of the furniture, bedding, and so on, and moved in at the end of two weeks on a Saturday afternoon in pouring rain. The last load arrived just before sunset. The muddy-footed coolies trampled all over the clean floors. Then the electricity conked out. The children thought it was fun. I felt otherwise, sitting in the dark, in the middle of the mess. An upsetting beginning.

Some time before we moved, I had dismissed the *baboe*, the nanny, because nobody liked her. *Kokki*, the cook, and *djongos*, the head-servant, came along with us. Although we weren't fond of them either, they did their work well, so grounds for dismissal were thin. None of us, however, felt at ease with them around.

Of course, I should have sent them away the very day twenty dollars disappeared from our *kast*, armoire. I asked everyone in the house about it. Naturally, no one knew anything. I thought I might have been mistaken.

A few weeks later fifty dollars disappeared. This time I was sure there was a thief in the house. I called the police. An investigation, including cross-examination, a thorough search, and even threats produced zero results. The money did not reappear.

I was more vexed with the idea that I could not trust the people around me than with the loss of the money. I was also disappointed, especially after the nice introductory speech I had given them the day we arrived, that everything would be left unlocked and that I would trust their honesty. Looking back, I realized I had put too great a temptation in their path, and thus the theft was partially my fault. From then on I locked all the cupboards.

I once heard a lovely story about "appropriations." The new telegraph line was being strung across Borneo. The natives, the Dayakas, watched from afar as the work gang erected poles and pulled and attached the wire. As weeks went by, the Dayakas ventured closer, but remained in the trees. The workers didn't pay any attention to them. Every day before sunset the workers would go to their bamboo tents a couple of hundred yards away, taking with them all their tools but leaving the huge copper wire rolls at the work site. One morning when they returned to the work site, they found one roll of wire missing, a big pile of bananas in its place, and no more Dayakas in the trees. The Dayakas had "bought" the copper wire roll and paid for it with bananas.

We loved our bungalow. The inside wall coverings were bamboo matting, which lent a warm, artistic atmosphere to the rooms. We had no pictures on the walls. Here and there, however, we hung a quaint seashell, some dried flowers, and the stuffed carcass of a giant lizard, a *gekko*.

The house lizards, the little *tji-tjaks*, lent a special living touch. They were our friends, racing around the walls and ceilings, chasing mosquitoes or some other insect, having no difficulty at all walking upside down. They were also excellent watch lizards. If any stranger or even a dog or a cat entered the house, the *tji-tjaks* would signal with their curious little warning sound: "tjik-tjik," or "tjak-tjak," depending on whether they were young or old grandfathers.

The children grew fond of them and decided to train one as a pet. Thus they were on the lookout to catch one. Yvonne succeeded in getting a hold of one by its tail, but, oh horror, the tail remained in her hand and the lizard got away. She burst into tears and let go of the tail. The little thing lay twisting on the floor for a long time. We squatted around it until *kokki* said we didn't need to worry because the *tji-tjak* would grow a new tail in about a week's time. Nevertheless, we had a small funeral for the tail. The funeral was small because the tail did not qualify as a pet, and only pets received grand funerals.

Among the regular *tji-tjaks* we also spotted occasional albino ones. We disliked looking at these. Their whitish-pink bodies were so translucent that we could see the eggs inside the females.

One day a praying mantis flew in and settled on the wall. A brave little *tji-tjak* went after it. A fierce battle ensued. Both were badly wounded and disappeared. We were left to wonder whether either had survived.

Our new surroundings grew on us. We became more and more fond of the large garden where the children could play, roll in the grass, and climb in the trees, and where I could pick as many flowers as I wanted. I still kept on the *kebon*, the gardener.

The *sawahs*, rice fields, around us were a special attraction for the children. They would disappear for hours among the tall rice stalks, walking on the narrow *galangans*, mud walls, between the terraces.

The bungalow badly needed a larger kitchen and a covered terrace. Wim had made some rough sketches, but because he was away most of the time, nothing came of them. During one of his longer absences, I called in two workmen who maintained they could build anything I wanted.

We outlined the kitchen and the terrace by means of bamboo rods placed on the grass. I called it a simple construction plan. Then I asked them how much stone and cement they would need for the three-foot tall supporting wall. I ordered half the amount, which turned out to be more than sufficient. We went through the same procedure for the roof tiles. Even my engineer husband was pleased with the result when he came home. I received a big hug for being such a good architect.

We had no gas in the house and electric stoves didn't exist. Cooking was done on charcoal, an excellent heat source but cumbersome to light for a cup of tea. For that, a small kerosene heater came in handy.

I watched *kokki* crouching next to the *anglo*, brazier, fanning the coals with gentle movements. The activities of the natives connected with the making of fire, the cultivation of rice, the carrying of heavy loads on bamboo rods, or even the manner in which they squatted on their heels without sitting on them seemed graceful and effortless, as though perfected through thousands of years of practice.

Our immediate neighbor was a small luxury hotel called Isola, formerly a private residence. It had only ten rooms, expensive but in the best of taste, with a nine-hole golf course, swimming pool, tennis courts, and grayish-violet Venetian glassware for the dining table and the chandeliers. We made an arrangement with the manager to use the swimming pool and tennis court. As the hotel garden was right next to our property, we could walk over in our bathing suits for our daily swim.

No matter how busy Wim was in Bandoeng, he tried to get home in time to play a game with the children before their bedtime. When all was quiet, we took our after-dinner coffee on the new terrace, discussed world events, and listened to the thousand noises of the night.

Letters from home came rarely because postal communication had been severed. Wim's parents in Holland wrote through friends in Switzerland, a neutral country. Laci, who was in Lisbon, forwarded Mami's letters from Hungary. Perhaps two months after the cessation of postal communication between Hungary and the Indies, I received a worn-looking letter from Aracs, our home in Hungary. The letter had obviously been opened and censored several times. It was four months old and had come via China. Amazing. In my mind I bowed to the great miracle of human cooperation, the international postal service.

Wim was often too tired for a game of chess after our coffee on the terrace, but I found a new partner, Langeler, a lanky, gray-haired Dutchman of about sixty who was another neighbor. He lived a couple of hundred yards away, in a bungalow among the natives. Once or twice a week, he would emerge with his flashlight from the darkness of the rice fields to challenge me to a game of chess. He usually won the first game. I soon discovered, however, that after a glass or two of whisky, I would win, and so I never failed to offer him a drink.

He was one of those complicated war cases. He had served in Bandoeng as a high government official. On retiring, he had sent his wife and children back to Holland while he took care of the numerous official and unofficial goodbye parties, which were elaborate after twenty years of service in the Indies. Once he was through with them, he sailed for home. His boat was approaching the Suez Canal when the Germans invaded Holland. The boat was turned back with all the passengers still on board. And here he was, sitting in the *sawahs*, awaiting the end of the war.

28

Langeler had a telephone and a radio, neither of which we possessed, so he became our principal and self-appointed news source. One day in June he came running, waving his hat and gesticulating frantically. He had great news: Germany had declared war on Russia. So Hitler had made an about-face and had also attacked the Great Bear. No small thing, to dare to open a second battlefront. Hitler was either terribly strong or crazy or perhaps he was both.

Toward the end of the year, Langeler came once more at an unusual hour. This time he was agitated and looked ten years older than the day before. It was December 8, 1941, the day after Pearl Harbor. The news was frightening. America, England, and also Holland had declared war on Japan. There was no question in our minds that the Indies would now come into the picture. We would be in the middle of it. Java was the heart of the Dutch East Indies. If Java fell, the Indies would be lost. And so would we.

The Japanese Invade

Christmas approached and it became more certain that Wim would not be able to spend the holidays with us. We were resigned to the idea.

On the afternoon of December 24, 1941, the children, our dachshund, Pinkie, and I were sitting in the garden. We were making a centerpiece for the Christmas table out of pine branches and red ribbon. We sang some carols, trying to create a bit of the spirit of Noel, so difficult under the tropical sun.

I had just told the children that the Angel would surely bring a Christmas tree tonight, because he never forgot good little children, when Pinkie shot out like a bullet toward the garden gate. We looked up, startled. The gate opened and in walked Wim. By then we were all running. Pinkie joined in the general rejoicing. Wild with happiness, he performed his famous high jumps, obviously feeling that his little body couldn't contain such a big joy.

While we were busy bombarding Wim with questions and giving him hugs, Pinkie expressed his excitement and joy in his own unique way. After tearing the Christmas decoration into pieces and leaving the shredded red ribbon as an offering at Wim's feet, he sat back, wagged his tail, and tilted his head up with a look of expectation.

Although having Wim home for Christmas Eve was wonderful, we celebrated the holiday with subdued joy. The Angel brought the tree on time, with real candles on it and small presents for everyone, but our thoughts were with those on the battlefield, with those who had no homes left, with those who no longer had daddies with whom to share Christmas.

In the next few weeks, bad news was followed by worse news: the sinking of the *Prince of Wales*, the surrender to the Japanese of one base after another on the Malayan peninsula, the nonstop Japanese advance on Singapore. Who would have thought this great English stronghold in the Far East, into which the British had sunk untold millions, was vulnerable from the land? The English looked to the sea, that's the way they would have invaded. The Japanese apparently knew that and approached unexpectedly from the north—from the land, not from the sea.

The daily paper printed only short news updates. Every day the news was the same: "The British Army, in order to reinforce its position, has withdrawn so-and-so-many miles." Everyone expected the British to make a strong stand in Singapore, but it fell after a week of fighting.

We Europeans in Java had the jitters. That the Dutch East Indies could hold out no longer than a few months at best was no secret.

When General Wavell and his staff arrived in Java after the fall of Singapore, our hopes ran high. He was billeted in a hotel two miles north of us, halfway between our place and Lembang, a lovely hill station. Somehow, his nearness gave us an added feeling of security. That feeling lasted only a few days. When Wavell, continuing his retreat, left with his high military command, we knew the Dutch East Indies was doomed.

Wim showed up again for a few days. He was now the liaison officer between the Dutch and the British Royal Air Force (RAF). The latter had been relocated to Sumatra. Wim flew from airfield to airfield in his new position. He apparently did such an outstanding job that after the war the British honored him with an Order of the British Empire (O.B.E.) decoration.

On the home front our spirits were low. The blackouts and frequent air raid warnings certainly didn't help to cheer us up. We wondered why the Dutch government wasn't evacuating the women and children to Australia when it was so obvious the Dutch could not hold the Indies against the Japanese.

Everybody was hoarding food and digging shelters. Langeler's was a veritable fortification. We, too, had ours dug: a simple, narrow trench covered with lawn bricks placed on bamboo matting, good enough to protect us from a side hit or shrapnel. As for a full hit from above? Well, we played the ostrich and simply refused to consider that possibility. Besides, few shelters would have withstood a direct hit anyway. The children reveled in the new game of hide-and-seek in and out of the trench. For them things were "happening."

I found my lonely evenings more and more difficult to bear. When the air raid warning sounded at night, I stayed in bed and didn't wake the children up to drag them to the trench. Holding my breath, I would stare into the darkness and listen to the silence that followed the siren. After a while I would hear the explosions. The Japanese seemed to be targeting the town itself.

Absurd thoughts went through my head: Would they drop a few bombs on us on their way to town? What was it like to be fragmented by a bomb? How many children had been hit during the London blitz? I saw nightmarish pictures: disembodied children, children torn to pieces, headless children walking around. I was so worried, so responsible, and so alone. One night as I went through my repertoire of worries, my mother's figure appeared. She sat down on my bed, smiled at me, and put her hand on mine. "All will be well," she said, without actually speaking. Her presence was so comforting that I fell into a deep, quiet sleep.

Wim, on his rare returns, usually managed to fly over our house, dip low, and circle above the garden. The children, who knew the sound of his plane, would rush out and wave frantically.

He was due for a short home visit from Sumatra when the news came that the Japanese had landed in Palembang on the Moesi River.

2
Wim
July 1941

Clouds of smoke billowed up from the airfield. Bomb craters pockmarked the field, but the pilot judged about half of it to be still usable. The plane came in for a nail-biting landing, screeching to a halt within a few feet of a large crater.

Fall of Palembang*

In his new role as liaison between the Dutch, the British, and the Australian air forces, Wim undertook his first trip in July 1941 as head of a team to install air bases on the islands of the Dutch East Indies. The group consisted of Wim as team manager, Frits Wilkens, who was to be Wim's right-hand man throughout the war years, as the electrical wizard, and a third Dutchman as the camouflage expert. In the months that followed, several British Royal Air Force (RAF) officers and others with other skills would be attached to the team.

The group's mission was to hunt for sites for air bases and, when they found a suitable location, to set the base up. Allied forces would use these bases to secure the Dutch East Indies archipelago against the Japanese military, which was sweeping down the Malayan peninsula. For the next few months, Wim and his group took numerous trips to the various islands, including Celebes (now Sulawesi), Bali, northwest Borneo, smaller islands in the far eastern part of the archipelago, and several trips to Sumatra, the largest of the Dutch East Indies islands.

---

* The information in this chapter comes predominately from Frits Wilkens's unpublished manuscript, *The Missing Years: 1940-1947*, and from a typed copy of Wim's report written in Dutch in 1947 on events of that time period.

Because of its limited range, the Fokker 18 planes the group generally flew required frequent stops for refueling, a process that took an agonizingly long time at each stop because the refueling was done by means of four-gallon metal containers. An added problem was the unreliable radio. When it quit working, the pilot would have to fly blind over the tropical forests, which looked like endless fields of densely planted green cauliflowers, with only an occasional meadowlike opening in the vegetation. Finding which grass-covered opening was the airfield they were heading toward could be hit or miss.

After the December 7, 1941, attack on Pearl Harbor, Wim concentrated on establishing air bases on the island of Sumatra. The town of Medan in northern Sumatra, which had a large airfield with long runways, was being considered as an important base. Wim and his team, with RAF engineers in tow, visited several factories there that could serve as backup service workshops. They also visited other smaller airstrips in the north and examined them for their potential.

Wim's official military ID

The team's main focus, however, was Palembang, located in the south-central part of Sumatra. With the area's abundant fuel supply, airfield, and nearby refinery installations, which Wim helped to build in 1937 and again in 1940, Palembang was a coveted military prize. The main new air base on the island of Sumatra, therefore, was to be located about forty miles north of Palembang. Previously an emergency landing strip, the future base was a huge natural field that was concealed from the road and difficult to detect from the air. Runways had been cleared of brush for the rapidly growing embryo airfield, which the military dubbed P2.

When completed, P2 was essentially a large jungle clearing where up to a hundred aircraft could be dispersed under the trees. The Japanese weren't aware of it for many months, despite their frequent flights over the area. Even Allied aircrew personnel who had been briefed on P2's location had trouble finding it.

After a brief Christmas interlude with Klara and his daughters in Java, Wim returned to Sumatra to tend to the installation of P2 and the other air bases in the increasingly tense and dangerous area. Wim's teammate, Frits Wilkens, recounts an unusual exercise at one of the northern air bases. Seven B17s were to take off from Palembang on a bombing mission to the Malayan peninsula and would have to refuel at an air base in the north of Sumatra. To accomplish this task efficiently, the local Shell man and his team, working feverishly, fashioned large funnels out of flattened gasoline cans and hammered together a series of bamboo ladders. When the B17s landed at the airfield in the north, not a moment was wasted.

"Four bamboo ladders were placed against each plane," Frits recalled, "the large funnels inserted into the fueling holes, and then relays of [native] boys ran up one ladder, each with a four gallon can of 100 octane fuel, dropped it on the funnel, and ran down the ladder on the other side. Another boy on top of the wing chucked the empty can down, while the next boy was coming up with the second can, and so on. Within an hour all seven planes were refueled and were lined up again for takeoff." The American commander was apparently impressed and said he'd never been refueled that quickly before.

With the British surrender in Singapore imminent, the Japanese turned their attention in earnest to Sumatra. At the beginning of February, Japanese air raids over the island intensified. Wim, in turn, accelerated his pace to get as many airfields operational in as short a time as possible. He crisscrossed the island in quick time, dodging enemy air attacks, as he tended to the developing bases. For each new base Wim had to determine what structures had to be built, what equipment and supplies were needed, what support services and personnel were obtainable in the area, whether an adequate road to the site was available, and so on. After assessing the site's needs and providing the wherewithal to fulfill those needs, Wim and his team made frequent flying visits to monitor progress and troubleshoot as problems arose.

When approaching the airfield in Medan in the north, on one such flight, they heard the warning sirens signaling an air attack. They flew off into the hills to hide and wait it out. With their radio out again and their fuel running low, they flew back close to the ground, practically skimming the tops of trees. With relief they found the enemy gone. Clouds of smoke billowed up from the airfield. Bomb craters pockmarked the field, but the pilot judged about half of it to be still usable. The plane came in for a nail-biting landing, screeching to a halt within a few feet of a large crater. A jeep came careening up, the driver waving frantically for them to follow. Skidding around and between craters, the plane made it to the safety of the shelter, where the ground crew quickly shrouded it in camouflage netting.

Brushing off their close call with a joke, Wim continued on as though nothing had happened. He met with a planter who said he had a possible location, fifty bulldozers, and one thousand men from the surrounding tobacco and sisal plantations ready to build the new airfield.

A mere sixteen hours after giving the good-to-go signal, dozens of bulldozers and hundreds of men were already at work on the airfield.

The following morning Wim and some RAF officers took off by car for Palembang. Their objective was to scout for additional potential airfield sites in the western part of the island, which was not reachable by plane at that time.

In the meantime Frits and the rest of the group were to return to Palembang by plane, with a stopover at another airfield on the way to check on progress there. As at Medan the day before, the air raid siren sounded as the group's plane approached the Pakan Baru airfield. Again they veered off. With no hills to shelter them this time, they hid behind a cloud, spotted an enemy plane, swerved frantically, and hid behind another cloud. They waited a little longer, and, when the all clear sounded, they quickly landed and nosed the plane into the bush since there were no shelters built as yet.

With no land transport available, the group set off on foot to the main base camp a mile and a half away. The built-up road connecting the airfield and the base camp was flanked on each side by a deep ditch. About half-way there, they heard the far-away whine of the siren again, followed by a stuttering noise. When they spotted a formation of twelve fighter planes heading in their direction, they reacted like chickens scattering at the sight of a dive-bombing hawk, some leaping into the ditch to the right, others to the left. Within seconds the swooping fighters were on top of them, re-leasing a hail of bullets. The projectiles chewed lines of holes in the sandy road above them. The fighters swerved in a tight circle formation and bore down on them again to spray them with a second volley. The planes flew so low that the crouching men on the ground could see the faces of the pilots. In a few minutes they were gone.

When Frits and the others climbed out of the ditch, they saw sev-eral columns of smoke spiraling upward over the airfield. "There goes my plane," the team's pilot said. "Better get your report ready for HQ."

The enemy was not finished with them yet. As they hurried on to the base, they heard the ominous rumble of Japanese bombers over the air-field. Explosions from the falling bombs followed. The men, about a mile away from the airfield by then, thought they were safe. They were wrong. From a break in the clouds, they saw six of the bombers splitting away from the others and heading straight for them. With no ditches here, the men dove into the low scrub, seeking shelter in the undulating terrain. Within seconds bombs rained down on them. Columns of mud and debris shot up in the air. The spray of muck and the deafening noise seemed to last forever.

When all was quiet again, several members of the group, in disarray and mud spattered, staggered to the base camp. Not until later was Frits Wilkens aware that he had been wounded. A piece of shrapnel had sliced a deep gash at the back of his knee. They found the base partly ablaze, with dazed, wounded men wandering about. When Frits told the camp com-mander that several of the RAF officers from their group were missing, the commander sent out a search party.

In the meantime Frits inspected the communication system, even walking another half mile along a track through dense jungle to the radio station where he repaired the severed telephone line. He returned to the camp to find that the search party had found the RAF officers and several native laborers who had joined the group earlier. One of the officers was seriously wounded; all the others were dead. The visit to this site had cost them dearly and all they had to show for it was the single repaired telephone line.

For the next fortnight Wim and his group worked on fortifying P2 and its ancillaries. They arranged with Shell in Pladjoe, where Wim had excellent connections with senior personnel from his years as construction manager there, to buy needed material, such as piping, cables, tanks. Two days later the train brought the ordered material plus the welders and other personnel to build the fuel tanks and lay a pipeline to the railhead. Within a few days P2 was ready to receive aircraft gasoline for the increasing number of planes arriving there.

British forces were now flocking to the area. Antiaircraft batteries arrived for P1, the more exposed air base near Palembang, which the Japanese knew about and had started to bomb. And quite a few Allied bombers arrived at P2, the air base the Japanese had not as yet detected.

And then came February 14, 1942, a momentous day, although Wim didn't know that when he awoke.

A widespread layer of smoke from the burning oil wells to the north on the islands of Borneo and Celebes, as well as from the spectacular fire at the fuel storage depot in Singapore, blanketed the area and provided cover for the Japanese paratrooper transport planes. On February 14, to the total surprise of the unaware Allied forces, over two hundred and fifty Japanese parachutists were dropped on P1, the more exposed air base near Palembang, and on the Pladjoe oil refinery. Intense fighting ensued, with P1 and the Pladjoe refinery changing hands several times. Losses were heavy on both sides.

In addition to the parachutists, and of much greater danger, was the fleet of Japanese warships and troop carriers steaming up the Moesi River. Headquarters in Batavia ordered the bombardment of this fleet with everything that could be mustered. Thus a continuous stream of planes took off from P2, dropped their bombs, returned, rearmed, and took off again.

With the attack of the Japanese on Sumatra, Wim's mission was irrevocably altered. He had been the builder; now he became the destroyer. To prevent the fuel, communication, transportation, and defense infrastructure from falling into the hands of the Japanese invaders, Wim had to destroy what he'd been instrumental in building.

With confusion reigning and contact with headquarters erratic at best, Wim took matters in his own hands. He and Frits Wilkens drove to the site that was to be another new air base near Palembang and warned the people there to retreat to P2. They arranged for transportation for the Palembang ground crew, who, during the panic surrounding the invasion, had been ordered by their command to *walk* to P2—a distance of forty miles.

Then Wim returned to the refinery to see about its destruction, should it become necessary. He was thwarted in this attempt by the local army colonel who adamantly maintained that if any destruction was to be carried out he could do it with his guns. Wim knew that was a ludicrous idea, like a kid firing a BB gun at a rhino, but he couldn't convince the colonel otherwise. Because the colonel outranked him, Wim couldn't proceed with his plan. The colonel was later court-martialed for incompetence.

After a sleep of only a few hours, they awoke at four-thirty on the morning of February 15 with the news that general evacuation had been ordered for all military personnel. On hearing explosions from the railhead in Palembang, Wim hurried to find demolition already taking place. Pulling rank on the lieutenant in charge there, Wim ordered the demolition stopped and the formation of the two remaining trains to haul refugees south.

The first train, after filling rapidly with panicky civilians and military, pulled out of the station. The last serviceable locomotive scuttled around to hitch up the remaining railroad cars. The stationmaster, who had earlier fled in fear, reappeared and swore to Wim by all that was holy that he would assemble and dispatch this second train. This train would be the last one to leave Palembang.

Wim drove the forty miles from Palembang back to P2, where bombers were still shuttling back and forth to, and dropping their deadly cargo on, the advancing Japanese fleet. Then came final orders from headquarters in Batavia: load all bombers up with as much fuel and as many bombs as possible and send them back to Java. In addition Wim was ordered to oversee the destruction of the P2 facilities and to organize the evacuation to the south of the remaining two thousand RAF men at the base. Two thousand men and only one train, the last train.

Wim ordered Frits to set the stop signals on the siding to intercept that last train on its way south and see what could be done to accommodate the RAF men from P2. When the train pulled into the siding, it was packed to the hilt with refugees. No room for the RAF men. What to do?

The train was already exceptionally long, but since the trip south was largely downhill, the train conductor was hopeful that it could pull some additional cars. Frits had the RAF men unload six flatcars filled with material for the base, which had arrived just the day before. In double time the cars were emptied, the material neatly stacked on the platform, making room for as many men as could fit on these cars.

After a great deal of maneuvering, the flatcars were hooked up and the men clambered aboard. With a flourish, Frits waved the green flag as a final salute to the conductor. Sounding a mournful whistle, the train, slipping its gears at first, then moving steadily, slowly pulled out of the station. The fleeing men were undoubtedly relieved to be escaping the advancing enemy. They were unaware, however, that their safety was ephemeral.

Frits returned to P2, which was deserted except for a handful of personnel and the remains of two planes, Hurricanes that had crash-landed a few days earlier. Wim was in the mess hall, outlining the demolition of P2 with the remaining British officers.

To avoid attracting the attention of the Japanese, Wim instructed the men not to set anything on fire. He sent a wrecking crew to tackle the power plants and their fuel supply. Because the engines were solid diesels and could not be easily wrecked, the crew ran the engines without oil, causing them to seize. They smashed the sensitive controls with crowbars. To destroy the fuel supply, they smashed holes in the drums. Dripping from the sticky, smelly diesel fuel that spurted out of the wrecked drums, they returned to Wim for further orders. More smashing of anything that could be smashed. Finally Wim called it a day. The demolition frenzy was over. What he had spent months planning and building was destroyed in a matter of hours.

Not allowing himself to dwell on or lament what could not be changed, Wim huddled with his men to decide on the next step. With no more planes available and the last overcrowded train dispatched hours earlier, the only way for them to escape the ever-advancing Japanese troops was to scurry off by car four hundred miles south to Oosthaven, at the very tip of Sumatra. There they hoped to catch one of the remaining boats ferrying refugees across the water to the island of Java.

By ten o'clock on the night of February 15, their small convoy—consisting of a truck loaded with bombs and detonators, a mobile workshop, a sort of minibus that could seat six, and a Chevy—set off on the road south through the jungle. At midnight they stopped briefly in a town that had been a main oil pumping station but now lay in ruins. The town was deserted, some of the houses already looted. Finding gas still flowing in one of the houses, they were able to partially warm their emergency rations before the gas petered out. On through the night they drove, Wim and Frits alternating behind the wheel of the Chevy.

At sunrise they reached a provincial center where they roused the local hotel owner to provide them with some breakfast, then they continued on through the sticky hot tropical day until they reached the next district town. The town's inhabitants seemed to be completely unaware that there was a war on, perhaps the consequence of the precarious communication network. Once the telephone line was cut, news traveled by word of mouth, with rumors rife.

The local guesthouse made a quick *rijsttafel* for them. The food almost made up for not having had more than a couple of hours of shut-eye in two days. Tired but at least fed, they pushed on south until they reached a bridge over a river. An excited engineer lieutenant there told them he had just finished weakening the bridge and was ready to blow it up at the first confirmed report of advancing enemy troops. Did Wim know whether the Japanese were indeed moving in from the coast?

Wim persuaded the lieutenant to remove his itchy finger from the trigger. He told the lieutenant that they had not encountered any Japanese on their drive south and to hold off with demolition. Wim's convoy plus other RAF personnel and a column of antiaircraft guns were heading south and would have to cross the bridge, Wim informed the lieutenant. The lieutenant shook his head regretfully. He doubted that heavy loads could pass over his severely weakened bridge. He turned out to be right. Both Wim's mobile workshop and later the British antiaircraft guns also heading south had to be abandoned on the north side of the bridge.

On they drove in the dark. First south to Oosthaven, their eventual destination, to check on the status of the ferry boats to Java. The British commander in charge of evacuation there reassured them that anyone who turned up would find room on one of the ferries. Then north a little way, to another new airfield Wim had started to build, where they found an army major waiting either to get the air base working or to blow it up, depending on developing events. Wim told the major they had bombs and detonators in their truck and would return with them after they had reconnected with their convoy.

North again, through the black night, back to the bridge. No movement or sound anywhere. Then two little pinpricks of light, approaching. Japanese? Wim hurriedly parked the car on the side of the road and the two of them crawled into the ditch. With relief they crawled out when they saw it was the local bus. Shortly after, their truck appeared. Back to the base where they left the bombs and detonators from their truck with the major and waited while the major wrote a report for Wim to bring to headquarters in Java. Then south for the final time to Oosthaven.

Driving along in the midnight black, Wim suddenly stomped on the brake, hurtling them forward.

"What?" Frits said.

"White reindeer, crossing the road. Didn't you see them?"

There were, of course, no white reindeer. Wim was so tired that he was seeing ghosts. They decided to switch drivers every ten minutes. Ten minutes later Frits thought he saw the same white reindeer crossing. At least they were in synch with their hallucinations.

As they approached Oosthaven, the sight of a threateningly red sky alarmed them. Had the Japanese firebombed the harbor? They rounded the bend and saw that the warehouses were on fire, but it was "friendly fire" by their own people, to deprive the enemy of their goods. Wim drove their trusty Chevy to the car compound and gave it a farewell pat, knowing that it, too, would have to be sacrificed, as would all the vehicles and all the supplies in the remaining warehouses—from parachutes, to cartons of cigarettes, to war matériel—to prevent them from falling into enemy hands.

As the sun rose on the morning of February 17, Wim and Frits boarded one of the last refugee-packed ferries, flopped down on the deck, and fell instantly asleep.

Four hours later they were on the Java shore where a train, filled with refugees and making many stops and starts, took them to Batavia, to headquarters. The general in charge listened to their account. With apologies for denying them a much-needed bath and bed, he packed Wim and Frits in a car with a driver, a bag of sandwiches, and a thermos of tea, and sent them at top speed on the four-hour drive to Bandoeng. The top commanders of the war in Java were waiting there to debrief Wim.

Because there was no communication with Sumatra anymore, the top brass was in the dark about the events of the past few days. The eyewitness account that Wim provided sobered the grim-faced commanders.

Among other things Wim told them of his concern that the oil refinery in Pladjoe had not been properly destroyed, thanks in part to the stubborn colonel who had declared he would blast it with his guns, like some Wild West cowboy. Orders were immediately given for a bombing raid over Pladjoe. Using his intimate knowledge of the refinery he had built, Wim made a sketch of the best targets for inflicting the most damage. Later Wim was disappointed to learn that even with the help of the sketch, the bombs had missed the main part of the refinery and knocked out only some of the large tanks.

Shortly after 2 a.m. on February 18, 1942, Wim's part as a witness to, and participant in, the fall of Palembang, and thus of Sumatra, was over. Exhausted, dirty, and haggard, but alive, Wim returned to the bungalow in the *sawahs* where Klara and his three daughters lay sleeping, perhaps dreaming of his safe return.

3
Klara
February 1942

He hissed and drew his body back. His hands moved quickly,
and suddenly I found myself facing the barrel of a revolver.

Last Days of Java

When I heard the news that the Japanese had landed in Palembang on the Moesi River, I thought of all the friends we had in Pladjoe, just across the river from Palembang. I knew that for the last month the Dutch had been destroying the refinery, along with all their other oil installations, to prevent them from falling into the hands of the Japanese. I wondered what this news meant for Sumatra and for Wim who was there.

Wim did not come home as expected. I waited a day. A terrible fear gripped my whole being. Had he been shot down? I telephoned his headquarters at the Bandoeng airfield. I was told they had been trying to reach him by radio for the past twenty-four hours. None of the airfields in Sumatra had answered. His commander assured me they would keep trying and let me know as soon as some news came through.

Another day passed, and yet another. Still no news. By then I could neither eat nor sleep. I tried to hide my great anxiety from the children. Once more I phoned headquarters, but all they could tell me was not to lose courage and to keep on hoping. That night I stayed up late, waiting for Wim, listening to the silence, and startling at the slightest noise, imagining it was a crunching sound on the gravel of the garden path. Did I hear footsteps or just a lizard scurrying by? Was that noise cockroaches rustling on the cement floor of the kitchen?

At midnight I drank a stiff glass of whisky and went to bed. I must have fallen asleep, because I awoke with a jerk, hearing my name being called. I sat up in bed. It was middle-of-the-night dark. A deep, bottomless silence surrounded me. I put on the light. It was one o'clock. Then again, clearly, I heard someone call my name. It was his voice. This was no dream. I flew out of bed, tore open the door, and fell into Wim's arms. He had come back. He was home. My heart was singing once again.

A few minutes passed before either of us could speak. He looked quite changed. His face made me think of Da Vinci's Christ in the painting of The Last Supper. Wim had had hardly any food and practically no sleep for four days. His eyes were enormously dilated in his emaciated, bearded, pale face.

He ate some food and the words came pouring out. He talked about the confusion and the destruction he had witnessed before Sumatra's final occupation by the Japanese. For four days he had been helping to evacuate civilians and military personnel. He himself had escaped from Sumatra with the remaining refugees on one of the last boats to Java.

He told me how the stationmaster at the last rail junction from where a train could leave for the boat to Java had panicked and had run away. Wim himself had taken over the job of directing the personnel to assemble a train.

At five in the morning, he fell into bed as if dead. What a wonderful man, I thought. Whatever he did he did wholeheartedly, never sparing himself.

With the fall of Palembang, the occupation of the whole of Sumatra was only a question of days. The Japanese seemed to be military geniuses. How many weeks, days, were left for Java? Everybody said the Dutch military power had been concentrated in Bandoeng for the defense of the island. That anything or anyone could stop the Japanese was hard to believe. Everybody was guessing what would come next.

Wim went back to work at the Bandoeng airfield. One day when he was home for lunch, we heard the sound of planes from afar. Wim jumped up. "Quick, into the shelter," he shouted. "There are a lot of them coming. This will be serious."

We ran into the garden, calling the servants to join us, and dove into our shelter. From the direction of Batavia, the sky was alive with black and silver dots. No alarm had yet been sounded in Bandoeng. The planes were flying very high, but Wim's practiced ear could discern that they weren't ours. The black dots formed a line heading toward the airfield in Bandoeng. Then, one after the other, with perfect regularity, they dive-bombed the field and the hangars. The sounds of the explosions reached us a bit later, each one followed by a cloud of smoke rising from the ground.

Twenty-seven fighter planes accompanied the fifteen Japanese bombers. Brave Dutch airmen in nine planes took off into the air to intercept the Japanese. The planes in the Japanese squadron, mission accomplished, were tracing a circular path in the sky, heading back to Batavia, when the Dutch planes reached them.

The fight took place directly above our garden. We couldn't help but peek out of the shelter, fascinated by this magnificent, flesh-creeping, modern gladiator show. Fascination soon changed to fear. The planes came. The ra-ta-ta-ta, pak-pak-pak-pak of their machine guns, the muffled popping of our antiaircraft, along with the roar of the engines made such a perfect hellfire above our heads that we thought the end of everything was near.

We huddled in the far corner of the shelter, as if that would have made any difference. Only Wim peeked out from time to time. Yvonne was crying. Maya and Robi were pressed against me, pale and silent. *Kokki* was in hysterics. The *djongos* was trembling, his face drained of color. With a cooking pot upside-down on his head, he looked like a ridiculous ghost.

The fight was over in a few minutes. We crawled out in time to see one of the planes coming down in flames. One of ours. The Japanese planes were gone, their noise fading away. The black smoke clouds hung in the air for some time. I swallowed my first war tears.

From then on the Japanese planes came every day. They bombed only the airfield and the munitions factory. From the radio and the papers, we couldn't make out exactly how things stood. Rumors had it that Batavia was in Japanese hands and the Japanese were pressing toward Bandoeng. Strangely enough, people in Bandoeng were still hopeful. "The town is well fortified," they told each other. "We can hold out for months, and by that time we'll have help from Australia and America." And the people seemed to believe it.

Our military occupied the entire neighborhood, including our garden. We were in the operational zone. A strong military guard, consisting of about twenty-five men, was stationed on the main road, less than a hundred yards away from us. The men dug a trench across the road in front of Tjan Jan's shop. The Chinese grocer watched the digging with an expressionless face. I went over to him for some groceries. Rice, potatoes, and some lemonade were all he had. I treated the military guards to Tjan Jan's last bottles of lemonade. The sergeant advised me not to wear a white dress. White made an excellent target for the Japanese planes, he said. He warned me that they were capable of machine-gunning even a single person.

The Japanese continued their daily flights, dropping their bombs over Bandoeng and returning unopposed to Batavia. The Dutch had no more planes, either on the ground or in the air. It was depressing.

Wim told me that most of our planes had left for Australia with the high military command and some of their friends. I begged him to go too, promising to look after the children whatever would happen. If he stayed he would only be taken prisoner and that wouldn't help anyone. He didn't respond. I had the impression he hadn't even heard what I had said. I suppose it was absurd to suggest that he leave us.

A few days later he brought two officers, a Scottish captain and an Australian colonel, home for dinner. We knew the Japanese would be here in a few days. We discussed the possibilities of escaping. The colonel had a small sailboat at his disposal, well provided with food and water. He offered to take the children and me with him to Australia. Wim could fly ahead. The sea voyage, he thought, would take from three to six weeks, depending on the winds. I was enthusiastic and prepared to take the chance, but Wim argued that the children wouldn't be able to withstand the hardships of such a long trip. Besides, he was sure the Japanese would bomb us out of the water. Rays of hope like winter sunshine, brilliant but ephemeral.

Four miles north of us, the Japanese bombed Lembang for an entire day. At dusk silence fell. The military guards had been changed in the surrounding fields. A native soldier, his uniform thick with mud, came into the garden, dug himself a hole under a tree, looked around with terrified eyes, and crept into it.

"*Bekin apa?*" What are you doing? I asked.

"I am frightened. I was in Lembang all day with my company, and we were being bombed the whole time. I saw the company's cook blown up. I have had no food since this morning."

I immediately brought him a warm meal, tea, and cigarettes. He recovered a bit, but his eyes were those of a hunted animal.

Our military occupied Isola, the luxury hotel next door. Military convoys rumbled nonstop along the main road to Lembang. I wanted to see what was going on and asked *kokki* to accompany me after the children were asleep. The night was dark. Outside our garden gate a light flashed in our faces without any warning. A sentry.

"Who are you?" he shouted. "What are you doing here?" Then he recognized me and let us pass. We were stopped several more times before we reached the main road, only about a hundred yards away. There we watched the camouflaged trucks, loaded with troops, guns, and tanks, roll by on their way to Lembang. A heavy attack was expected the next day. If the defense failed, as every defense so far had failed, the fight would continue closer to Bandoeng, about where we were standing. Our place would be the battlefield, the front. Strangely enough the thought did not disturb me.

Wim came home about ten o'clock, pale and obviously under great stress. He didn't want his dinner. He didn't even want to sit down.

"Can you be ready in half an hour?" he asked. "We're going."

"Yes, of course." I was joyful. I flung open suitcases and threw things in helter-skelter. "When does it leave?" I asked.

"When does what leave?"

"The plane. Or are we going by boat?"

"What are you talking about? Where do you want to go by plane or boat?" He sounded cross and agitated. "We're simply going into Bandoeng for a few days until the nasty show here is over. Tomorrow they'll be fighting in our garden. And after the fight the Japanese will march in. It won't be safe for you and the children to stay here."

What a blow. I had been hoping for Australia. Nevertheless I was ready in half an hour. A couple of sailor's duffel bags were added to the suitcases. Wim would not hear about me taking along his good London-made civilian suits. They seemed to belong to a dead world now.

I got the half-asleep children out of bed, wrapped them in their bathrobes, and out we went into the dark night. Wim had parked his car in the hotel's garden. Several sentries stopped our funny little procession before we reached the car.

While driving to Bandoeng, Wim explained that we would be taken in by Beatrix Laan, a friend in whose house a number of people were already gathered, mostly Dutch Shell employees and their families who lived in outlying areas. We arrived at the house where two young women greeted us and told us that the other women and children were in bed. The men were out on night duty, burning documents and blowing up munitions. Wim left to join them.

For a while the two women and I discussed the situation. They thought it was safer for us to be huddled together in town rather than scattered in the countryside when the Japanese marched in. It sounded reasonable. Nobody knew how the Japanese would behave. Most of us knew very little about them, misconceptions only, gleaned from *Madame Butterfly*.

The children and I lay down, two in a bed, among innumerable trunks and suitcases. As soon as I shut my eyes, I started worrying about the things I had left behind, the things I should have taken along: the material for the children's dresses, the typewriter, the silver, the cases of whisky. And where on earth had I put our money? I got up, went through my bag, and found it. But then I decided the handbag was not the best place for the money. Much too obvious. It would be found right away. Where could I hide it? I tried one spot after another and finally slipped it into the leather case of Wim's Leica camera.

Next morning at six we were all down for breakfast. The men had not yet returned. We were sixteen Europeans in the house plus a few servants. Soon the men returned, one by one. They were tired and depressed after having dynamited material all night long. In their opinion the resistance wouldn't last longer than two days.

The siren suddenly sounded. Soon we heard planes overhead, followed by explosions nearby. Down we went into the shelter in the garden. Ten minutes later we were back in the house. Someone telephoned the news. The post office and the quinine factory had been hit. Thirty dead. The Japanese were no longer restricting their bombing to military targets.

A few minutes later the siren sounded again, followed by more bombing. From then on no half hour passed without an alarm. The bombing continued. We had no planes with which to fight back and few ack-ack guns. They proved useless anyway, so our side gave up even trying. We had no way of knowing how long the bombing and strafing would last.

Nobody went down into the shelter anymore. Numb with fear and with no hope left, we had only one wish: to see the end of this infernal game.

Late in the afternoon the planes stopped flying. A strange silence enveloped us. Our men hurried to town for news. They returned with grave faces. It was over. We were capitulating.

Wim drove out to see whether our place was still standing. He went first to Isola and found it had been badly damaged. He stumbled over a number of dead bodies lying scattered in the hotel, targeted by the Japanese dive-bombers. Our bungalow next door seemed intact, except for half of the roof of the servants' hut.

While retracing his steps from our place, Wim crossed the garden of the hotel and came across the general in charge. They had a brief conversation in the heavily damaged hall where the Venetian chandelier once hung and where it now lay in ruins, its pieces scattered all over the floor. The general gave his last order: "*Wij moeten de strijd staken.*" We have to give up the fight.

Wim later told us how vividly he felt that he was taking part in a historically important drama. Drama it was indeed. How dramatic and traumatic we would find out only later.

A Buick inched by. Inside were a Dutch captain and another Dutch officer. They carried a large, unfurled white flag. The car continued in the direction of the enemy.

Unconditional Surrender

Wim returned from Isola and told us about the white flag, the symbol of surrender. We assembled in the living room and turned on the radio. In a calm voice the governor general of the Dutch East Indies told us that the fight was over and the Indies had to capitulate. The Japanese exacted unconditional surrender. The governor general appealed to the population to bear the inevitable with calm and dignity and counseled obedience to the Japanese authorities. When he finished speaking, the Dutch national anthem was played. We all rose, eyes glistening with tears. Silence followed, both on the radio and in the room.

I felt completely isolated in my thoughts, remembering the past. After World War I we in Hungary went through the miseries of the Romanian occupation. This time it might be even worse. The occupiers were Asians, their minds and morals a closed book to us Europeans. I escaped to the terrace for a few minutes. When I returned, drinks were being served and a general thank-goodness-it's-over feeling prevailed. An hour later, the governor general's message was repeated, but we turned the radio off. Who needed to go through that again?

Night fell. The lights were switched on and the blackout curtains were raised. The first Japanese order came through the radio. Everybody was to stay indoors and all lights were to stay on. After the continuous blackout of the last months, the blaze of lights had a reassuring effect. For a while we sat on the terrace. A heavy silence fell over the town. High above in the dark-blue tropical sky, the stars appeared unchanged.

Next morning orders were given by telephone for the men to surrender all their weapons. We were afraid they themselves would be held, but within an hour they returned. Uninterruptedly, lists of names were being given over the radio. Names of those who had disappeared, those who had been found, those who had died. We took turns, with paper and pencil in hand, noting down the names of friends and acquaintances.

Several times during the day, the Dutch military headquarters repeated the order to all commanders in outlying posts to lay down their arms. By evening all the posts had surrendered except the one in Atjeh (now Aceh), commanded by a well-known, tough military man. Apparently he was going to continue to fight. The Dutch themselves, as colonizers, had not managed to pacify the province of Atjeh in Sumatra until the beginning of the twentieth century. The Atjeh people were the most independent and freedom loving of all the peoples in the archipelago. They were rumored to have eaten their last missionary as recently as 1903.

We all hung around. There was nothing to do that day but wait for orders. The children were remarkably good. They were in a new house with plenty of rooms and corners to explore. And, of course, something was "happening" again.

A motorcycle passed in the street. We ran to the verandah. It was our own police patrol. The radio announced that the first Japanese troops would arrive the next day. We kept guessing as to the future. We suspected that all the professional and military personnel would be interned. As for the rest of us, we thought we would be sent home and life would continue under Japanese control more or less as before. If ever a guess was wrong, this one was it.

The next morning the men were called to headquarters and were told to bring blankets, pillows, and a change of clothing with them. Only Lagaay, who was a retired lieutenant, and Frits Schouten, who was a civilian and the husband of blonde Elsje, stayed with us women and children.

At three o'clock, during siesta time, a truck stopped in front of the house across the street from us. A number of Japanese soldiers, small men in worn-out uniforms, alighted and, accompanied by indescribable shouting, stormed the house. Five minutes later we saw the owners come out: a man in pajamas and a woman in a dressing gown, obviously aroused from their nap. Both carried suitcases, blankets, coats, and whatever useful items they had been able to grab in a hurry.

The soldiers stormed the next house, and the performance was repeated. Clearly, people were being thrown out of their homes. In a few minutes it would be our turn. I went to warn the women. Some were already packing. I quickly went back to our room, dressed the children, and stuffed whatever I could into the suitcases.

I was still packing when the house resounded with the noise of rifle butts banging on the front door. My heart jumped into my throat. The Japanese did not seem to be too gentle. I looked around quickly to make sure I had everything. Where had I put the money? Oh, yes, in the camera case. Surely a good hiding place. Who would look for money in a camera case? But what if the Japanese wouldn't allow me to take that suitcase out of the house? I pulled the money out of the camera case and just in time hid it in my blouse.

The front door opened, followed by heavy steps and lots of shouting. Our veteran, Lagaay, probably nervous but outwardly calm, led the Japanese up to the bedrooms. He showed one into my room. Others flooded the house. They were all over the place, opening—none too gently—drawers, cupboards, wardrobes; throwing the contents on the floor; looking into and behind everything; inspecting every corner. All of this was accompanied by wild gesticulations and loud shouts in Japanese. They made Lagaay understand, by pointing to the front of the house with a waving motion and then to their watches, that in five minutes we had to be out of the house. The children were frightened and rushed to the room next to ours where there were several women and children and no Japanese as yet.

I remained alone with the Japanese soldier who had come to inspect our bedroom. While kneeling and packing on the floor, I looked him over furtively and saw a squat, wide-shouldered man, with abnormally long arms and bowlegs. He was dirty and seemed exhausted. He sat down in an easy chair behind me and watched me pack. I was about to close the suitcase with the precious cameras inside, when he got up, said something in Japanese in what sounded like a ventriloquist's voice, and pulled the Leica out of the suitcase. The same Leica from which I had removed the money a few minutes earlier.

He inspected it left and right, this way and that, snapped it a few times, and hung it around his neck. Apparently he liked it. I waited. Nothing happened. I asked him in Malay, French, English, German, and Dutch to give me back the camera. He only grinned, showing lots of strong, healthy teeth. I grinned back and pointed to the Leica and then to the suitcase. He shook his head. Then I became angry and repeated my gesture with a stern face. *That* he understood. He hissed and drew his body back. His hands moved quickly, and suddenly I found myself facing the barrel of a revolver.

A most unexpected surprise. I didn't think he would really shoot me, but who could tell? I felt extremely uncomfortable. To get rid of this wild man at the price of a Leica camera suddenly seemed a good bargain. But he didn't move. He stayed in the room.

I closed the suitcase with the two other cameras still in it and rose to leave the room. He jumped at me from behind and tried to put his arms around me to touch my blouse in front. My reaction was quick. I hit his hand high in the air and, with calculated calm, I took two steps toward the door. He followed me and jumped again, repeating his gesture. I repeated mine. All this in silence, except for the hissing.

My knees were jelly. Dear God, if I could only get out of that room. With two quick strides, I reached the door. He came after me, but I was out by then and in the next room. Did he suspect where my money was hidden or was he after something else?

A roar came from another Japanese. Time was up, we had to leave the house. Where to? Nobody knew. In any case out of here and into the street.

It was raining. Robi was crying and holding onto my neck for dear life. Maya and Yvonne behaved sensibly, holding each other by the hand and clinging to my skirt. I carried the suitcase in my free hand. We stumbled out the door with the others.

On the street we discussed what to do. Somebody suggested a friend's house nearby where we could talk things over, provided that the Japanese soldiers had not as yet stormed it. We moved on and soon reached the house. The Japanese had come and gone, taking all the money and some wristwatches with them.

I suggested our place, some five miles out of town. We knew from Wim's reconnoitering on the day of capitulation that the bungalow was still standing. The idea, however, was rejected. It was too far from town, too isolated and therefore dangerous.

Finally we agreed that Schouten and Lagaay would go back to the house we had been thrown out of and try to smuggle the two cars out of the garage. We could then drive to the Kortewegs' house, which was only a short way out of town, half as far as our bungalow. The Kortewegs were part of our group and were anxious to know what had happened to their house and possessions.

The men succeeded in getting the cars out. We squeezed into them and were on our way. Driving through town, we saw crowds of people ejected from their homes by the Japanese, dragging bundles, blankets, and clothing. On the highway to Lembang, we had to drive in first gear because we met the Japanese troops coming in. Progress was slow. They looked tired, dirty, badly dressed, but marched in good order, led by mounted officers.

We arrived at the Kortewegs' home to find it unoccupied. The gas was still functioning and a quick cup of tea — good thing I had taken tea along — somewhat restored our frayed nerves. Soon afterwards Wim arrived with the other husbands. They had been sent back from headquarters. When they returned to town, they found the Japanese in the house instead of us women and children. Sheer guesswork had brought them out to the Kortewegs'.

We were about to make ourselves comfortable when a truck stopped in front and Japanese soldiers stormed the house. We braced ourselves, expecting to be thrown out again. Luckily there was an officer with them who knew some English. Our men talked with him, playing on his sense of honor, emphasizing the well-known role of Japanese chivalry toward women and children. Surprisingly, it worked, and they went away, but our position was not secure because another truckload might come by at any moment and order us out.

A frightened-looking elderly man, his wife, and his twenty-five-year-old daughter came to the door, asking to be taken in. The daughter told us a Japanese soldier had assaulted her and that she had barely escaped being raped. He got away with her jewelry. After dark another couple arrived with a child. We were twenty-two by then.

The evening was spent in speculation. Nobody knew what to do. We were undoubtedly going to be evicted the next day. All the villas in the area had already been evacuated. We tried to make ourselves as comfortable as possible in easy chairs, on sofas, on beds, on the floor, anywhere we could stretch out a bit. Nobody dared to undress.

The frightened-looking elderly man turned out to be the director of the Bandoeng quinine factory. He suggested we go to the factory with him the next morning, where we might be able to find shelter.

We left in the gray light of dawn, fearing that once day broke the Japanese might forbid all private traffic on the road and might confiscate the cars. Unmolested, we arrived a little before six in the morning. Dutch officials let us in. The Japanese hadn't been to the plant as yet.

In the deserted offices we dozed for a while on chairs, desks, and trunks. Later some of the employees came in. We asked about the reported hit on the factory during the bombing. A pale-faced young man told us that only the shelter in the courtyard had been hit. Only the shelter, with all the people in it. "They all died," he said. "All of them, including my wife and child." He broke down as he spoke.

The chief mechanic, Mr. Cramer, and his wife, who were living next door to the factory, put their house at the disposal of the refugees. They were wonderfully hospitable, cheerful, active people. Mattresses and blankets were brought over from a nearby orphanage, and we dispersed to different rooms. Ten women and children in one, six men in another, and a few more here and there, most of whom were sleeping on the floor.

More refugees arrived. We were now thirty-two at the table. Everybody helped with the cooking. Food was available again. The market was alive after two days of suspension. Bread was scarce, but we hardly noticed it amid all our troubles.

The next day the Japanese took over the factory and closed its gates. Our cars, parked in the plant's courtyard, became captives. The Japanese didn't interfere with the houses of the employees, however, and we stayed where we were. Nevertheless, we were careful not to show ourselves on the street, where continuous yelling and the thumping of marching troops resounded.

The military men were again called to headquarters. Again with blankets, pillows, clothes. This time we knew we wouldn't see them for some time. Maybe a long time. A big truck rolled in through the back gate to pick up our men. A last embrace. A last kiss. The men jumped into the truck. A last wave. "We'll be back in a few weeks," shouted Wim, as the truck drove out of the gate. Three and a half years would pass before they would come back, and then not all of them.

A few days later we received word that the Japanese had moved out of the house in town. We went back immediately. Like the giant in "Jack and the Beanstalk" who smells human flesh, we went around smelling the Japanese everywhere. To our surprise we found that not that much was missing, except all the men's clothes, drinks, and edibles.

Our *kokki*, cook, whom we had taken to town with us, and who had been left to cook for the Japanese, had also disappeared. Had the Japanese taken her along? If so, it was not for her looks. Or she might have returned to her husband, our *djongos*, manservant, whom we had left to guard our bungalow.

I couldn't go looking for her because there were strict orders not to leave town. Those orders had been transmitted by radio in Japanese and Malay only. Another order was that every civilian who wanted to keep his car had to pay a license fee of a hundred guilders, about fifty dollars. Of course they omitted adding that the cars would be confiscated anyway within a week, whether the money was paid or not.

Two days passed in tension as we awaited news from our men. We occupied ourselves with little jobs to keep busy and help the hours pass. Hair washing was one of them. While drying Maya's hair, I noticed little black spots on the towel. On closer examination, I saw that the spots were moving.

Apa itoe, baboe?" What are these, *baboe*?" I asked the nanny. "Rice bugs, perhaps?"

"Oh, no, *njonja*."

"Do you know these bugs, *baboe*?"

"Yes, *njonja*."

"What are they, then?"

"They are lice, *njonja*." She laughed.

Lice? For heaven's sake. Lice on my child's head. I had never heard of black lice before. So the Japanese had left us some presents after all. I sent to the drugstore for some "hunting water," as it is appropriately called in Dutch. After a thorough inspection, we discovered that all four of us had the bugs. With expert fingers, *baboe* deloused us. Everybody in the house chuckled. Smiling at our heads wrapped in babushkas, they inquired with merriment what the daily catch was. The merriment burst into loud laughter, though, when Elsje Schouten started scratching her head. She had them too.

We found out where our husbands were being interned and that we would be allowed to visit them twice daily. Feverish activity broke out among the wives, everyone preparing her husband's favorite dish. When the food was ready, off we went down the long road, carrying our heavy load. From now on we had to rely on our legs, as neither taxis nor the two-wheeled, pony-pulled carriages, called *kreteks,* were available.

The men were being held in an unused, neglected school building, surrounded by barbed wire. One of Wim's comrades, a pilot, functioned as the gatekeeper. The yard was crowded with brown Dutch uniforms. Their eager eyes trained on the entrance and the street, the men watched for the arrival of their wives and sweethearts.

Seeing Wim as a captive gave me a strange feeling. Wim, the man of freedom who found every place, every country too small after a few months' stay.

The men were cheerful and convinced that in a few weeks' time they would be sent home. In the meantime they had organized a canteen, which Wim ran. They used their own money. Two officers were allowed to leave the compound to do the daily shopping. We did their laundry and brought them a hot meal every day. After a week the Japanese changed the rules, and we were allowed only one visit a day.

I was worried about *kokki*. We had heard rumors about the natives looting around Lembang. I decided to risk leaving town, although nobody could tell whether the ban on travel had been lifted or not. I persuaded Frits Schouten to accompany me.

We found the bungalow deserted, the grass waist high, our *djongos*, who was supposed to be guarding it for a fat tip, nowhere to be found. We forced the door open and the disturbing sight of looting greeted us. Not that the place was in complete disarray. Except for the candle drippings on the floor and the rotten foodstuff on and in the icebox, the rooms looked almost as we had left them, except that the trunks, armoire, cupboards, and pantry were open and empty. Clothes, shoes, suitcases, china, silver, linen, blankets—everything was gone.

I almost burst into tears. What to do? Frits Schouten suggested going to the Dutch police, whose headquarters were in the bombed-out hotel, Isola, next door. We went and found Pinkie, our dachshund, there. The dog had been left in the care of the *djongos*, who had obviously abandoned him. The military police had adopted him. Pinkie was beyond himself with joy at the sight of me and performed his characteristic high jumps.

Within two days the police produced our *kokki* and *djongos*, who trembled with fear. They brought back two baskets full of small items: pots, pans, some china, some linens. They denied having stolen anything. They had only been "guarding" the items for us, they said. As for the clothes and valuables? They didn't know anything about them. Because I had no proof of their guilt, that was the end of the story.

I decided to move back and live in the bungalow. Friends in town said I was crazy. I would be alone, with no protection whatsoever. I never felt alone in nature, however, and this city life was nothing for the children. I talked it over with Wim during my next visit to him. He saw my point. A day later I moved back.

I was touched by the children's joy at seeing their old home again. It was as if we had been away for years. They rolled in the grass, climbed the trees, rediscovered every corner of the garden and every nook of the house. Here they felt safe and happy.

Back in the Sawahs

The bustle of the first day back in our bungalow surrounded by the rice fields left no time for reflection or the realization that a new life had started for us, a life without Wim. When the children fell asleep after the long day's activities, and only the croaking of the *sawahs'* frogs, the shrill chirping of the cicadas, and the dark-blue night remained for companions, I sat on the terrace for a long time, trying to figure out the future.

Wim's watercolor illustration of our bungalow, Bandoeng, 1942

I wished I had somebody to talk to, or, even better, somebody to ask for advice. I could have used a little encouragement. But there was nobody. I had to direct all the queries to myself: How long was this going to last? What was in store for us? How could we live without any income? What would they do to Wim? How was Mami in Hungary? The questions kept chasing one another in my head. I went to bed that night with my brain twisted into a big question mark.

Because the Japanese didn't recognize the International Red Cross, communication with the outside world was impossible. I had no friends in Java except for the new acquaintances in town. This bungalow on the hill surrounded by the rice fields and with its magnificent view was peaceful but lonely.

I would have to adjust to this new life. I had to steel myself against loneliness. "No self-pity, old girl," my inner voice said.

Food was the first concern, because looters had emptied the pantry. The bombing of Bandoeng, coupled with the arrival of the Japanese troops, had depleted food stores everywhere and disrupted the food distribution system. Formerly life out here had been easy. The shops had delivered anything we wanted from town. Besides, we had Tjan Jan, who only two weeks ago had looked on with such an expressionless face as they dug a trench in front of his shop. That all seemed like years ago. In the past I also had *kokki* go into town once or twice a week by bus to the excellent Bandoeng market. All that was finished. No more bus service. No more market for us.

I went over to Tjan Jan's. The shop windows were boarded up. His wife, a plain, fat, friendly Chinese woman wearing slacks, told me that during the confusion of the occupation, their house and store had been looted. She did not complain about it, merely stated the facts with resignation.

"Have you got any rice, Mrs. Tjan Jan?" I asked.

"Lice?"

"No, rice to eat."

"Yes, I can give you some lice to eat."

I had momentarily forgotten that the Chinese have difficulty pronouncing the "R," and after our Bandoeng experience with lice, I shuddered at the mention of the word. She sold me a few pounds of rice and some sugar, but she had no oil or oil substitute.

I went a little further up the road to a dairy farm owned by a friendly Indo-European, Mrs. Willy Westbroek. She sold me a chunk of butter and promised me milk every day as long as I came by and picked it up myself.

With these few edible treasures, I hurried home and made a good meal for Wim. Once I had left Bandoeng to return to our bungalow, I obviously wouldn't be able to visit him every day, so we had agreed that the *djongos* and I would alternate days—one day the *djongos* would bring him his meal, the next day I would do it. Biking the five miles to town was easy enough as it was all downhill, but coming home, pushing the bike uphill three out of the five miles, was tiring, especially during the heat of the day.

When the meal was ready, the *djongos* left with the food, clean clothes, and a note for Wim. He returned a few hours later with the food, the clean clothes, and the note. The prisoners were no longer allowed any visits or food. From now on they would be fed by the Japanese and would have to wash their own clothes.

I didn't believe the *djongos* and went over to Langeler to try to call the camp. I succeeded in getting Wim on the phone. He confirmed the news. He asked me to call him every day. Of course I agreed. Who knew how long the luxury of being able to phone would last. The Japanese regulations were getting ever stricter.

In the evening Langeler came over for a game of chess. He was a peculiar man. We spoke about the uncertainties of the future and I casually mentioned my meager funds. He thought to comfort me with a detailed account of his financial position, which was so sound that he would be able to stick out this sort of vegetating life for ten years, if necessary. He assured me he had really nothing to worry about and asked me to safeguard two diamond rings for him. He said he was afraid of burglars. The stingy old coward.

His preoccupation with money affected me. When he left I found myself counting my cash and drawing up a budget. I figured that one hundred guilders (fifty dollars) a month would take care of the household, including half the rent for the bungalow. I assumed that, under the circumstances, no landlord would expect full rent. I later learned nobody paid rent anymore. One hundred guilders was less than a third of what we had been spending. I had two thousand guilders and thought, therefore, that I was safe for twenty months, even if the Japanese didn't pay out anything to the prisoners' wives. Twenty months. That was more than a year and a half. This situation couldn't last that long. I was convinced that before long we would all be safely and happily back in Hungary.

Reassured, I went to bed, but the thought of burglars, now that I was responsible for Langeler's diamond rings, bothered me. I got up, found my old hockey stick, and put it next to my bed. Like a person who talks aloud when alone in a dark and unfamiliar room, I encouraged myself. If any burglar dared to enter, I vowed, I would hit hard, aiming my weapon at his head.

The next day Langeler came to show me the first issue of a new newspaper. The Japanese had suspended the publication of all newspapers except this one, which appeared in Malay. Its theme, as expected, was the new Nippon spirit—namely, Asia for the Asians. Except, of course, that the Japanese meant Greater Asia for Nippon. This much we got out of the paper, but not much else because the written Malay was different from the pidgin Malay we were familiar with. Langeler, with great diligence, worked at translating it with the help of a dictionary.

In spite of my outward calm, my nerves were in a tight knot. I could feel them around the middle of my body. I had an ever-present butterfly in my stomach. I could hardly eat. Every bite stuck in my throat when I thought of Wim. And when did I not think of him? Because I couldn't send him food any longer, I gave up tea, coffee, and smoking. I hoped this little self-denial, through the unknown chemistry of a spiritual transformer, would be reflected on him in some favorable way. Maybe this decision, however, was only self-centeredness on my part. I couldn't enjoy a cup of coffee and a cigarette with the thought that he might not have either one of them.

The Japanese dismissed European civilians from their jobs, with the exception of a few whose services they still needed. I went to see Elsje and Frits Schouten, who were now living together with the Kortewegs. Frits Schouten was working for the Japanese and received one-sixth of what he had earned before. He was glad to get anything at all.

According to a new order, all aliens—all Europeans were now aliens—had to take out identification cards, for which the men had to pay one hundred fifty guilders and the women eighty guilders. The Japanese simply wanted to extract money from us. Rumor had it that those who didn't apply for the cards would be sent to internment camps.

Because complying with this order meant three hundred twenty guilders for us, I went to discuss the matter with the Schoutens. They said I'd better put down the cash and get the cards. So down I biked and stood in line for hours at the Bandoeng town hall. At the very place where formerly we had been received with much courtesy and helped with promptness, now native clerks ordered us about, taking their time about attending to business, not caring whether we stood there for hours. So began the first little humiliations.

The Dutch police were still quartered at Isola, but not for long. Their interpreter, who spoke fluent Japanese, called on me to warn me that in a few days all the Dutch would be leaving the hotel and the Japanese would be taking their place. I bought a book of Japanese grammar from him, thinking it might come in handy one day.

Because I couldn't get Wim on the phone anymore, I went to the Schoutens regularly, hoping to get some news. One day Elsje gave me a smuggled letter from Wim. He wrote very comfortingly and asked me not to worry about him.

Elsje told me that the men had been transferred from the old school building to an empty juvenile penitentiary outside of town. As the men were being led through the town, a number of women somehow heard about it. In groups they followed the men at a distance to see where they were being taken and also to pick up the matchboxes the men were casually dropping. The boxes contained tiny scraps of paper, messages to wives and relatives. The women deciphered who they were for, and took them to their destinations. That was how I got mine. The solidarity of the women was admirable. The guards caught a few of the women and beat them right there in the street.

The next day, during lunch, the *djongos* hurried in to say that two Japanese soldiers were in the garden. I went out to ask what they wanted. They didn't reply but grinned and continued their walk around the house. They were from the Japanese garrison now occupying Isola. I told *kokki* to ask them with signs whether they wanted to eat or to have something to drink. They didn't answer, grinned, and left.

Later the *djongos* reported that three knives and three forks were missing from the kitchen table near the open window. Was it the Japanese or the *djongos* who had spirited them away? It was hard to tell.

Our landlady, Mrs. Merz, who lived in a bungalow a few hundred yards away from us, sometimes came over in the evening to break the monotony of both our lives. She was a character, an interesting seventy-year-old woman who had traveled extensively and had lived for years on the Riviera. She spoke good French and passable English, was divorced from her doctor husband, and had a daughter whom she adored and who was living in Australia.

Mrs. Merz rolled her white hair in curlers every night and had a number of large, picturesque straw hats that she wore at a coquettish angle. She had a way with plants and flowers. Whatever she touched grew and blossomed. In Malay they would say she had *tangan dingin*, cool hands.

When she was not puttering in her garden, she was busy painting. She was surprisingly talented and made remarkable progress. Her meals were peculiar and cooked at any hour of the day or night. She ate when she felt like it. Rules, regulations, or orders were words banned from her vocabulary.

She was a great collector of things. Her junk room would have been the pride of any junk dealer. She liked showing me her treasures.

"Why do you keep that old padlock?" I once asked her.

"It might come in handy one day."

"And this torn umbrella?"

"Wait till I fix it."

"But will you fix it?"

"That remains to be seen. Don't be such a fussbudget, anyway."

She also had a red-hot temper. She didn't mean to harm anybody with it, and it died down as quickly as it flared up, but her native gardener, a sensitive man, trembled when she turned it on him. Still, he stayed on because she had a good heart.

Mrs. Merz took her daily siesta in the garden on a lounge under a big bamboo bush. One afternoon she awoke to the sound of a rifle shot and something falling in her lap. A Japanese, standing a few feet away, had shot a bird in the bamboo above her head. She was so upset about this double outrage—the interrupted siesta and the dead bird—that she gave the Japanese hell. In Dutch, of course. Not understanding a word, he picked up the bird, grinned, and left the garden.

The Straw Hat

Mrs. Wonder, a school teacher, moved with her little son Jan into one of the empty bungalows on Mrs. Merz's property. Tall, with sharp blue eyes, independent ways, and a sense of humor, Mrs. Wonder was a promising neighbor.

She had been living on Lembang Road, but being on the highway became more and more dangerous since the start of the occupation. Japanese soldiers would drop in any time. Such visits were unpleasant because the Japanese were inordinately fond of wristwatches, jewelry, cameras—anything that was valuable and small enough to slip into a hip or coat pocket.

Lembang had been the scene of many a recent tragedy, just before and since the occupation, caused either by the natives or by the Japanese storm troopers. The European population had fled to Bandoeng before the arrival of the Japanese troops. In those uncertain days the natives engaged in wholesale looting. They carried away anything useful. Doors and windows were dismantled, locks unscrewed, and water faucets carted off. What they did not want or could not carry away, they destroyed.

I took a look inside the looted home of a well-known Lembang artist. The home had been exquisitely furnished. Now I was saddened to see that the handcrafted Chinese furniture had been hacked to pieces. His paintings, some still hanging on the walls, had been slashed. His collection of priceless china smashed. It was a depressing sight.

The conduct of the natives and the general vandalism proved to be too much even for the Japanese. In Lembang they hanged about a dozen looters, ordered all loot to be brought back to a central location, and warned that if any stolen goods were found in anybody's possession, the culprits would be hanged.

That was the kind of language the mob understood. The stolen goods poured back. A large, empty storehouse was allocated to hold the returned loot. In less than twenty-four hours, the building proved too small. An acre of land around the storehouse was fenced in and it, too, quickly filled up with goods.

Mrs. Wonder and I decided to go in search of the goods that had been stolen from us. We set out at seven in the morning. The walk of more than five miles was uphill, but the grade thankfully gentle. Halfway there we passed the Lembang Hotel where General Wavell had stayed during his short and unsuccessful visit. A Japanese sentry stood in front of the hotel. I reminded my companion to greet him, as the Japanese authorities required us to do.

The sentry stood motionless, his gun lowered at his feet. As we passed him, at a distance of five or six yards, we said "good day," and nodded our heads slightly. He took no notice of us and we continued on our way.

When we reached Lembang we had no difficulty in finding the storage area. The Dutch military police, functioning under Japanese directions, were at the entrance and let us in without any fuss.

"If you ladies find anything that belongs to you, just take it with you," one policeman said.

We were dumbfounded at what we saw. A cemetery of Dutch middle class wealth spread before us: big divans, club chairs, precious books, standing lamps, tea sets, piles of oriental rugs, bedding, men's suits, ladies' evening dresses, sewing machines, refrigerators, typewriters, silverware. Everything and anything that could be found in a well-furnished house was there by the dozens.

We walked around searching for about an hour but didn't find any of our belongings. In a depressed mood, we headed back. Because the road back was downhill, the walk promised to be easy and uneventful, despite the great heat.

Mrs. Wonder wore a wide-brimmed straw hat as protection against the sun. I wore none. She had offered me a hat when we set out in the morning, but for some inexplicable reason, I hadn't accepted it.

As we neared the Lembang Hotel, I reminded her again about greeting the sentry. Our conversation died down when we sighted him. At a proper distance we performed the little ceremonial greeting, exactly as we had before. This time, however, the sentry responded with a terrific bellow. The Japanese roar, coming from the belly, had a disconcerting effect on us Europeans.

We stopped, frozen in our tracks. Another yell from the Japanese and a gesture summoning Mrs. Wonder. She approached him reluctantly. He gesticulated some more and shouted even louder. From his gestures I realized he wanted Mrs. Wonder to remove her hat. She either didn't understand or didn't want to understand and kept on standing erect and motionless in front of him.

After a few more shouts, the Japanese lost his temper, grabbed his gun with the bayonet fixed at the end of it, and jabbed it toward her, piercing the brim of the big straw hat from underneath. He jerked the hat off her head, swung it around a few times on the tip of the blade, and let it fly in a wide sweep some ten yards away.

Mrs. Wonder, a good head taller than the sentry, looked down at him. Her blue eyes flashed with indignation as she angrily retorted in Malay that women did not remove their hats when greeting and that she was surprised at such behavior. Of course, the sentry didn't understand what she was saying, but seeing the anger in her eyes and hearing the not-too-gentle voice, he felt his authority threatened. With a quick movement, exactly as the Japanese who took away my Leica camera had done, he drew back his right arm and shot it out lightning fast. He gave Mrs. Wonder such a slap in the face that she almost fell over.

All this time I was standing on the spot where we had originally stopped. I didn't want to desert her and walk on when I saw she was getting herself into trouble, but I didn't want to go any closer either for fear of getting involved. Sensing that the situation was becoming critical, I called to her in Dutch to walk away before she received another slap. She shouted back that she was outraged and wanted to register a complaint to somebody about the brutal behavior of the sentry.

Good heavens. Didn't she understand that we had lost our rights to expect decent behavior? In fact we had no more rights at all. The Japanese were the conquerors. They could and would do what they wanted and that was that.

"Don't be a fool," I called to her. "Come away before it's too late. They might arrest us both and what will happen to the children then?"

A group of Japanese officers were sitting on the open porch of the hotel, enjoying the scene. One of them called out to the sentry and he piped down.

Mrs. Wonder turned around, walked over to her bayoneted, sad-looking hat, picked it up, and joined me. Amazing woman, I thought. If the officers themselves had picked up that hat and presented it to me with their apologies, I wouldn't have dreamed of taking it back.

Without saying another word, and with simulated calm, we continued on our way. The whole scene had lasted no longer than two minutes.

I looked at her out of the corner of my eye. The veins on her forehead protruded like bluish earthworms. Half of her face was red and swollen. A thin streak of blood ran down from the corner of her mouth. Her eyes were full of rage and tears, but she wasn't crying. I respected her for that.

When a bend in the road hid us from the sentry, we sat down in the shade and I did my best to comfort her without getting too emotional. For all my sympathy I couldn't help asking why she wanted to retrieve that poor shamed hat of hers.

"It's a good hat," she said. "I'll mend it and it'll be wearable again." Good old Dutch common sense and practicality.

Soon we heard about many more slaps, administered only to white women. The count ran into the hundreds, then into the thousands. Not only a slap in the face, but real beatings, lasting five to fifteen minutes.

The causes varied: greeting a Japanese with glasses or a hat on, not putting down a parcel before greeting, wearing slacks, not dismounting from a bicycle while passing a sentry, smiling while greeting, not bowing low enough. In effect, anything we did was reason enough for a thrashing.

We knew little about the Japanese. We believed them to be a hard-working people who led simple lives and were courteous and well mannered. Instead we were confronted with their brutish behavior. Not only was this behavior perplexing and disturbing but painful and humiliating as well.

The Samurai

One morning while I was giving Yvonne her lesson, the *djongos* came running in to report that a Japanese had entered the garden and was coming toward the house.

I ran into the bedroom, hid my money in my blouse in front, and was back with Yvonne when we heard a knock on the door. Proper, civilized knocking, no banging or kicking. An unusually tall, slender, good-looking Japanese entered, his shirtsleeves rolled up high on his strong, brown arms. For more than a second, we looked at each other. Strangely enough he inspired no fear in me and I felt no enmity in his gaze. I addressed him in Malay. He shook his head. I tried English.

"Yes. Little," he said.

He looked around the room, scrutinizing every object. I patted the money in my blouse. I felt a flutter in my insides. Would he discover the remaining silk of Wim's parachute, which I had started to cut into pieces the night before? The Japanese had ordered all Dutch military equipment in private possession to be delivered to Japanese headquarters in town. The parachute silk was of excellent quality and would make lovely blouses and underwear for us and for friends. I had decided to use it rather than give it to the Japanese.

He looked back at me. "Where man?" he asked.

"No man," I replied, adopting his pidgin English.

"Where man?" he repeated with more emphasis.

"Man gone, prisoner of Japanese."

He responded with a grunt. I motioned him to a chair. He sat down, grinning. Yvonne, frightened, watched him with big eyes. Maya and Robi were in the garden.

The most difficult conversation of my life followed. The little he knew of English was indeed very little.

"How children?" he asked.

"Children good."

At this reply of mine he grinned again, hissed between his teeth, and tried anew.

"How number children?"

"Three," I said.

He nodded and hissed. I felt it was my turn to ask something, or to hiss perhaps. I searched my mind desperately for some question.

"Hungry?" I ventured.

"No."

That was that. Now what? "Captain?" I enquired.

"No."

"Lieutenant?"

"Yes, yes," he said. He thrust out his chest.

While racking my brain for the next suitable question, I came up with the idea of producing my Japanese grammar. More hissing and grinning when I pronounced a few words in Japanese.

After a while the conversation stalled again. The world atlas came to my rescue. I had been giving Yvonne a geography lesson when he entered.

He turned the pages and stopped when he saw a map of the entire eastern hemisphere. He pointed to Japan and said, "Japan here."

It was my turn to nod. Then his fingers traveled to Indochina and to Burma. "Japan here," he said.

"Yes," I said.

Then he got excited, jumped up, pointed to Australia, spread his fingers, and counted aloud in English. "One, two, three, four, five, six. Six weeks, Australia. *Dai, dai* Nippon. Big Nippon. Asia, Australia, all Nippon. Life, work, good under Nippon."

"Yes," I responded meekly.

My visitor turned and departed as unexpectedly and unceremoniously as he had come. When he left I called the *djongos* but got no reply. *Kokki* didn't answer either. I looked for them but couldn't find them anywhere. A while later I discovered them sneaking back from the rice fields.

"Why did you go away? Why did you hide?" I asked them.

"We were afraid of the Japanese."

Cowards, I thought. But now I knew that I wouldn't be able to count on them in an emergency.

Two days later in the morning, while I was tending to my sick camellia bush, the garden gate flew open and a military-uniformed man with big riding boots strode in. I hardly recognized my shirt-sleeved Japanese. He had put on his Sunday best. Kepi, tunic, white gloves, sword—nothing was missing.

I stood where I was while he approached stiffly, stopping at a proper distance and making a bow. Then he advanced a few steps and made another bow. Two more steps and a third bow. Then he straightened up, saluted, and delivered the following little speech, hissing properly before starting.

"I know you wife captain. I pay respect wife captain."

Then he saluted again and bowed once more. I was taken aback by this unexpected "respect."

"Thank you," I said. "How do you do?"

I bade him come in and called the *djongos*, who hadn't disappeared this time, to bring us some lemonade. We sat on the porch, sipping our cool drinks. He asked whether he could do anything for me. Of course I wouldn't have accepted any favors from a Japanese and was about to decline when an idea shot through my mind. Putting my pride aside, I asked him whether I could see my prisoner husband.

"No. Cannot," he answered. "You write letter. I bring letter man."

There was no sense in doing that because I could still smuggle tiny notes to Wim through friends. Besides what would Wim's reaction be if he were to receive a letter through a Japanese channel? Weighing all this up mentally, I thanked him but politely declined his offer.

He stayed for only about ten minutes. Then he got up, saluted, and was gone. I had to admit that I appreciated this courtesy call, which undoubtedly had not been easy for him to undertake. But I also hoped he would call it a day and not feel the urge to express more of his "respect" in the future.

Two days later I received a telephone message from Elsje Schouten to come to Bandoeng. Phone messages were transmitted now through the dairy up the road because Langeler's phone had been cut off.

I bicycled down at lunchtime. Elsje, disconcerted, met me at the door. I saw she hated to give me whatever news she had. The news wasn't good. The Dutch officers had been moved from Bandoeng to the former Dutch garrison town of Tjimahi, some twelve miles away.

What a shock. Although we couldn't visit the men or send them any packages, knowing they were nearby had been a comfort. When the men went out in small heavily guarded groups, a flock of women followed at a careful distance. Whenever the women saw a lax guard, they would manage to pass close to the men and smuggle a few notes to them.

A few of the women would walk behind the men and would pick up odd objects lying on the road: a carefully rolled cigarette, a string bean, a matchbox, a banana peel. These would contain notes the men intended for their wives. The men had become clever at secreting their messages.

Unfortunately, the Japanese guards sometimes caught the women as they intercepted the men's notes and would beat them on the spot. The men were so disturbed by witnessing these beating that many of them asked the women not to follow them.

Another way of sending messages was to sing or shout them. Only the essentials. "Marjolein Bander, birthday greetings. Suzanne van der Heide, need underwear badly. Anneke Smitt, don't worry, everything okay." The women following the men listened to the messages and passed them on. Similar to native drum signals, these verbal messages would travel from friend to friend until they reached their destination. Alas, I hadn't heard from Wim in a long time.

When Elsje saw that I had digested the bad news, she handed me a tiny note. A thin cigarette paper containing no more than three sentences. It was Wim's goodbye message. He was well. I shouldn't worry but stay cheerful. "Thanks for looking after the children and God bless you. Everything will end well," he wrote.

Elsje left me alone to read the tiny letter. I sat down and gazed at the note in my hand. The tears blurring my sight would have rolled down my cheeks had Elsje not entered with a cool drink and a smile.

We sat for a while and she gave me news about our mutual friends. Then I put the slip of paper in my blouse (in front, of course), thanked her, and went home.

At seven in the evening, when the children were in bed, I checked as usual whether all the doors were locked and whether my hockey stick, my only weapon, was near my bed. I reread the letter. Or rather, I stared at Wim's handwriting. Then I sat down at the piano.

A loud knocking-banging at the porch door nearly frightened me off the piano stool. Who can it be? Is it the police? Or just Mrs. Merz? But she wouldn't knock like that. Is it a house search? Are the Japanese here? Should I open? Should I not open?

As these thoughts zigzagged through my mind, I picked up the flashlight and went to the door. I pulled the curtain aside and shone the light out, straight into the face of a smiling Japanese, the same officer who had paid his "respect" a few days before.

For heaven's sake, what does he want at night? Is he drunk? Should I open? Of course not opening was not an option. I opened the door about a foot and asked him what he wanted.

"Want speak," he said

"What do you want to speak?"

"Speak."

"Do you just want to talk?" At least he didn't smell of liquor.

"Yes."

"Only talk?" I asked firmly, putting up my forefinger and slowly pronouncing every syllable.

"Yes."

"Come in, then."

Here he was again and our painful conversation had to be faced anew. I got out my Japanese grammar again and for two hours we "conversed," me asking him questions, and he answering "yes" or "no." I was the geisha. I tried every conceivable subject but felt I was banging my head against a brick wall. Sports, music, literature, home life, marriage, cooking, education—all were strange to him. He knew little about Fujiyama, and the subject of cherry blossoms was quickly exhausted.

I did find out he was twenty-six and had been in the war the last four years, mostly in China. He had not had a home leave all this time. He told me proudly that he had killed two Chinese with his sword. He also told me that he was a samurai. With that he jumped up and showed me the sword he had inherited from his great-great-grandfather, also a samurai.

Copper cherry blossoms embellished the hilt of the beautiful piece of metalwork. I admired it dutifully. He pulled it out and showed me how sharp the blade was. Our kitchen knife seemed a blunt piece of metal in comparison. As his glittering eyes caressed the blade, he grinned mysteriously. I had the idiotic notion that he might go crazy and slice off my head to prove how sharp the blade was. I hastily asked him to put it back in the sheath.

He did as asked and sat down again, but he still seemed excited. "I kill two Chinese this sword," he repeated.

"Not sorry for Chinese?" I asked, perhaps tactlessly.

"No."

There we were, exactly where I did not want the conversation to turn. "You like war?" I asked.

"Yes. War good."

"You like if bomb kills women and children?"

He thought that over a moment. "No," he said.

"You like when bomb fall on your head and you dead?"

"Yes. I like. I go God." He pointed up to heaven. Here lay their strength—fanaticism.

Shortly after nine o'clock he left. I had a splitting headache.

A few days later, while I was playing the piano in the evening, the familiar knock came again. I opened the door to find two Japanese this time. My young lieutenant hissed, showing almost all his teeth, and pointed to the other fellow with a broad gesture, introducing him as his "good friend."

I let them in and noticed the "good friend" was rather oddly dressed: military tunic, pajama pants, and bathroom slippers on bare feet. He was a captain and a doctor. He spoke no English but claimed to speak German. It proved to be a miniscule amount of German. I had never spoken pidgin German before but learned quickly. To make the time pass I served them tea.

"You take sugar?" I asked.

"Yes."

"Milk?"

They burst out in loud laughter. The question must have seemed as strange to them as the Tibetan custom of putting goat's milk butter in tea does to us.

After tea the "good friend" said they would like to see the children. I told them the children were already in bed, but as they insisted on seeing them, I went in first to prepare the children. I told them that these two officers were good Japanese and they loved children. "Try to smile, please," I added. "They won't hurt you. Don't be afraid."

In came the two men. Like three frightened puppies, the girls crouched in their beds. Poor Robi's lips were trembling. I was afraid she would burst out crying, but she swallowed her tears and pasted on a miserable grin. The Japanese shook hands with each child. The doctor produced a can of California peaches from his pocket and presented it to the children. Obviously this gift had been looted from some Dutch storage bin. The gesture, however, showed kindness.

Back on the porch I had to continue my role of entertainer. If I didn't speak, they kept silent. I couldn't help laughing when the lieutenant asked me how old I was.

"To you I am as old as I seem," I answered evasively.

"Thirty," he said.

I hadn't thought that Japanese men were flatterers. However, he could just as well have guessed fifty, for they were as unable to gauge the ages of Europeans, as we were to guess theirs.

After they had left I noticed a package of cigarettes and a box of matches on the table. These items were valuable because they were unobtainable. Clearly they were meant as a gift. In the short period of the occupation so far, we had learned of this Japanese custom. If a small gift was accepted, larger presents generally followed, perhaps ending up with a banknote on the table. In the eyes of the Japanese, these gifts, either silently or protestingly accepted, meant a bargain had been struck. There was no doubt about the price the European woman had to pay.

However, taking into account that the Japanese were the conquerors and considered women inferior, this way of negotiating a deal seemed a civilized and fair way to try to win the affections, or whatever we choose to call it, of the fair sex.

Perhaps my guests had no ulterior motive, but to make things clear to them, I handed back the cigarettes and the matches at their next visit.

My good-looking lieutenant came twice more. The second time he was in a hurry. He wanted me to translate some German instructions for using the camera he had recently acquired.

The next day the big red-rising sun flag at the top of Isola's tower was gone. The *djongos* reported that the Japanese garrison had left. I couldn't suppress a sigh of relief.

Those dark-blue-sky, million-starred, cricket-chirrupy, heavenly scented, lonely evenings were all mine again.

chool

Since the start of the occupation, all schools had been closed to European children. Half the children didn't receive any instruction at all. The other half tried to pick up private lessons when and wherever possible. The Japanese forbade having classes with more than five pupils in any one group.

Mrs. Wonder, who had mentally and physically recovered from the sentry's slap, was a godsend to our neighborhood. She taught several classes a day. Yvonne, who was in second grade, was now in one of her classes.

One morning Mrs. Wonder, looking tired and discouraged, came to see me and asked me to take over teaching second grade. I tried to protest, but she didn't let me finish.

"Don't tell me you don't know Dutch well enough, or that you have an accent, or that you have never taught small children before. Even if all those things are true, this is wartime," she said. "Furthermore, as a sign of my complete trust in your ability, I will send my Jan to your class," she added.

What could I say? The fees were small, but I could use the money. Still, I had doubts about my ability and spent half the night figuring out how to tackle this new task.

The next morning I arose at five, tidied my bedroom and the dining room, and went to work in the garden as usual. Because I had dismissed the *djongos*, I had to do his work myself. At breakfast Yvonne, Maya, and Robi were excited about the turn of events. Again, something was "happening." Because the dining room was to serve as the classroom, they hurried to finish their meal.

At 7:30 sharp the children arrived:

Wim, a sturdy, fair-haired boy, somewhat spoiled.

Jan, Mrs. Wonder's son, a lovable, original, independent boy, with an occasional terrible temper.

Puckie, my little Brunhilde, with such a pretty face that you couldn't take your eyes off her and two thick, long, golden braids as exist only in fairy tales.

Puckie, No. 2, just the opposite from Brunhilde in appearance: tiny, dark-haired, and a boy. He came from the dairy farm. My daily milk supply was the fee exchanged for his lessons.

Jan Al, the clown of the class, came with his father, who clearly didn't like the idea of the change of teachers and didn't trust my teaching ability.

To put Jan Al's father at ease, I told him that I respected his feelings and that, if I were in his place, I too would prefer to send my son to a Dutch teacher. I added that Mrs. Wonder might know someone else in the neighborhood.

He was polite and suggested we try it for a month and if he wasn't satisfied, he would take his son away.

"There won't be any hard feelings?" he asked.

"Of course not," I hastened to reassure him.

My sixth pupil, one above the number allowed by the Japanese (I took a chance there), was my Yvonne. She was fond of company and overjoyed with this new development. She took over the hostess role, showing every child to his or her seat with motherly solicitude.

I don't remember how I got through that first day of teaching, but I know that the arithmetic lesson ended with pearls of perspiration on my forehead. The problems didn't seem to be beyond my capacity—after all, it was only second-grade math—but those darn multiplication tables came to my mind in Hungarian, my mother tongue. In order not to get the two languages mixed up, I spent many an evening repeating the tables aloud in Dutch.

Mrs. Wonder suggested I limit the lessons to the essentials: reading, writing, a bit of grammar, and arithmetic. I was ambitious, however, and enlarged our field of studies with Bible stories (the life of Jesus), English, and physical education, in which Maya and Robi also took part. Needless to say, physical education was the most popular. I suggested the children come a quarter of an hour earlier every day to give us time for a fifteen-minute exercise session.

The fifteen minutes proved too short to really enjoy a game. As the children were constantly clamoring for more, I told them they could come on Friday afternoons for gymnastics and games. Furthermore, I told them, their friends were welcome as well and it would be free of charge. The latter was particularly good news because money was scarce.

Two months after the classes had started, Jan Al's father came with his wife. They were effusive in wanting to personally thank me for the excellent instruction and loving care Jan Al was getting from me. They also wanted to be sure I would keep him in the next grade as well.

I tried not to show how pleased I was and how proud of this recognition. I had worked hard and had committed myself wholeheartedly to the job, but the little voice inside me told me it would be vain to pocket the thanks with such joy.

The final exam was planned for the end of July. August would be vacation time. I asked Mrs. Wonder to come give the exam. As a qualified teacher, she would know whether we had satisfactorily covered the second-grade material. I invited the parents to attend as well.

The night before the exam, after the girls had gone to bed, I made a cake. Because white flour was practically unobtainable, it would have to be a cornmeal cake. The baking process was slow and unusual. My oven was a round tin box on a charcoal brazier. So that the cake would receive heat from above and below, I spread glowing coals on top of the box lid. I couldn't sit back and take satisfaction in my clever baking solution, however, because I had to fan the coals nonstop and replenish them frequently from another brazier. It took two hours of fanning and moving hot coals to bake the cake.

The next day my pupils arrived with their parents. The exam, presided over by Mrs. Wonder, went without a hitch, with everyone passing. The children received congratulations and handshakes from the grownups and a small present from their parents.

By this time the Friday afternoon playgroup had congregated in the garden. We had athletics, games, races, and gymkhana. I served tea and the cake to the parents and cool drinks, cookies, and sweets—a real treat in those days—to the children. The school year was officially at an end.

We set the first of September as the start of the next term. I would teach third grade and also have a class for first graders because Maya was ready to start school. Within a week I had four pupils for the first grade.

Even with my successful new experience, I wasn't confident about how to introduce first graders to reading and writing. The Japanese had not yet closed the Bandoeng library, so I biked to town, hoping to find a guidebook for teachers.

Going to Bandoeng had become a risky excursion. The five-mile trip downhill was easy, but pushing the bike uphill for half the way on the return trip, with the sun beating down, was another matter. In addition you were never sure of coming home at all. Any Japanese, under any pretext, might beat you or arrest you.

At the library I found a book on Maria Montessori's system. I learned that the main idea was to teach through play. Nothing easier. I loved to play with children.

Mrs. Wonder, as helpful as ever, supplied me with books, notebooks, and pencils, which she had saved from the school where she used to teach. I also bought a triplex board and a dozen blades for my jigsaw.

On the first of September the third graders came in at 7:15 for their lesson, At 9:45 they had gymnastics in the garden together with the first graders, who came in for their lesson from 10:00 to 12:00.

The first graders spent the first few days becoming acquainted with each other while I assessed their intelligence level. Then I produced the wooden board and the jigsaw. I drew a capital "A" on it and had them take turns sawing it out. They spoiled a few and broke some until they finally got a good one. I held it up high in the air and we looked at it from all sides.

"It's a beauty," I said. "But it has no name. We must call it something. Something easy. For example, 'A'."

So we called it "A," and we put it in a bamboo basket. Then we played with flowers and pebbles to master the rudiments of arithmetic.

The next day the first child to remember the name for "A" was allowed to color it. And color it he did. All eyes watched as the "A" was dressed in sky blue. When the artist had finished, we started sawing the next letter. Soon we had pink, purple, yellow, red, and green letters lying on the table, and we attempted to form words with them. The competition was keen to make more and more words and to decipher each other's words.

When we ran out of capital letters, we started on the lowercase letters. Our bamboo basket filled up bit by bit. We played with the letters and then "imitated" them, using pencil on paper. After four or five months of this game, without noticing it and without any special effort on anybody's part, the children had mastered the rudiments of reading and writing.

Then I received a surprise.

Robine, who was four and a half years old at that time, was too young to join the first graders. Feeling left out of the "game," she sat on the verandah next to the schoolroom, listening to what was going on. Sometimes I found her with Maya in the garden, sitting under the bougainvillea tree with a schoolbook in her lap.

About six months after the start of classes, Robi came to me with the first-grade reader and said, "I can read, Mami."

"Oh, really, Robi?" I said, humoring her. "That's great. Come and read the first page."

She read it fluently from beginning to end. My first thought was that she had learned it by heart from having heard it read so often by the first graders. I asked her to read the second page, then the middle of the book, then the end of the book. She could read the entire book. She hesitated slightly here and there, but she had taught herself to read. My clever little "Benjamin." I gave her a big hug and a small bar of chocolate as a reward. She would have probably appreciated the opposite more, that is, a small hug and a big bar of candy, but chocolate had practically disappeared from the market.

The third graders were also doing well. I had added geography to the curriculum. We started by lighting a candle to represent the sun. Next we turned a globe around on its axis near the candle, illustrating night and day. Then we traveled with the globe around the candle. Soon the children grasped how we arrived at calculating the year and the seasons.

After that we examined the globe. When we became acquainted with the continents and oceans, we started traveling by sea and by land, by boat and by train, by car and by bullock cart. I varied the stories and made them colorful. Any qualified geography teacher would probably have shuddered at my method, but I achieved my goal: the children became interested in the world.

Every day at noon, after school was finished, I took my three girls for a swim. A friend about a mile up the road had a swimming pool. We all contributed a small sum toward the upkeep of the pool. Yvonne and Maya were already pretty good swimmers, and Robine could do about ten yards in deep water without a flotation ring.

In the afternoon the girls would play in the garden or walk on the *galangans*, the low mud walls in the *sawahs*, while I gave private French and English lessons for ten to fifteen American cents per lesson. With money scarce, ten cents was better than nothing.

Including the Friday afternoon games, I was giving forty-seven lessons a week. My oldest pupil was Mrs. Merz, who came twice a week from eight to nine in the evening to learn English. When on dark nights I saw her oil lantern swinging back and forth in the *sawahs*, I would pick up my lantern and go out to meet her. She was seventy, and the mud walls were narrow. I didn't want her to slip and sit down in the muddy water of the rice field.

The lesson usually stretched to ten as we talked about places in Europe we both knew well. At times her English was fluent. But there was one thing that we never talked about in French, English, or Dutch. We carefully avoided mentioning the rumor spreading like fire in dry grass that the Japanese intended to put women and children into internment camps.

Day by Day

The noose was tightening around the necks of the Europeans. More and more civilian men were being rounded up and put into internment camps. Even those who were in the service of the Japanese and who wore special armbands proving their privileged status, which supposedly gave them personal protection, were being arrested. Seemingly on purpose, the Japanese carried out raids randomly to make everyone feel jittery and insecure.

People were being arrested on the street. A truck would stop, native police would jump out, grab the men, put them in the truck, and off they'd go. People were being arrested in their offices, in their homes, without warning, any time of the day or night. A few hours after such a "whisking off," you would see the frightened wives or relatives carrying small bundles of clothing, hurrying from one police station to another in search of their loved ones, hoping to hand these parcels over to them personally or at least to their keepers. Some succeeded. Some did not. Many got slapped. Others escaped unhurt.

The continual beatings were odious to us, whereas the Japanese seemed to find them a normal form of behavior between superiors and subordinates, even among themselves. The natives also hated being beaten. They were not used to such treatment under the Dutch. In fact, under Dutch rule any native who had been slapped could go to court and sue the white man who had slapped him. Now, however, beatings became the rule. Consequently, many natives grew to fear and hate the Japanese.

More and more rumors circulated that women and children would be put into internment camps as well. In Bandoeng a number of streets had been evacuated for the new campsite, or so we heard. Everywhere in town you could see these evicted people, carrying their belongings, dragging their furniture and belongings, not knowing where to find a place to live. Those receiving an evacuation notice usually had twenty-four hours to clear out, although sometimes they received only a couple of hours' notice. A number of the evicted camped in the street, rain or shine, until somehow someone took them in.

Native policemen under Japanese command came almost every week to every house, searching for this or that, checking to see who had a registration card and who didn't, and looking for radios. All radios belonging to the families of the prisoners of war had been confiscated months before. All other radios had to be brought to a center in town where they were adjusted to receive only the Java station. Anyone caught listening to a foreign station on a nonadjusted radio was whisked away by the Kempeitai, the Japanese Gestapo. The person would return a few days later after having had a "treatment," usually a punctured eardrum.

I knitted six pairs of socks for Wim. I sold the only remaining pair of Wim's shoes the looters had overlooked and bought a new polo shirt and some vitamin pills for him. Then I took my courage in my hands and biked to Tjimahi, about twelve miles from Bandoeng. Our husbands were being kept in the *treinkampement*, the former Dutch military barracks, in Tjimahi. Elsje gave me a sketch and directions to a house where some six or seven European women were living. These women were involved with smuggling packages and letters to their prisoner-husbands through the hospital or through a reliable native.

I arrived at the spacious main square, planted with rows of tall coconut palms. The square was totally deserted. I dismounted and took out Elsje's sketch to get my bearings in order to locate the house, when, as if spring-ing out of the ground, a Japanese soldier stood in front of me, bellowing. He had been hiding behind one of the palm trees.

The rage in his eyes was unmistakable. I lowered mine, knowing this was expected from women facing Japanese men. I tried not to show my fear, thinking all the time with terror that if he were to beat me and take me to the military police, I might be detained for days and the children wouldn't know what had happened to me.

I didn't have the faintest idea why he was roaring at me because he was doing it in Japanese. I waited patiently for the outcome without making the slightest movement. When he'd stopped shouting and had made no move-ment to beat me, I calmly picked up my parcel. Without saying a word, I pointed to the nearest house some twenty yards away and walked with the parcel and the bike toward the house with measured steps. My back tingled as his eyes pierced me from behind. I prepared myself for an attack.

I reached the gate, which, wonder upon wonder, was unlocked. The Japanese hadn't moved. When the package, the bike, and I were safely in the courtyard and the gate was bolted, several European women fell around my neck, jabbering excitedly and hugging me.

"How lucky you are," they said. "About five minutes ago, we saw the same Japanese soldier beating another woman. European women aren't allowed to walk around in Tjimahi because of the garrison. We unlocked the gate when we saw you were in trouble, hoping you'd take refuge here, beaten or unbeaten."

How wonderful this solidarity. And how lucky I was to land in the very house I was looking for.

I handed over the parcel to Elsje's friend, who promised to get it to Wim. She also gave me the disturbing news that our men would probably be moved again to another place. No one knew where or when. I hoped the package would reach Wim in time.

I biked home safely and was grateful to do so.

A few days later Elsje and Frits Schouten came out for a visit with a big bunch of orchids and congratulations for me. Wim had asked them in a smug-gled note to remember my birthday. At times, small things are big things. The Schoutens also brought news of the Cramers, the chief engineer of the quinine factory and his wife who had been so hospitable to us when the first Japanese occupation troops had chucked us out into the street. The Japanese still employed Mr. Cramer at the factory, because they couldn't manage without him. They had dismissed all other Europeans.

Frits Schouten heard from him that on a Saturday, payday, the native workers gathered at the usual place in the plant, waiting for their pay. On some pretext the Japanese paymaster refused to pay out their wages. Mr. Cramer stood up for the workers and told the paymaster the workers had to be paid. The Japanese, apparently feeling his dignity was at stake, slapped Mr. Cramer in front of the whole gathering. The natives looked on silently and filed out of the building, never to return. The following Monday the work couldn't proceed as usual. The Japanese were forced to hire unskilled, untrained replacements.

There was such a lot of talk of epidemics that I decided to get the children and myself inoculated against typhoid, cholera, and dysentery. I had to have this done at the Pasteur Institute in Bandoeng.

Because we had no means of transportation other than our legs and the bicycle, and because I couldn't take more than two children with me at a time, I had to make several trips before the inoculations were completed. These trips developed into real excursions. On the way home we always stopped at a little milk shop where they still sold iced cocoa. The children got a bottle each by way of compensation for the shot in the arm (which they bore without crying), for the inevitable Japanese shouting or hissing, and for the weary uphill trip in the heat of the day. The children loved the iced cocoa so much that they were overjoyed when we had to return to the Pasteur Institute after the Japanese ordered the inoculation of the whole population against Asian plague.

On one such trip to town, I treated the children to a ride on a little horse on the way. They, of course, loved sitting on the horse. Pegasus couldn't have soared higher in the air than did their imagination.

The pony ride gave me an idea. Asmaji, a rich native who lived a few hundred yards from our bungalow, had some horses but no meadows to graze them on. I offered him our large lawn as a grazing field. In return the children rode the horses, led by a native boy.

This bareback riding went on for weeks until one day one of the horses threw Yvonne off and bolted. That stopped the riding. I was afraid of a serious accident. The children were disappointed, but I just couldn't risk any broken legs or arms because there was no doctor in the neighborhood and no transportation to the hospital.

I had dismissed the *djongos* some time before because I couldn't afford to keep both him and his wife, who was our *kokki*. She was willing to stay on by herself, but she was getting more and more restless and had a bad temper. I still believed that they had been the looters of our home during the days of the capitulation, so I told her to go. She brought a new *kokki*, a gnarled, old-ish woman with big ears, an open smile that showed teeth stained from betel chewing, and laughing eyes. Her name was Manggoen.

We quickly became fond of Manggoen, of her gentle ways and her sense of humor. She was an eastern Javanese, a race very different from the Sudanese of west Java. She was a fine cook and had a dainty way of decorating her dishes, knowing that food should please the eye as well as the palate. When I had time I would squat beside her at the charcoal bra-zier and learn some of the mysteries of Oriental cooking. The art of mixing spices lay in her blood. Spices to her were living things. She would say, "No *njonja besar*, grand lady, you can't mix pepper with *koenjit*. They don't like each other. You can put *djahe* with it. They are friends."

On long, dark evenings when the children were asleep, we would sit and talk. She would tell me about the many spirits who influenced every-one's lives. About the moon, the Lovely Lady, whose cycles of wander-ing in the sky divided their year into thirteen months. About death and afterlife. And about all the punishments awaiting people for the wrongs committed in this life.

The Javanese were Muslims, as was the majority of the native popula-tion of the Dutch East Indies, but Hinduism, from which the sons of Allah had converted them, had left many traces in their beliefs.

Wim had told me that whenever a refinery was being built, the head of a buffalo had to be buried in the ground under the most dangerous spot of the plant in order to frighten away the evil spirits. The management knew that if this were not done, they wouldn't get any natives to work in the refinery. The proper ceremony had to be observed on such occasions. A *hadji*, a man who had made the pilgrimage to Mecca, would be invited to lead the invocation and recite the prayers while the buffalo's head was being buried. When the burial and the prayers were concluded, the refinery management would give a *selamatan*, a festive meal, for the fifteen hundred to two thousand workers.

Rice was the mainstay of the diet and was considered precious and as having a life force. Manggoen told me that the rice had a spirit and, therefore, out of reverence, should not be kept on the ground. I took the hint and let her buy a low stool on which the big basket of rice, our daily food, was placed.

One evening, squatting native fashion in front of me, she said she wasn't happy because no prayers were being said in our house. I told her that I prayed every night with the children before putting them to bed.

"Yes, *njonja besar*, that might be all right, but we ought to pray to Allah," was her reply.

"How do you wish to do it, Manggoen?" I asked.

Following her wishes, we assembled the next Friday after sunset in the little service kitchen. In front of the rice basket, she placed a low stool covered with a colorfully embroidered cloth, which I had frantically just completed stitching. On it we placed a cup of freshly made *kopi toebroek,* black coffee, a lump of brown palm sugar, some cookies, a fingerbowl half-filled with water with some flowers floating in it, and a tiny brazier with hot coals.

Manggoen knelt down in front of this "altar," tilted her weight back, and sat on her heels, the Muslim position of prayer. I bade the children do the same. They surrounded the altar in a half circle, with me standing behind them. Manggoen started murmuring her prayers in Javanese. Then she raised her voice, slowly repeating the term *salamalecum* three times as she sprinkled incense on the glowing coals and bowed her head deeply. The heavily scented incense smoke filled the room.

Manggoen continued her prayer in Malay so that we could understand. She asked Allah to safeguard Wim in captivity and to bring him back soon, healthy in mind and body. What delicate feelings for such a simple woman, and what a golden heart. I stealthily wiped away my tears. I didn't want the children to know about the big ache in my heart.

When the prayer was finished, we followed Manggoen into the bedroom, where she circled Wim's and my bed with the smoking brazier in her hands. Twice a week we prayed in this manner to Allah because it made Manggoen happy.

On full-moon nights we usually threw a *Mondschein*, moonlight or full-moon, party. Mrs. Merz would join us as we sat on mats spread out on the steps of the bungalow, facing the rising moon, which looked like a fairy-tale cheese in the dark blue sky. For a short while we would stare at the Lovely Lady in silence and awe, breathing in the sweetly scented tropical night air. Then Manggoen would serve tea and cookies, the highlight of the party for the children, and she would entertain us with innumerable stories.

One night after such a full-moon party, I had gone to bed when I awoke suddenly to Manggoen's cry under my window: *"Njonja, bulan sakit!"*

While struggling back to consciousness, I caught only the word *sakit*, ill.

"Who is ill?" I asked, full of anxiety.

"Bulan sakit, njonja," she repeated. The moon is sick.

That was more than I could understand, so I jumped out of bed, put on my bathrobe, and joined Manggoen in the garden. She pointed to the moon. And there she was, sick indeed, a perfect eclipse.

The natives seldom go to bed when there is a full moon, because, as Manggoen explained, they had to entertain the Lady. She was being entertained this night, too. You could hear the drums gently beating in all the surrounding villages down the valley.

I comforted Manggoen as best I could, trying to explain what an eclipse was. She didn't believe me, but she wouldn't say so. I gave her a cup of coffee and a few cookies and stayed up with her for a long time. At about four in the morning, the moon started to get better. Manggoen was comforted, and I could go back to bed for another hour.

Frits and Elsje Schouten came out with their Tjimahi friend in her new Pontiac, which she had named Blue Bird. The friend brought me the good news that she had been successful in smuggling my last parcel to Wim. Because the Japanese were confiscating all cars, even from those who worked for the Japanese, she hoped to hide the car in Mrs. Merz's empty garage. Mrs. Merz agreed to garage the car, so they removed all the tires and took out the battery.

Frits Schouten also asked me whether I would hide a tin box for him. It contained Shell employees' receipts for money they had taken since the capitulation, payments the Japanese were not supposed to know about. He didn't feel safe keeping the receipts because he might be subjected to a house search at any time. I told Frits I would take care of it.

When they left, Mrs. Merz and I talked it over. She suggested we bury it in her garden. We would have to proceed carefully, however, because not only her gardener and every other native in the neighborhood but almost every tree and bush had eyes and ears.

The following morning she had her gardener dig a large hole in an odd corner of her spacious garden and told the man she wanted to plant a tree there. The hole was left to air and dry out in the sun for a few days. Then she had him fill it with earth again and dig a new hole somewhere else. She told him she had decided to change the place for the tree. The same thing happened to the second hole. Because everyone knew Mrs. Merz often changed her mind, we hoped her gardener would not find anything strange in this continual digging-a-hole business.

At least that's what we thought.

A third hole was dug close to Mrs. Merz's bungalow and left alone for a few days. Then, on a dark night, I crossed the *sawahs* with Frits Schouten's tin box under my arm. Mrs. Merz joined me at the most recent hole. On our knees, working with our fingers only because a spade or shovel would have made too much noise and talking in whispers interspersed with muffled laughter, we buried the tin box. We planted a tree on top of it and then placed slabs of sod around the tree to hide the signs of fresh digging in case of a house search. So many people buried valuables those days that freshly dug-up soil was suspect. For about a week we alluded to our digging adventure when we met, then we forgot about it.

Nearly each day brought some unpleasant surprise. Native police came to confiscate flashlights and all weapons, which now included long garden knives used for cutting the grass.

Our dentist told me that he had gone to Tjimahi with his wife, hoping to get a glimpse of their prisoner son. Japanese soldiers picked them up in the street and brought them to a police station, where he had to watch as they beat his wife.

The Japanese didn't pay out anything to the military or civilian prisoners' wives. The banks had been closed. We had to live on our cash reserves, by selling our personal belongings, or by our wits.

Because we had lost most of our valuables during the looting and because I didn't want to spend all my cash reserves, I was trying to cover our daily expenses from my own earnings. These expenses had been reduced to a monthly fifty guilders, about thirty dollars, in spite of the rapidly increasing prices for foodstuff. One sacrifice I had to make was to give up the piano, which I had been renting for three guilders a month. I played long into the night preceding her departure. The following day my heart nearly broke when I had to say goodbye to her.

My Dutch pupils paid five guilders, or about three dollars, a month, if they were able to do so. Those who couldn't, received free tuition. Puckie with the webbed fingers gave me a liter of milk a day, which was wonderful. The private lessons brought in twenty-five Dutch cents, about ten to fifteen American cents, although I often had to bike to town to give them, five miles each way.

We ate meat only twice a week but had plenty of fruits and vegetables. I had a large section of the lawn converted into a vegetable garden and worked in it every day. It was fun to see things grow about twice as fast as in Europe. At times, however, mysterious things happened to the plants. For example, out of one hundred twenty strong, healthy tomato plants, heavy with green fruit, only twenty survived. The rest died within a few hours without any visible cause. Some said the soil was not suitable. Others thought the plants had suffered sunstroke.

The peas were doing beautifully, as were the beans. I had five kinds of beans growing, varieties unknown in Europe. Eggplant, leek, and sweet potatoes were all doing fine, but the leafy vegetables were not successful. My first harvest of peanuts was a joy for all of us. Growing our own vegetables helped reduce our monthly expenses and kept us supplied with nutritious food.

Not only did my plants grow quickly, but so did my jam business. This enterprise started when I gave away a jar of homemade jam as a birthday present. It was better quality than any jam you could buy in the shops, and my birthday friend came back asking whether she could buy another jar from me. At first the idea seemed strange to me, but later I thought, why not? My friend brought other buyers, and soon I had quite a clientele. The jam business was more lucrative than the lessons, but irregular and tiring because I had to cook the jams at night, having no free time during the day. I tried all sorts of fruit combinations: mangos, pineapples, strawberries, mulberries, papayas, green tomatoes, and oranges.

My busyness kept me from thinking too much about the future. The days and weeks went by without any contact with our men. No more letters could be smuggled to or from the prisoners. We learned through the *kabar angin*, the whispering wind, that our men had indeed been moved from Tjimahi. I had been alone for nine months now, and the loneliness weighed heavily on me.

Song of the Sawahs

The ever-rustling, swishing, whispering rice fields surrounded us. Many faces has the *sawah*. Many moods. It is Mother Nature who speaks through her. Mother Earth. Nothing male about it. The natives know that. No man is allowed to touch her forthcoming child, the rice plant.

The men have to make the soil fertile, ready to receive the *bibit*, the seed, as it is called in Malay. After that, the *sawahs* are taboo to them.

The field is under water for at least ten days when the plowman arrives with two water buffaloes and his antediluvian wooden plow. It is good to scratch the back of Old Mother with the help of her own child. No man-hammered metal should touch her crusty skin.

Man and buffaloes are knee-deep in the mud. Slosh, slosh, slosh, they advance slowly. When a corner comes they will have to turn. "Du-du-du-du. Du-du-du-du," the man calls, and the buffaloes change direction. Slosh-floff, slosh-floff, slosh-floff. The turning of the mud with the plow continues until well into the afternoon. By then it is difficult to see where the mud stops and the man and animals begin. All is gray-brown muck.

The man detaches the plow and massages the spinal column of each beast, starting from the neck. When he comes to the tail, he gives it a hard pull, bracing himself with both feet against the buttocks of the animal. The buffalo almost purrs with delight.

The man then lets them loose, and they roll voluptuously in the mud. Hooves pointing to the sky, the animals turn from side to side and snort with satisfaction. The man gives them a shower with clean canal water, and home they go. The beasts also have souls. Besides, they work better if well looked after.

The plowing will be repeated a few days later. The soil remains under-water, the irrigation canal gurgling from higher terrace to lower one.

And now the women take over. Fully clad in long sarongs and long-sleeved *kabaya*, blouses, they enter the flooded fields. The wet sarongs stick to their legs. The wet sleeves hinder them in their work. But no, they don't shorten their sarongs or pull up their sleeves. You should be decently dressed when working with Mother, lest she become offended and the harvest be poor. Did you hear her sigh? Like the rustling of a gentle breeze.

Young girls, just children, bring the bunches of tender rice plants, their tops cut off, and throw them into the flooded field at well-aimed distances from one another. The women, their starched *slendangs*, batik scarves, cleverly twisted, folded, and knotted into coquettish sun hats, with not a pin anywhere, line up. Each one takes four rows. They undo the rice plant bunches and push two delicate plants into the watery mud, about three inches apart. They keep the rows remarkably straight, retreating as they go. Their speed is dizzying. With a stopwatch in hand, I once checked. The slowest planted forty in a minute. The fastest did as many as sixty. Do they whisper to each plant? Is there a short grace to be said when four rows are completed? Who could tell?

One terrace after the other is planted. The ripples circle away as the last woman steps out of the water. The hillside is now a giant terraced mirror with thousands of toothpick-thin plants stuck upright on its surface. The sun paints it red and dark green before retiring.

The women go home, change, and wash their planting outfit. It is sa-cred, respected, and not used for any other occasion.

The *sawahs* frogs seem to know the timetable, because after the plant-ing is finished, they settle in the muddy water to croak away their endless love-croaks and happy tidings of good, warm weather. The women come back and work the rows, going forward this time, heaping up, with three fingers, a tiny mud-mound around each and every plant.

Their slim figures are reflected in the *sawahs* mirror as they file home, one behind the other on the narrow *galangans*, the low mud walls between the terraces.

The *sawahs* are left in peace. They remain underwater for ten days, are drained, then are flooded again.

The frogs croak, the *sawahs* fish thrive in their special little pools, and the rice stalks begin to grow, their blades fluttering in the breeze. At night they whisper to each other and even sing aloud if the wind is willing to lend an accompaniment.

Soon the ears appear, looking up, searchingly at the blue sky. Do they think they can solve the mystery of heaven and life on earth?

With bent heads and blushed countenances, they swing in the wind. The birds notice them, and flocks descend to pick at the golden heads.

A little boy lies on his back in the high bamboo structure in the *sawahs*. It has an *atap*, a dry palm-leaf roof, to protect him from the sun. He lazily pushes a bamboo handle with his foot, which jerks the long strings of swinging palm leaves stretched crisscross above the rice fields. The birds are frightened, and with loud chirping they flutter away.

Another little boy, crouched on the *galangan*, seems to be playing with tiny mud balls. He rolls a number of them. Then he places one at the end of a yard-long bamboo stick, gives it a swing, and "pang," it almost hits the one cheeky bird still picking at the ears.

Under the glare of the hot sun, the rice heads bend deeper.

Harvest time has come.

The owner of the field determines the day of the picking. The women of the *kampung*, the village, thirty to forty in number, depending on the size of the field, gather early in the morning. A little clearing is made on one of the terraces and a primitive altar is erected. It is draped with precious sarongs and surrounded by offerings of food and flowers. Rice, one must never forget it has a spirit too, is in a basket placed in the middle of the altar. The *hadji* arrives, says a prayer, gives a benediction, and the harvest may begin.

The women work fast with curiously shaped wooden knives gripped between the third and fourth fingers. Each ear is cut separately and then held together in bunches. Each woman deposits her bunch on her own little pile. By noon the harvesting is finished. The women pick up their bunches and file past the owner, depositing with him five out of every six bunches.

The sixth is their earnings, their payment for the planting and harvesting. The faster they pick, the more they can earn, and so they all pick fast.

On one of the terraces, a tiny bamboo lean-to has been erected, with an *atap*, a roof. For ten days the rice guard, an honored position, will live there. During the day he spreads the bunches of rice out on the field to dry in the sun. At night he piles them up in neat, even mounds. If rain threatens, which he can spot from the approaching clouds, he piles the rice up under the *atap*. After ten days the rice is taken to the owner's granary.

In the fields the plowman has cut down the headless rice stalks and taken them away. He comes once more with his buffaloes and allows them to roam through the fields and eat whatever they find. They have two days. Then it is another's turn. A scantily dressed native boy of about eight or nine appears, a three-yard-long bamboo pole in hand, followed by the village's flock of long-necked brown ducks.

With loud chattering, the ducks invade the terrace. "What a lot of grains are still to be found," they exclaim. "Those stupid buffaloes didn't pick up anything. This is delicious. Shall we try the next terrace as well?"

Two enterprising ducks ready themselves to jump off the *galangan* to the terrace below, but the little boy raises his long, flexible bamboo rod in warning. With heads cocked to one side, the ducks look at it. "Well, perhaps we'd better not go today. Tomorrow he will take us there anyway. Tarsch, tarsch, tarsch...." They are well-trained ducks. They respect the pole.

Late in the afternoon the boy makes his rounds of the terrace and picks up the eggs. He fills a whole basket. The ducks, like a regiment, line up by themselves. This time a drake is in front, leading. The boy follows at the back. The ducks know the way home. Every day for a week or so, they come back to feast on the terraces.

The rice guard has left some time ago with his mound of rice for the owner. The buffaloes have had their feast, and so have the ducks.

The *sawah* is exhausted. She gave all she had. Now she will rest.

The evening breeze picks up a few stray rice straws, whirls them around, and drops them again. The setting sun paints the sky red.

All is peace and satisfaction.

Tropical Nights and Days

It was the sixth day of the most unpleasant, aggravating, enervating, strong, dry, hot wind. It blew day and night. The mistral and sirocco were teases compared to this. The heat was unbearable. The irrigation canals between the rice fields had dried up. The parched soil was cracked, and so were Manggoen's heels. My flowers, thirsty and limp, shook in the wind and bowed their heads. Everyone was irritable. The children quarreled a great deal.

Night fell at last. Before putting the children to bed, I gave them another cold shower. When all was quiet, I settled on the porch with a book.

Five minutes later a pleading little voice peeped, "May I have some water, please?"

According to house rules, the children were not allowed to ask for anything after lights out, but in that trying heat I disregarded the rule and brought them a big jug of cold water.

When all three had drunk, and all three had received another good night kiss, and all good nights were repeated—"good night Daddy, good night Nagymama, Grootvader, Grootmoeder, good night Uncle Laci, Uncle Gabor, and Lizi, and all good friends"—I settled down again to read.

Yes. Good night, Wim. Where are you and how are you? My longing was so intense, I saw him clearly, standing in front of me. My heart bubbled up with love. I stretched out my hands. He vanished.

A chirping cricket broke the silence of the night. I knew the children would never fall asleep with that darn cricket making so much noise in their bedroom, so I got up again, put on the light, and hunted for the noisy intruder. By then she had shut up, bothered, I suppose, by the light. I found her under Yvonne's bed, but by the time I got near enough, she had hopped to a spot under Maya's bed. I went after her again. She jumped on a chair and from there to under the table. The children sided with the cricket and against me. It took me five minutes to catch her.

Finally I caught her in the dust cloth, which I shook out through the open window. When closing the shutters, I pinched my finger on the rusty hinge, which I had been meaning to oil for the last three days. Of course everyone had to inspect the dark purple blister.

"Now really, good night," I said. Putting out the light, I went back to the porch.

I read no more than ten lines when the cricket piped up again. Damn it! She must have slipped out of the dust cloth and had been laughing at me when I shook out the empty cloth.

"All right, Buzzy, you won the first round, but I'll catch you this time," I said to myself, keeping my temper in check.

The renewed hunt was well organized and all took part in it. At last I held her between two fingers. No duster this time. We inspected the cricket closely. She was a beautiful specimen.

"You aren't going to kill her, are you?" Yvonne asked anxiously.

"Of course not," I said. "She is a nice little creature, but she should make her music in the garden, not here."

"How does she make music?" Robi asked.

"She rubs her legs here, against her wings, this way . . ." I loosened my hold on the cricket to demonstrate how she did it, and away she hopped again.

"Verdomme!" I swore in Dutch and sat down on the tiled floor, feeling defeated. Perspiration broke out all over my body, trickling down from my forehead and along my back. Even my knees were wet and itchy. The hammering in my head was so loud I thought my head would burst.

On all fours I went after that cricket, murder in my heart, and caught her. No inspection and no natural history lessons this time. Holding her tightly, I walked out into the garden and released her. The wind had abated. I took a deep breath of hot, dry, scentless air and walked back in on leaden legs.

"Good night once more, and now, really, go to sleep, children," I said.

I buried myself in my book, trying to ignore the heat. A few minutes later, a tiny, anxious voice, as if from very far away, cried out, "Mami, a mosquito." It was Maya this time.

I got up for the fifth time. I put on the light once more, killed the mosquito, sprayed the room, and put the light out.

Back on the porch, I couldn't read anymore. I took an aspirin and sat for some time in the company of my loneliness. I thought of home. It was St. Catherine's day, my mother's name day, the twenty-fifth of November. It would be cold in Budapest. Perhaps the first frost had already sprinkled white powder on the roofs. A wood fire would be burning in the huge, white-tile stove. I could hear it crackling. Friends would be dropping in, filling the room with bunches of chrysanthemums, good wishes, love, and light, happy chatter. Many happy returns, my dearest Mami. Will I ever see you again?

November became December and my thoughts turned to the approaching holiday. The sixth of December, Saint Nicholas day, *Sinterklaas* as the Dutch call the saint, was drawing near. According to Dutch tradition, the fourth-century bishop, who was fond of children during his lifetime, would come in person on that day, accompanied by his black servant, Zwarte Piet, and bring presents to all children. His messages, in rhyme, would be hidden in the presents. It was through these primitive poems that the good saint would praise or admonish each child separately. If for some reason he couldn't come in person, he would send the presents and the messages. I worked on these poems at night, drawing Sinterklaas on each letterhead and composing the celestial messages.

The night was quiet around the bungalow. The rice fields whispered their eternal stories in the delicate breeze, when all of a sudden a warning siren broke the magic. I got up, shut the windows, and pulled the blackout curtains into place. By the light of a well-camouflaged ten-watt bulb, I continued drawing Sinterklaas on his white horse, trotting on the roof of a house. My mind, though, was on the siren. Was this only a practice blackout or were the Americans finally coming?

A few days later a mysterious native dressed in European clothes and wearing dark glasses came by saying that Wim had sent him. He said he was one of the truck drivers who took vegetables into the prisoners' camp and had managed to talk to Wim. The native said Wim was well but rather pale and depressed and in need of cigarettes, clothing, sheets, towels, and so on.

I believed his story except for the sheets. I was overwhelmed with concern. I went into the bedroom to gather some items, when doubt crept into my mind. Wim would surely not have sent an unknown native to me without some sort of note.

I returned and questioned the man. "Why didn't you bring a letter from the captain?"

"The Japanese have taken away all paper and pencils from the prisoners," he replied.

This definitely sounded suspicious. It might be true that all paper and pencils had been confiscated, but unlikely that Wim, or for that matter all of the other officers, wouldn't have kept one small pencil and some paper somewhere.

"I am going to give you some paper and a pencil," I said to the native. "Go back to the captain and ask for his signature. If you return with it, I will give you the clothes and a good tip on top of it."

"Oh, that is impossible, *mevrouw*. There is no time for that. The prisoners will leave camp within an hour and nobody knows where they will be taken. Write him quickly a note. I will take it along with the package."

This definitely didn't click. We had heard that the prisoners had left Tjimahi a few days earlier.

Should I write a letter? I so much wanted to be in touch with Wim, tell him I was all right and the children were fine, but writing seemed risky. If the fellow was a scoundrel, he might deliver the letter to the Japanese, and Wim and I might get into serious trouble for the clandestine correspondence.

Then an idea occurred to me. I took a snapshot of the children and wrote on the back that we were all well. Without signing it, I handed it to the man, repeating my promise of a good tip if he came back with Wim's signature.

He looked sheepish and disappointed when he left, grumbling about my not trusting him. Of course he never came back. The next day I mentioned the encounter at the dairy and heard that the same native had called at every house on the hill where prisoners' wives lived and had collected bundles of clothing from the credulous women.

The dairy, the home of my little, dark, web-fingered Puckie, was the center point on the Lembang road. It was also our information bureau. The people there knew everything and helped everyone. Besides the dairy itself, several bungalows on the large estate housed various families, all Indo-Europeans and all related to one another. Willie Westbroek, whose husband was also a military prisoner, was in charge. Good-looking, small, dark, close to forty, she was common sense and kindness itself. Her older son, thirteen, and daughter, fifteen, came to me for private lessons.

The matriarch of the dairy, an old lady, was a bird lover. She had some twenty-five cages hung around her bungalow, some on the walls, some in the surrounding trees and bushes. A number of these birds were so tame that she kept their cage doors open. They flew in and out, made their nests in the cages, and laid their eggs there. Her most valued winged creatures were the talking beos, black velvety-looking birds, no bigger than merles, with an orange flap on each side of their heads. They had nothing of the cockiness of the parrot and delivered their repertoire in a soft, gurgling tone.

The old lady told me that some Japanese had visited the place and while the soldiers were whistling to the birds, the beos started showing off their skill: *"Dag mevrouw,"* the first one gurgled. *"Doe je best, Amerika,"* a second one chimed in. *"Cheerio Churchill,"* came from a third cage. The Japanese asked the nearby servant girl what the birds were saying. "They are asking for food," was her quick-witted reply.

The rumor that women and children were being sent to internment camps turned out to be true. Those being interned were being housed in the empty homes in the evacuated quarters of the town. Written notices summoned the first batch of women. A notice in the local papers also stated that all European women were "welcome" in the camp. Housing and food would be free, as would Nippon's protection.

Most of us found this invitation hilarious, but to many women who lived on only what they could get from the sale of their belongings, the move seemed attractive. Those living outside of Bandoeng were especially interested in finding some protection against burglars.

Burglaries had been increasing so rapidly that the natives themselves organized a sort of civil guard in every village. Our night watchman frightened me badly the first time I heard his steps on our terrace in the middle of the night. When I found out who he was, I gave him a cup of coffee and some cookies every night. I noticed he slept on the terrace for a few hours each night from then on.

I called on Mr. Wester accompanied by two new Hungarian acquaintances, Viola Boronkay Ankerman and Klemi Pajzs Meyer, both of whom had fled from Medan in Sumatra and whose husbands were imprisoned with Wim. Mr. Wester was the Swedish consul who represented the interests of Hungary in the Japanese-occupied Dutch East Indies. Wester advised us to go to the local authorities in Bandoeng and have our registration cards changed from Dutch to Hungarian nationality. Doing so, he said, might keep us out of camp, at least for a while.

A few days later we went to the Bandoeng town hall and waited for hours. Native officials pushed us around and sent us from one clerk to another. Suddenly I caught sight of Wester, who had come to the town hall on some business. He was about to slip into the chief clerk's office when I tugged on his sleeve. With a smile, I thrust our papers into his hands. He had no chance to say no. Within an hour, which otherwise might have taken the whole morning, all was ready and we were in possession of our corrected registration cards.

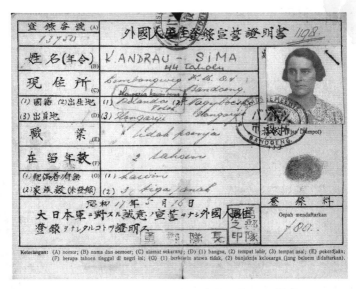

Klara's registration/ID card, Bandoeng, 1942

Wester also told us that he was no longer representing the interests of Hungary. The Japanese had appointed a certain Mr. Trethan to do this. My immediate reaction was that Mr. Trethan would obviously be representing Japanese interests and not Hungarian ones if he was an official of Nippon.

Nevertheless, I called on Trethan, who lived outside Bandoeng in a native quarter with his native wife. He was polite but one hundred percent pro-Axis in his feelings. A big blackboard in his entrance hall scribbled full of Japanese writing was obviously meant to catch all eyes. Cheap, I thought.

Trethan explained that Java was a first-line battlefront, and, consequently, the military authorities ruled over civil ones. These authorities had not decided as yet whether Hungary would be considered a neutral or a pro-Axis country, or whether Hungarian women married to Dutchmen were Hungarian or Dutch. Trethan told me that were I to get a summons to go to a camp, I should contact him in his office in Bandoeng and he would see whether anything could be done about it.

As I was near town anyway, I decided to visit the women and children's camp to see what it was like. The third-rate houses that had been evacuated to create the camp were rapidly filling up. Twenty to thirty people were now living in a house where one family had lived before. A two-car garage sheltered four to six people. Laundry hung on every porch. Tiny gardens were filled with furniture and odds and ends that the overcrowded rooms couldn't hold. Small children sat outside on chamber pots. Women cooked over charcoal burners. In short, the sight was dismal. On the perimeter of the camp, natives were hammering poles into the ground for the barbed-wire fencing and bamboo wall that would surround these quarters.

I knew that many women had moved into the camp voluntarily because protection, food, and living quarters were being provided for nothing, but my reaction was that anything was better than being herded together this way. I didn't mind working fourteen to sixteen hours a day as long as I could keep our freedom and our privacy and protect the children's dream world among the whispering *sawahs* and my lovely flowers in the big garden on the hillside.

More Things Happen

The number 13 isn't considered unlucky for nothing. On December 13 I received a camp summons. So the inevitable had arrived after all.

How were we going to live in captivity? What did it feel like to be a captive? Suppose they shut the gates and starved us to death? I wouldn't mind anything, were I alone. But the children. These were my dark thoughts while I biked to Bandoeng to find out whether something could be done to avoid going to camp.

First I wanted to talk to Trethan in his office, to see whether he could and would help me as he had promised. For a few minutes, while parking my bike in front of the former Dutch government building, I watched the people going in. At the gate a native policeman stopped those entering, checked their papers, then let them proceed. Next the visitors entered a small waiting room where some four or five Japanese soldiers were sitting. Here the visitor had to bow deeply in front of each soldier. One of the soldiers would examine the visitor's papers. If they were found to be in order, the visitor could ascend the stairs to the official she had come to see.

Such a strong feeling of rebellion and loathing seized me at the thought of going through this comedy of deep bowing and more bowing that I mounted my bike and left. My Hungarian temperament was probably responsible for this, but I just couldn't make myself bow deeply to a number of ordinary soldiers in order to get to Trethan. And who knew whether I would even obtain his help. I could have gone to his home later in the afternoon, but my summons was to report at the camp by twelve noon.

This first summons was only for checking papers and getting a date to enter the camp. If Trethan could help me, surely he would do so even if I had a date, I mused. So, slowly and reluctantly, I pedaled toward the camp.

I must have been deeply buried in my thoughts not to notice the sudden sharp turn the boy on the bike in front of me made. I ran straight into him and we both fell down. The two bikes, the boy, and I were all in a heap. We disentangled ourselves, and, ignoring our bruises, anxiously examined our bikes. They didn't seem damaged. We apologized to each other and went on our way.

From afar I could see the high camp fence. In front of the gate, a small building housed the camp officials. The recently called-up women, with summons and identity cards in hand, had formed a line outside. I took my place at the end of the line. After about half an hour's wait, I was directed to a bald fellow at a window. He looked neither Japanese nor Malay, but a little of each race.

He went through my papers and asked me what nationality my parents were.

"Hungarian," I said.

"Go home," he said.

Go home? Surely there was something wrong with this melonhead. Did he know what he was saying?

"Go quickly, before he changes his mind," whispered the woman behind me.

Still perplexed, I asked the man for some document showing my status in case of a street arrest or house search. He scribbled something in Japanese on a scrap of paper and stamped it with a big rubber stamp. This stamp was worth more than any writing or signature. The East had respect for rubber stamps.

I fled from there as quickly as I could, wondering who had decided 13 was an unlucky number.

On the way home I dropped in to see my Hungarian acquaintance Viola Boronkay. Although she hadn't received a summons, she had decided to move into camp voluntarily. I couldn't understand why. I wished her and Klemi, my other Hungarian acquaintance, good luck. We said goodbye and I sped on to Elsje Schouten. For five minutes we celebrated my freedom with an orangeade.

I arrived home to hugs and rejoicing at the news that we were still free. Pinkie took part in the rejoicing by performing his high jumps, though this time he had no Christmas wreath to shred.

We didn't make a wreath at all that year, but almost all my Christmas preparations were completed for the feast of the Nativity: homemade sweets (I had made fondants and peanut brittle, which I also made for others for some extra income from time to time), cookies, the refurbished tree ornaments, and real candles. All this I had done clandestinely, of course, because in reality the Angel was supposed to bring the decorated tree on Christmas Eve.

Besides making these preparations, I was taking care of Yvonne, who had not only the usual three-to-four-day tropical fever but was producing alarming wheezing sounds, as though she had bronchitis or asthma.

The last time I had gone into Bandoeng in search of Christmas candles, a native in the street had spat at me. This was my first public insult. At the beginning of the Japanese occupation, a small fraction of the native population behaved abominably toward Europeans. In out-of-the-way places they murdered many a white planter. By the time the Japanese regime had become firmly established, however, the natives received more beatings than they did good wages. Even the small hostile anti-European groups apparently realized how much better off they had been under the Dutch.

The Japanese hadn't taken over the country to run it as it had been run before, or at least to try to do so. They had taken it over to exploit and destroy it, or so it seemed. All business came to a standstill. Almost all commercial enterprises and banks were closed. A great number of the tea and coffee plantations had been destroyed. And the famous quinine factory, the biggest in the Far East, was working at only five percent of its former capacity while malaria was a greater danger than ever.

Christmas Eve was here again. Yvonne was still in bed, so I sent just the two other girls over to Mrs. Merz. Manggoen and I decorated the tree and put the small presents under it. Then I joined the girls at Mrs. Merz's. Manggoen was left to light the candles and, when she had done so, to call us. Soon she came running and shouting from afar, "Maya, Robi, the tree has come." She loved her role in this mysterious make-believe game. Her heart was as young as a child's.

We took Mrs. Merz with us and entered the house through the bed-room where I picked Yvonne up in my arms and we all walked to the lighted tree.

The Christmas tree, the symbol of Peace on Earth was here again. Where was Peace?

Robi's eyes nearly popped out in awe. Maya trembled with excite-ment. We sang "Silent Night" and remembered Daddy and all our good friends in a short prayer. Then they opened the gifts.

Afterwards we had a light supper and played some games: The chil-dren went to bed later than usual. When all was quiet I chatted for a while with Mrs. Merz about past Christmases. After she left I sat alone for hours, listening to the howling wind tearing along the *sawahs*.

The next day, Christmas Day, we heard of more arrests in the streets of Bandoeng, of people being picked up haphazardly, of more beatings, and of long hours of bowing in front of the Masters of the East.

And so Time brought us New Year's Eve.

Following an old family tradition, we made, accompanied by laughter and merriment, a life-sized doll that personified the Old Year. His body consisted of two pillows with my coat around them. The old man's thighs were rolled-up blankets and his lower limbs were Wim's riding boots. The head was a stuffed pillowcase with a charcoal-painted face, topped off with a big-brimmed hat and a long, white cotton beard. He held a small doll in his arms that represented the New Year. Once he was ready, we put the old man in an easy chair in the corner of the room.

Mrs. Merz came over in the evening for the melting of the lead, an amusing way of fortune-telling. To the children's delight, she was startled when she first saw the old man in the corner. The children felt altogether grown-up that evening because they were allowed to stay up until ten.

Everyone received a cup of cocoa and a few cookies. We took turns melting the lead and pouring it into a bucket of cold water to divine the future. I acted as chief fortune-teller because I knew the wishes of all present and could interpret, accordingly, the odd shapes that the hot metal took in the cold water.

After the children's bedtime, Mrs. Merz and I sat up to greet the New Year. She became sleepy, however, and dozed off. I tiptoed to the clock, pushed the hands to midnight, and woke her up, wishing her a happy New Year. After helping her home through the *sawahs*, I returned home, reset the clock, and alone watched the New Year creep in. Welcome 1943.

Next morning we received a lively present: four beautiful puppies from our longhaired, stray mongrel, Bobby, who had attached herself to our household some months earlier. What a joy that was for the children.

We spent New Year's Day between petting and praising Bobby for the lovely family she had produced and making a calendar for the next twelve months. Inserting the days of the week and the months was easy, but who knew the date Easter fell on? I had to bike down to the Catholic church to find that out.

All the children's free time was spent watching Bobby and her family. The girls had never seen puppies suckling and were upset when they became rougher and rougher at it, pushing each other out of the way to a more profitable teat or tugging at the rosy nipples ferociously if they didn't yield milk right away. We named the puppies Lady, Beertje (Little Bear), Sleepy, and Fuzzy.

When their eyes were open, we enjoyed playing with them. For fun we would place them in a row about ten feet away from us, each of us facing our own puppy. Then we would call out our puppy's name, clap our hands, and whistle to induce them to come to us. Whichever puppy reached its mistress first was declared the winner of the race. At the beginning it looked more like a tortoise race.

Then a lot of unpleasant things happened.

Robi cut the sole of her foot deeply when she stepped on a piece of broken glass. I was unable to stop the bleeding for hours. I sent for the Dutch doctor, a great friend of the Japanese, who lived a half mile uphill from our place. Instead of coming, he sent word that I should take her to the Bandoeng hospital, an impossible task in the dark and with no transportation available. So I left the tourniquet on her ankle and sat up with her all night, holding her leg vertical while she slept. The next day the bleeding stopped, but I kept her in bed for a few days because her whole foot was sore from the deep wound.

Next Mrs. Merz came over in a flurry and asked me to come over and have a look at her garage. Burglars had broken the lock on the door and had taken the new tarpaulin that had covered Blue Bird, our Tjimahi friend's car. We had the lock repaired and engaged a night watchman. Had we been wiser and less optimistic, we could have spared ourselves the trouble, because the next morning Blue Bird herself was gone. Strangely enough, nobody knew anything about its disappearance, not even the night watchman.

A terrifying night with Maya followed. At about eleven I heard her moan. I went over to her bed, thinking she had had a bad dream. She was red in the face and extremely hot. I took her temperature: 103°. She started vomiting and complained of a stomachache. Her temperature shot up to 104°.

For a brief moment I considered putting her on the bike and taking her down to the hospital, but I had no light on the bike and the police had confiscated our flashlights some time ago. I was also worried that the shaking might burst her appendix. Worst of all, I had no one to talk things over with.

I changed the cold-water compresses on her head and on her tummy as often as I could without disturbing her sleep. The minutes crept by. The hours would not pass.

At four her moaning seemed to have lessened and she was not as hot as she had been. Her short puffing breaths changed into regular, quiet breathing. At five she didn't seem hot at all. By six, when the sun came up, she was back to normal.

I kept her in bed all morning, and at noon, after school let out, I took her to the doctor in Bandoeng. "Absolutely nothing wrong," he said. "It must have been a fever trick of the tropical climate, or just an upset stomach."

A new Japanese order came to advance the clocks an hour, to match Nippon-time. Japanese soldiers would walk into any house and check whether the order had been carried out. Whenever they found a clock showing the old time, the owners were beaten and the clock confiscated.

For several weeks I had been negotiating with the post office, with Trethan, and with Wester, to ask the Japanese officials to allow me to send a telegram to my brother Laci at the Hungarian legation in Lisbon. I hoped the telegram would go through diplomatic channels.

When all obstacles had been removed, I produced a much chewed-over draft of the telegram. The Japanese authorities objected to its wording, which said that I and my family were well. The Japanese argued that I didn't know whether my husband was well or not. For that matter I didn't know whether he was still alive. Such realistic talk made me wince. I feared that if only the children and I were mentioned in the message, Laci might think that Wim was dead.

The Japanese did not want Wim mentioned. There was no alternative and, thinking that some news was better than none, I sent off the telegram saying that the children and I were well. Laci would surely find a way to communicate the news to our mother and our brother Gabor in Hungary. I didn't know until after the war that my worry about the wording of the message had been for naught because Laci never received the telegram.

Mrs. Merz, upset, came over to recount that three native policemen had appeared at her bungalow, asking whether she had buried anything. She said no, having forgotten about the tin box of Shell receipts and our merry night-digging party. The policemen said they would search the garden.

"Go ahead," she replied.

The three policemen thumped the ground here and there with a long iron rod. Within five minutes they were under the little tree we had planted over the buried box. The men started digging and the box came into view. They ordered Mrs. Merz to lift it out and take off the lid, apparently afraid it might contain a bomb. They seemed disappointed at the contents, but took the box and the receipts with them. So the trees and bushes had eyes and ears even in the dark of night.

"What will happen to us?" Mrs. Merz asked me.

I didn't know, of course, but I calmed her down, saying we would cross that bridge when we got to it. Not very original, but comforting. I told her that if the police questioned her about the receipts, she could put all the blame on me. I hurried to Bandoeng to warn Frits Schouten about what had happened.

For days we lived in a sort of panic, jumping at the sight of every person opening the garden gate, but nobody came to take us away. The days passed. The weeks went by and so many other things happened that slowly we forgot about it. Apparently, so did the officials.

Yvonne's health wasn't good. On the advice of our Bandoeng doctor, I decided to have her tonsils removed. On the day before her ninth birthday, we were summoned to be in the hospital by 7 a.m. She was not allowed to eat before the operation. Soon after sunrise, therefore, we got on the bike and coasted downhill, our tummies rumbling.

In the hospital I was allowed to take Yvonne to the children's ward and put her to bed. Another hug, another kiss, then I fled lest the supreme effort she was making to keep back those heavy tears should fail.

Two hours of waiting followed. It seemed endless. I walked up and down in that little waiting room, memorizing the floor linoleum pattern by heart and counting the legs on the chairs. They all seemed to have four. After what seemed like ages, dear Elsje Schouten came to help with the waiting.

Finally the door of the anteroom of the operating theater opened, and the surgeon, looking more like a butcher with soapsuds up to his elbows and bloodstains on his apron, announced that the operation was successful. Not a word more. Rather curt, I thought. I stood there, expecting some little detail or a comforting word. "You can go home," was all that the doctor added. All right, all right, I replied wordlessly, but my heart will stay here with my child whether you like it or not, you hard-hearted, dried-out-soul of a doctor.

When passing the children's pavilion, I peeked into the ward from the garden and saw Yvonne's little brown head on the pillow. A nurse told me she had been given an injection to sleep.

I biked home.

We spent the afternoon with Yvonne's birthday preparations: baking the cake (as before in the tin box over the charcoal), wrapping the presents, and decorating Yvonne's chair with flowers. Decorating the birthday person's chair is a lovely Dutch custom that thrilled the children every time.

The following morning I went to pick Yvonne up. She was pale and wouldn't utter a word when she saw me. I hired a *kretek* to make the trip home easier for her. We had covered about a mile when she burst out crying and buried her head in my lap. I was afraid her crying might cause the fresh wound to bleed, so I started telling her a fairy tale to distract her. By the time we reached home, I had told her a number of them and she had forgotten about crying.

The rest of the day passed in a happy birthday mood. Everybody was amused by Yvonne's whispering voice. She wasn't allowed to eat the birthday cake, however, so we saved it for later.

Then a bit of sunshine in the form of a telegram from my brother Laci. Trethan gave it to me in Bandoeng. I hurried home with the treasure in my pocket. Outside of town I settled in the shade of a lone palm tree and reread it a few times. It said that everybody was well at home. Maybe it was an answer to mine, I thought. This slight contact with the real world made me feel as if we were living on the moon.

Then something sad again: Cingi Pipeke died. She was a blind, dear, little field mouse, just a few days old. A native boy had found her in the *sawahs* and given her to Yvonne. A small cardboard box, padded with white cotton batting and covered with a mosquito net, was her bed. Out of wax paper we made a tiny funnel and tried, unsuccessfully, to feed her diluted cow's milk. On the second day, a drop of blood appeared from one of her nostrils and a little later she was dead. Yvonne was heartbroken.

We arranged a beautiful funeral, with lots of flowers. Hers was a first class burial.

On the anniversary of the Japanese occupation, Mrs. Merz and I sat down together and, for fun, enumerated the advantages of the Japanese regime as far as we and our households were concerned:

No bread and no flour, only ersatz
No butter
No canned food of any kind
No toothbrushes and no toothpaste
No shoe polish
No dress material and no knitting wool
No rubber or elastic
No needles
No writing paper, no pencils, no notebooks
No wine, no liquor
No matches
No soap

No kerosene, no gasoline
No cars
And no windows, just bars, on many houses

Strangely, we had grown accustomed to these conditions. We didn't mind a bit not having bread. We had gotten used to the ersatz bread. Made of cassava flour, corn flour, and goodness knows what else, we found it to be chewy and heavy, but we liked it.

We grew to like the strong aroma of coconut oil, which replaced butter for cooking. We smeared lard instead of butter on bread. Instead of soap, Manggoen did the laundry using the water of soaked wood ashes. For bathing we used the soaked roots of a plant that produced a good lather.

I bought a few five-gallon cans of kerosene on the black market, which I hoped would see us through the war. We used little kerosene because most of the cooking was done on charcoal.

The old system of keeping the fire going replaced matches. At night we buried the hot coals in ashes. Manggoen was our vestal virgin. If the coals went out, as they sometimes did, Manggoen would walk to the nearest neighbor, a few hundred yards away, and get some glowing coals from their fire. The custom was established that for a few glowing coals, you paid twice the number in black charcoal. Only fair and inexpensive, I thought.

With cotton thread still available in a few shops that had stayed open, I bought a lot and knitted eighteen panties for the children. Panties were the most important item in their wardrobe since they wore practically nothing else all day.

For Easter I sewed new dresses for the girls from the flowered curtains in the living room. A good soul from the dairy helped me with the machine stitching. Besides giving the girls new dresses for Easter, I hid colored eggs in the garden for them. Yvonne was sure she saw the Easter bunny.

The Japanese army had forbidden their officers from visiting European women. I suppose they were afraid of sentimental ties. We heard of a Dutch woman who had had a baby by a Japanese officer. He brought her bunches of flowers while she was in the hospital. Later, however, the baby was taken away from her to be cared for by a Japanese woman. Because the child was a boy, he was eventually sent to Japan, to the father's family.

High bamboo fences surrounded several newly erected brothels in town. The Japanese soldiers were brought to them in trucks and given a few hours of leisure before the arrival of the next truckload. The women in these houses were mostly natives, but I was told that some imported Japanese women were among them as well.

The Japanese military women we saw in the streets in their navy blue uniforms were anything but pretty. No Madame Butterflies among them. The majority of them were short, heavily built, and inelegant, many with grand-piano legs.

A telephone message came from Elsje Schouten to come to town. I biked in. In tears she told me that her husband Frits had been arrested and that she would follow him in a month or two. As a special favor, though, they would get family internment because Frits had worked for the Japanese. This meant that Elsje would be allowed to stay with Frits in the same camp, together with other couples. We said goodbye to each other and hoped to meet sometime, somewhere, after the war.

The Hungarian doctor Ujlaki of Bandoeng had also been locked up. Not long afterwards his wife was locked up as well.

Our ranks were thinning. Of the twenty Hungarian women in Bandoeng married to Dutchmen, fourteen had already been called up. When I asked Trethan why we six were still free, he said the decision depended on the quality of the whisky the Japanese who signed the summons had drunk the night before.

Another great surprise: money had come from my brother Laci by cablegram through diplomatic channels. I went to the bank with Wester, the Swedish consul. Everything seemed in order for me to withdraw the money. After having signed numerous papers, I was standing at the cashier's window when a high bank official gave the order to stop the transaction. I was told that because my husband was Dutch, I would have to put in a written application for the money. This was sheer nonsense, of course. They wanted to keep the money but decided to confiscate it in a "civilized" way since diplomatic sources were involved.

The end of July arrived and again we held our official school exam, the same as we had the year before. The day ended with games, gymkhana, and cool drinks. We all hoped to open the new school year a month later, on September 1.

The day after the exam, the tail end of a tornado hit us. The rain came down in torrents. The wind tore at everything in its path. We watched as a few of our roof tiles sailed over the treetops. A minute later the ceiling of the closed-in porch started to leak. Soon water was dripping everywhere.

The big drops, hammering on the roof, would have made the Salvation Army drum sound like the simple tapping of fingers on a table. Bursts of lightning and thunder punctuated the infernal noise of the wind and rain. The children, frightened, followed me from room to room, not suspecting that I didn't feel at ease myself. We salvaged what we could. They weren't sure whether seeing pools of water on their beds, wading ankle-deep in the soft rainwater in their bedroom, or being wet from head to foot was serious trouble or just funny.

The sky was black by then. The electricity conked out and I was trying for the third time to light a candle. A sudden flash blinded us, followed by a crash that almost punctured our eardrums. "That's Mrs. Merz's old wairingin," Manggoen cried out. The natives consider the wairingin tree to be sacred. They believe that if it is chopped down or gets hit by lightning, disaster is sure to follow.

For an hour the storm played havoc. Then it stopped as suddenly as it had started. Great silence followed, as though Nature were catching her breath. Everywhere and everything was dripping. We lit a few charcoal fires. I made hot tea and gave some to everybody. Then we tried to clean things up.

Mrs. Merz came over to report that her wairingin had, indeed, been hit by lightning. Split in two. We wondered whether we should believe in the folktale that disaster would be sure to follow.

Two weeks later we again had a lovely *Mondschein* party, not suspecting it would be our last in freedom, or at least relative freedom. We had been leading a strange, lonely life in the *sawahs* for a year and a half now. For over a year there had been no news from Wim. All we heard were rumors. Rumors that many prisoners had been taken to Japan.

4
Wim
March 1942

*Thousands of prisoners were crammed into the cargo holds of the hell
ships, sometimes with not even enough room to sit much less lie down for
the duration of the voyage, which often lasted two or three weeks.*

Internment in Bandoeng

The Dutch governor general's message of capitulation came over the radio on March 8, 1942. Following it, a strange calm settled over the town. For Wim it meant that his personal intense struggle of the last several weeks against the inevitable was over. He and the other men assembled and burned sensitive records, then returned to their families to wait by the radio for further instructions. During the next few days, the military men were called up several times, once to relinquish their handguns, another time to assemble and stand around but then to go home again, none the wiser for what would come next.

Finally, on March 12, Wim and the other air force officers received orders to bring a change of clothes, a blanket, a pillow, and eating utensils and report to a former school. A hastily erected barbed wire fence surrounded the abandoned and neglected building. On the first night Wim and the others slept on the bare, hard floors of the various classrooms. A plea for help resulted in the arrival, the next day, of a string of taxis and cars filled with the men's wives bringing mattresses.

The Japanese told Wim and the others that they would be interned until further notice, while also promising that normal life would be restored as quickly as possible. They were given forms to fill out, to state what their jobs had been before the war, a hopeful sign. Several of the engineers who had worked for oil companies were whisked away, presumably to their old jobs. Thus many of the remaining ones believed their captors' assertion that life would return to normal in a matter of weeks. Who of them could imagine that it would be three and half years of ever-worsening internment conditions before they would be free again, if they survived at all?

A nearby army barracks served the men rice in various forms for each of the three meals: a thin, gruel-like rice cereal for breakfast, plain un-adorned boiled rice for lunch, and plain boiled rice plus a watery soup for dinner. For the first week the women were allowed to visit their men twice a day and bring them cooked food and clean laundry. By the second week, visits were restricted to once a day. In short order the men organized a can-teen, run by Wim. Two officers were allowed to leave the "school" daily to do the shopping, which improved the cuisine considerably.

The uncertainty and the inactivity made the men restless. On the twen-tieth of March, several of the officers, all graduates of Delft University, found a way to liven things up by organizing a celebration of the founding of their student fraternity. With sherry flowing freely from bottles a few of the wives had smuggled in in their food hampers, the men took a brief break from the reality of their situation.

Shortly after their fraternity party came news that they would be trans-ferred to another camp, a former juvenile detention center on the outskirts of Bandoeng. Surprisingly, the Japanese sent trucks to move the mattress-es, while the men, carrying the rest of their belongings, marched the three miles to their new home.

In a small office of the detention center, the prisoners discovered a working phone. For the weeks that it continued to operate, it was a lifeline to their former lives and families and to what was happening in the out-side world. For Wim it made his family seem less distant, especially now that Klara and the children had moved back to their place in the *sawahs*. Because the isolated bungalow had no phone, Klara called Wim from the dairy. On April fifteenth she called him so he could wish his daughter Maya a happy birthday. At that time Wim also told Klara the bad news that visits would no longer be allowed.

As at the school, a nearby army barracks supplied the meals, the same nutritionally inadequate menu as before. The men, however, enlivened the meals with curry powder and other spices brought in by Chinese vendors, who were allowed into the compound to sell items such as condiments, cigarettes, and soap. The latter was important because, with the end of allowed visits from their wives, the men had to do their own laundry.

The vendors also served a crucial communication function. When the Japanese had discovered the live phone, they had abruptly killed it. The Chinese, therefore, stepped into the breach by agreeing to take out the prisoners' messages for a good tip, as long as they were written on tiny scraps of paper.

Other than the Japanese captain's daily morning visit to hand out instructions to the Dutch colonel, who was the senior officer of the camp, the Japanese were practically invisible. The Japanese guards stayed outside the gate and out of the affairs of the men. The prisoners were in charge of the camp's internal routines.

Escaping was relatively easy, but the punishment, if caught, was extreme. To set an example, the POWs were forced to watch as three recaptured escapees were bayoneted to death.

To stay occupied, the prisoners developed an extensive, self-styled, open university. May became the month of classes. Courses were offered in a variety of topics by whoever felt qualified to teach them, for example, foreign language instruction or lectures on electrical engineering or the intricacies of the Paris metro system. Elaborate programs were published to keep prisoners informed of the smorgasbord of lessons available to enrich their lives or at least to stave off depression, anxiety, and ennui.

Amusement came in the form of Wim Kan, a Dutch cabaret entertainer who had been touring Java with his group when the army roped him in. While leading an impromptu sing-along, he sprinkled it with his well-known patter, jokes, and songs. The evening was such a success that the colonel approached the Japanese captain and asked him to allow Wim Kan to go to his home and gather up some of his cabaret material for future shows. With his sheet music and joke material, he would be able to provide regular shows for the prisoners and, not incidentally, for the Japanese. The latter liked the music but, luckily, didn't understand the pointed camp jokes.

Thus, accompanied by a Japanese guard and with his fellow-prisoners' ribald cracks ringing in his ears, Wim Kan visited his house. And his wife.

In the next show he inserted a comment into his patter that the guard had even allowed him to see his wife in private, adding, "But it cost me five guilders, which is the first time I had to pay for it!"

Wim, noting other high and low points and events of their time in this second camp, listed the following:

Inadequate meals resulting in an increase of smuggled-in food

Setting up of a canteen, which provided milk, butter, eggs, cheese

Relinquishing of all badges and decorations

Shaving of heads because the prevalent theory held that the Japanese wouldn't beat bald-headed men and shaved heads helped to combat lice

Turning in of binoculars, knives, batons

Turning in of civilian clothes

Witnessing incidents of women being beaten when retrieving dropped notes from the men

Participating in exercise/sports in the form of gymnastics and soccer

Camps in Tjimahi and Batavia

By the end of May, the prisoners were on the move again. They were given only one day to get ready and could take along only what they could carry. Frantic activity ensued as everyone tried to fashion halters or straps to carry their suitcases and other gear as backpacks for the march to the new camp. No trucks this time, so the mattresses had to be left behind. Their destination was Tjimahi, a garrison town about twelve miles from Bandoeng. The men would be housed in the barracks of a former Dutch military training camp.

Wim quickly wrote a good-bye note to Klara, telling her he was well and that she shouldn't worry and should try to stay cheerful. He ended the tiny note with the words, "Thanks for looking after the children. Everything will end well." He had to be optimistic. He refused to dwell on dark thoughts of what could happen. How lucky he was to have married a woman on whose strength he could count.

The men mustered early the next morning but were kept endlessly waiting. The column finally started to move under the midday broiling sun. Bellowing Japanese soldiers herded the prisoners like cattle and warned the townspeople to keep their distance. Despite the short notice, the whispering wind had disseminated the news of the impending move. At the first main intersection, hundreds of women waited, waving wildly, calling out the names of their loved ones, some crying. The din was deafening. Keeping their own emotions in check, the prisoners could do nothing more than wave back.

They marched for hours without a single stop. Undoubtedly the Japanese guards were afraid that if they did stop, the women would gain access to the men. As it was, the soldiers chased the women away, even using whips to lash the ones who came too near. Many of the women followed the men the entire twelve miles until the prisoners reached their destination, one of the newer barracks on the outskirts of Tjimahi. Because the camp was already half occupied by other groups of officers and a company of infantry, Wim's air force group had to adapt itself to the existing routine.

The bathing facilities in Tjimahi, which included real showers, were an unexpected luxury. Even the latrines were better than the ones in Bandoeng, with running water abundantly cascading through the narrow troughs over which the men squatted.

In place of the mattresses they had been forced to leave behind, the men slept on stretchers made of mats woven from coconut husk rope attached to wooden supports. Unfortunately, however, these soon became infested with lice.

At first there was nothing like the open-university classes they had set up at the Bandoeng camp, so the men whiled away the hours by playing bridge every day, all day. They kept this up for several months until one by one they became sick of it and quit. Having overdosed on the game, Wim stayed away from bridge for the rest of his life. Many were happy when the university classes started up again. They helped to break up the monotony of prison life.

Wim also learned some Japanese. Besides mastering Japanese numbers and a list of characters and their sounds, he memorized basic military commands, such as, *attention, assemble, at ease, forward march, stop, salute, double-time*, and the like. The men subsequently drilled using Japanese military commands.

In early June Wim received a postcard from Klara written in Malay, probably the only language allowed by the Japanese authorities. Roughly translated, it read:

4 June [1942]

Dear Biga,

Here everything is fine. Children are healthy, I also. Yvonne gets piano lessons from me.

I hope your food is better now. Maybe I can send packages with food later.

Lots of love and strength from the three children and me.

Klara

During the months in Tjimahi, Wim kept close watch on the progress of the war. From news on a contraband radio (he mentions BBC) and perhaps from news brought in by the Chinese vendors, Wim jotted down all rumors and reports of what battles were being waged, where troops were being deployed, and which side controlled militarily strategic areas. He hoped to draw a favorable conclusion regarding the imminent defeat of enemy forces from this information.

For those who still had money, shopping for food and amenities was possible. Every week the men could place a written order, and a few days later in would enter a convoy of donkey carts, delivering fresh fruit, spices, sugar, condensed canned milk, butter, matches, cigarettes, soap, paper and pencils, shaving cream, razors, and even shoe polish. Who would have thought there would be a need for the latter?

Notes or packages could also still on occasion be smuggled into the camp. Wim was heartened when he received such a package from Klara, containing six pairs of knitted socks, a shirt, and vitamins. He marveled at what it must have cost her in stamina and courage to bike from Bandoeng and find a way to get these to him.

To allay her concern for him and to make light of the prison conditions and his confinement, Wim sent a note to Klara on August 21, which she never received:

Thanks 2 postcards June and July and note 8/13. Am perfectly healthy, fit, and in good spirits; here sort of sanatorium life,

*with very simple menu—rice + rice + rice + (apparently) just
enough vitamins (therefore, pills being saved for possible
future harder times), result weighing now 67 kg. Lots of
sunning and plenty of time for misc. studies and hobbies—
among others, planning and detailing future Aracs building
alteration and addition to your heart's desire. Glad to note any
worries either side out of question and quite unnecessary.
Both keeping up spirit, form, etc. etc. till next "testmatch."
Tell also to kids. Endeavoring picking up some Hungarian
from Viola's husband.*

In October they were moved again. This time to an enormous barrack complex in the center of Tjimahi, surrounded by gigantic wairingin trees. The occupants of this camp, who were mostly Indo-Europeans, that is, of mixed Indonesian and European extraction, had established useful links with the natives outside the camp and had set up, with the tacit approval of the Japanese, a daily *passar*, or market. The various *kongsi*, casual groups that came together for mutual benefit, would order in bulk and produce delectables to augment the meals for one or two cents a portion.

This relatively comfortable life, however, was short-lived. Soon after arriving in this second camp in Tjimahi, the men were assembled and again told to list their professional qualifications. Engineers and air force personnel were automatically classified as being "technical" and were issued red ribbons to be worn at all times.

A few weeks later the order came to be ready the next day to entrain for Batavia, with only one bag or suitcase allowed per person. The following morning the Japanese marched them to the train station and herded them onto a string of third-class coaches, a superior means of transport compared to the cattle trucks usually used. They were accorded this luxury, the Japanese lieutenant explained, because they were *shoko*, officers. The Japanese had respect for the hierarchy of command.

They traveled all day, reaching Batavia by nightfall. After a quick half-hour march from the station, they were once again incarcerated in a school, this time one in the Chinese district in downtown Batavia. Their camp was an island prison surrounded by the roiling life of Batavia's Chinatown. Although an architecturally interesting building, decorated with wooden scrollwork, the school was infested with lice, apparently brought in with the wooden bed boards on which the men would be sleeping for the next several weeks.

Shortly after arriving, they were told they would soon be sailing to Japan, selected for this honor because they were "red bands," that is, technical people. But because of the long journey ahead, they would first be inoculated against various tropical diseases and checked for dysentery. The three Dutch doctors in their group, who were assigned to inoculation duty, assured the six hundred prisoners that the vaccines were safe, having been manufactured by a well-known pharmaceutical firm in Java. The check for dysentery was another story.

After all the men had received their inoculations, Japanese military nurses set up long tables with rows of glass dishes. The men were lined up in columns in front of the tables. Through an interpreter the first man in line was told to drop his pants and bend over. When he hesitated, a few kicks persuaded him to comply. As all looked on with apprehension, one of the nurses pushed a glass rod into his behind, pulled it out, and smeared the sample onto a glass dish.

The intention was to determine whether dysentery bacteria would develop in the culture. Although the men would undergo this procedure many more times, what the Japanese did with these cultures was a mystery. The Japanese never used them as an early diagnostic tool.

The living conditions at the Chinese school were cramped. The food, however, which was contracted out to a Chinese group, was good, with a varied menu. In addition the prisoners didn't feel isolated. Day and night the sounds and mysterious, pungent aromas of the East surrounded them as the turmoil of daily life swirled around the high walls of the school.

To Changi on Singapore Island

On January 4, 1943, Wim and the others, each allowed only a single suitcase or bag, boarded a miserable-looking ship in Tandjong Priok, Batavia's harbor. They recognized it as a ship that had been sunk at the harbor entrance in the last days of the fighting before the capitulation. If this old tub was to be the transport to Japan, they would need heaven's help to survive. The situation, however, was not as dire as it seemed. The ship, after it had been raised, had been minimally repaired and had then been filled with empty kerosene drums to increase its buoyancy. They also learned that the ship was bound for Singapore, not Japan, as they had feared. Thus somewhat reassured, although they wouldn't have had a say in the matter even if they hadn't been, they were shepherded none too gently onto the leaky boat. They huddled together down in the hold, breathing in the nauseating odors of kerosene and copra, the latter having been the ship's last cargo.

By evening, bursting from bladder pressure, they were allowed on deck. Following a mad scramble, they lined up shoulder to shoulder at the railing. With groans of relief they watered the Java Sea below. As Frits Wilkens noted, had there been a wind, the spectacle might have resembled New York harbor fireboats aiming their arcing water jets at a marine vessel fire.

Located on deck at the stern were a dozen latrines built over the side. Long lines of men formed to use these facilities for other urgent needs.

When the ship reached Singapore, the prisoners were again allowed on deck. The sight was depressing. Perhaps the Japanese wanted them to see the devastation as a way of rubbing salt into the wounds of their defeat. Endless piles of rubble lined the docks, evidence of the fighting that had taken place before the British surrendered Singapore, "the impregnable fortress of the East." Disembarkation took several hours. The men were encouraged when they saw a convoy of trucks lined up to transport them. They didn't know where they were going, but at least they wouldn't have to trudge there on their own steam.

In the light of the setting sun, the trucks wove their way through Singapore's dock area and through a Chinese town. Continuing on, the convoy drove through darkening jungle as night fell. At the bottom of a hill, the trucks stopped. Visible in the moonlight, a huge building resembling a medieval castle loomed above them. They had arrived at one of the main barracks of Changi camp, a gigantic prison camp in which British and other POWs were concentrated.

After the fall of Singapore in early 1942, the Japanese ordered the surrendering captives to make their way to Changi on foot, some fifteen miles to the east of downtown Singapore. Because of the vast number of prisoners—an estimated fifty thousand British, Dutch, and Australian troops in the first week—Changi was never a prison in the usual sense.

Most of the prisoners were housed in the damaged buildings of the former British barracks, the whole located on four hundred acres of land surrounded by barbed wire and ditches. As in earlier camps, their own commanding officers controlled the prisoners. The Japanese rarely entered the compound, instead patrolling the camp's perimeter outside the barbed wire fence to guard against any prisoners foolish enough to attempt an escape.

As the men jumped out of the trucks in front of the castlelike building, a voice with a pronounced British accent said, "Who is in charge here?"

As senior officer of his group, Wim stepped forward. "I am," he said.

The British colonel, the commanding officer of the compound, told the new arrivals to follow him. Once the trucks had disgorged all the prisoners, the Japanese disappeared. With a grin the colonel said, by way of explanation, "We don't like them here after dark."

Because it was too late for food that night, the colonel showed them where they were to bed down and told them that breakfast was at 7 a.m. Tomorrow, he promised Wim, they would get things organized.

Next morning's meal turned out to be the same watery rice gruel they had received in previous camps, but accompanied to their delight by a tablespoon of sugar. Then the colonel summoned Wim and his trusted unofficial adjutant, Frits Wilkens, to camp headquarters, where he laid out the operation of the camp for them. The colonel told them that as long as the prisoners "behaved," no one escaped, and no trouble arose with the guards, the Japanese allowed the prisoners to govern themselves.

After the irregular life the men had led in the camps in Java, they were relieved to return to a disciplined military system where the chain of command was respected and infractions were punished. Theft, insubordination, and more serious criminal acts were dealt with in typical military fashion, with punishment consisting of reprimands, extra work, detentions of various lengths, and arrests.

As much as possible, the camp was run as a regular peacetime military establishment. Because the barbed wire fence was far away and the Japanese stayed out of the camp, doing so was not as difficult as it might have been. The day began with regular roll call during which groups were assigned to carry out the necessary work of the camp, such as garbage collection and disposal, building maintenance, and work in the vegetable garden. Although some of the infantry officers refused to participate, Wim persuaded most of the other officers to roll up their sleeves and volunteer a few hours of work a day as a way, if nothing else, of breaking the monotony of their lives. Work in the vegetable garden, besides being an antidote to boredom, produced valuable additions to their meager diet of rice, some dried fish, some oil, and a daily tablespoon of sugar.

Entertainment and the arts were well developed at Changi by the time Wim and his group arrived there. The prisoners had developed and ran two flourishing theaters. Nearly every night groups offered entertainment of one kind or another, such as a boxing match, a sporting event, a cabaret night, or a musical show.

In the British section the men had built a stage in a hollow between the hills. The slopes of the hill made a perfect amphitheater. The productions were elaborate and included music by the camp's concert group, female impersonators, and even a chorus line. Frits Wilkens noted that one particular show had been an enormous crowd pleaser. The show started with the orchestra playing an overture.

> Then, to roars of approval, the opening scene: to the theme song "Let's Go to Town," the company arrived in a . . . train. Admittedly, only a two-dimensional affair of cardboard, but most impressive, with the singers and players hanging out of the windows of the coaches. More delights were to follow: the leading ladies dressed in gorgeous dresses and a chorus line that would have put many a London theater to shame.

While doing some work in the compound, the men discovered a serviceable distillation vessel in an old workshop. Because the sick bay badly needed alcohol for disinfecting purposes, one of the doctors suggested trying to use the vessel to that end. Chemists and engineers consulted with each other and came up with the idea of fermenting kitchen garbage, especially potato peels when these were available. Progress was slow, so an appeal went out for individuals to donate a third of their sugar ration to the cause. The men responded favorably and soon several bottles were set to bubbling.

On d-day (i.e., distillation day), the vessel was put to the test and, to cheers of approval, a fairly clear liquid dripped into the receiving vessel. After running the liquid through a few more times, the distillers were pleased with the resulting alcohol. The doctors gratefully accepted the alcohol for use in the sick bay, where they were treating an increasing number of cases of pellagra, dysentery, and beriberi.

As the distillation process was underway, Wim and his staff were debating what the Dutch officers could do to show their appreciation to the British officers for their help in organizing and reestablishing military order among the Dutch prisoners. Flush with their success, the amateur moonshiners hit upon the eureka idea of throwing a cocktail party for the British officers. Invitations went out to the seven British officers Wim and his officers had the most contact with, as well as to the British commanding officer. Surprisingly the CO, intrigued, was the first to accept.

Two bottles of alcohol from the daily crop were set aside. Although the men didn't know the alcohol's strength, they estimated it to be about seventy percent, so diluting it 2 to 1, they reasoned, would produce a fairly good ersatz gin. Limes could be bought over the fence.

They figured on three gimlets per person, with ice. The block of ice, which a Chinese vendor brought to the fence, had shrunk somewhat by the night of the party, but enough remained for a decent-sized lump in each drinking utensil. The latter consisted of a motley array of mugs, cups (some without handles), and a few real glasses. The party was such a success that the CO invited Wim and his group to a return dinner party to be held two weeks from then.

With great anticipation the Dutch officers awaited the dinner in what had become a competition in ingenuity, with a good dollop of national pride thrown into the mix. The evening started with great ceremony. After a few minutes of animated conversation, the guests were summoned into the mess where a long table had been set for sixteen: the eight hosts and their eight guests. In front of each place setting, which consisted of a fork and a spoon, was an artistic scrolled menu describing a seven-course meal: appetizer, soup, fish, roast, entremets, dessert, and cheese and biscuits.

The menu listed the exotic wines that would accompany the seven courses, from gooseberry wine to Adam's tipple (what that was was anyone's guess). In actuality all the wines were a steady stream of plain old H2O . . . but served with great finesse.

Each course was elaborately shaped to represent what it purported to be, with the fish dish looking like a fish, the roast like a roast, and so on.

But to the Dutch officers' amusement and chagrin, every course except the last consisted of rice in one form or another. The last course was indeed cheese, or at least what the Japanese considered cheese: curdled soybean milk, that is, tofu. The competition was probably a tie, but if imagination were to be factored into the score, the British officers' dinner would have to be declared the winner.

On the Hell Ship

In the eyes of the Japanese, the Allied prisoners had disgraced themselves by becoming POWs. Surrendering rather than either fighting to the death or committing suicide was considered a cowardly and dishonorable act. The Japanese believed, therefore, that the POWs deserved whatever brutal treatment they might receive. Beatings, starvation rations, poor or no medical treatment, summary punishment—these became standard operating procedures for the Japanese conquerors. The rations the prisoners received provided only half of the calories needed to survive. Most lost weight and many became ill. The prisoners were not considered individuals with rights. They were expendable.

For many of the prisoners, Changi was a way station, not a final destination. With Japanese men fighting in and occupying the many areas of the ever-expanding Japanese empire, Japan needed more manpower, more laborers both abroad and at home to support the war effort. Many of the Dutch prisoners from newly conquered areas were first sent to Changi, then shipped off to Taiwan, Burma, Thailand, or Japan as forced labor to build roads and railroads and to work in Japanese coal mines, factories, or shipyards.

For Wim and his group, the relative lull they had experienced in Changi for the past four months was about to end. They would soon be on their way to Japan. In April 1943 they were told that a contingent of a thousand Dutch prisoners would be shipped to Japan from Changi. Wim was tapped to organize and lead the group, which was to consist of ten officers, ten ensigns, and the rest noncommissioned officers and privates. For balance, Wim chose three navy, three air force, and four army officers. Ensigns were distributed in similar fashion among the three military branches.

After the usual preparations of injections, (butt) sampling, and long sessions of counting by both Wim and the Japanese to ascertain that the group was one thousand strong, the men assembled on the vast open space in front of Changi jail. They were then loaded onto a long line of trucks for the winding trip south to the Singapore docks.

Singapore had not changed any during their stay at Changi. The sight of broken-down trucks, burnt-out *godowns*, or warehouses, rubble, and general desolation was as depressing as it had been four months earlier.

Spilling out of the trucks, the men again assembled and waited and sweated under the sizzling tropical sun, while the Japanese, accompanied by lots of yelling, counted, recounted, and once again counted the prisoners. Finally, convinced that there were, indeed, one thousand men, the Japanese gave the order to board the *Kyokku Maru*, a seven thousand–ton freighter. The destination was Japan.

As Wim noted in his report:

When the Japanese authorities in Changi, Singapore, on April 20th, 1943, ordered the formation of a POW working party of "red bands," or technicians, of which I was to be the senior Dutch officer, it was only possible to get this party up to the required strength of 1000 men after the Japanese authorities—quite well knowing about the poor condition of the last Dutch troops in Changi—had specifically stated that up to 30 percent of old and perhaps "not fit" men had to be included.

This party of 1000 men was to be sent overseas as a working party, but partly for "light duties only," for which the older and unfit men were to be employed.

On April 25th we sailed from Singapore on the SS *Kyokku Maru*, a 7000-ton freighter, with a party of 1500 POWs: the aforementioned
1000 Dutch, including 10 Dutch officers
300 British, including 3 British officers
200 Australians, including 2 Australian officers

The *Kyokku Maru* was one of a fleet of freight ships the Japanese used to transport POWs out of Singapore, Hong Kong, and the Philippines for work in Thailand, Taiwan, Burma, Manchuria, Korea, and Japan. These ships were called "hell ships" not because Allied submarines torpedoed or Allied aircraft targeted these unmarked ships, ships that provided no indication they were transporting POWs, but because of the horrific conditions endured by the prisoners onboard as they were shipped to their forced-labor destinations.

Thousands of prisoners were crammed into the cargo holds of the hell ships, sometimes with not even enough room to sit much less lie down for the duration of the voyage, which often lasted two or three weeks. Many stood or squatted hour after hour from sunup to sundown and through the dark nights. With no ventilation, the heat was stifling, the air fetid. Sanitary facilities often consisted of buckets that were hauled up, emptied overboard, and lowered again. The stench from the teeming mass of sweating, unwashed men, punctuated by the odors from the slop buckets, especially as the dysentery-afflicted made use of them, was overpowering.

On many of the ships, the prisoners received only a small handful of cooked rice twice a day and a cup or two of water. With not enough air, inadequate food and water, and unbelievable heat, many succumbed. Some died of dysentery or other illnesses, others suffocated or went mad. By some estimates a third of the prisoners of the Japanese who died in captivity died at sea, either from the horrendous conditions on the hell ships or from attacks on the unmarked freighters by Allied forces.

As Wim and his group embarked, they noted that there were twelve latrines on the deck of the *Kyokku Maru*. Twelve latrines for fifteen hundred men? And how many would the Japanese crew and sailors preempt for themselves? Promising, however, was the sight of provisions being loaded onboard. From the markings on the outside, the men determined that the boxes contained frozen Australian lamb.

The prisoners were jammed into a space between decks where the Japanese had built an extra floor. The space was so cramped that the men could hardly sit upright. There would be no room to lie down to sleep. The men, eerily quiet, sat as ordered, stupefied by the heat and the fear of what would happen next. They waited and waited.

Then a loud yell in Japanese, "*Shoko*, hurry, hurry." Wim and the other officers disentangled themselves from the mass of sweating humanity and climbed on deck where a Japanese officer and interpreter instructed them on the rules of the trip, including the information that they would be fed two meals a day to be prepared by their own cooks. Wim had been careful to include the Changi kitchen crew when he drew up the thousand-men roster, so that was no problem.

Besides the lamb, the food supply consisted of huge piles of fresh vegetables, sacks of beans, sweet potatoes, and various unidentifiable greens.
Although the portions, perforce, would be small, the variety of the provisions meant more nutritious food than most had consumed in months.
Even huge piles of food, however, wouldn't last long when feeding fifteen
hundred mouths (the thousand Dutch plus the three hundred British and
the two hundred Australian prisoners) twice a day.

More immediate problems than food were the use of the latrines and
the need for fresh air. After much reasoning Wim persuaded the captain
that twelve latrines for fifteen hundred men meant the latrines would have
to be in use twenty-four hours a day. So from day one until the end of the
trip more than three weeks later, two single-file lines of men, one on each
side of the deck, shuffled along slowly, eagerly inhaling the fresh sea air
as they made their way to the latrines.

As the ship proceeded northward, plowing its way through the waters
of the South China Sea, the Japanese guards became bored and retreated to
the foredeck, leaving the running of the ship to the sailors. A few days into
the journey, the Japanese crew relaxed the rules somewhat, allowing prisoners up on deck for air for short periods of time, as long as they stayed
within the strict boundaries of the aft deck.

Wim and his fellow officers took turns sleeping on the aft deck, along
with as many of the other men as could fit. The majority, of course, still
had to stay in the airless, rank-smelling, jam-packed hold. Later we would
remember Wim's black humor account of sleeping on deck, with the men
packed so closely together that they formed a single mass. They'd have to
turn as a solid unit, Wim said, because there wasn't even a hairbreadth's
space between them. There was certainly no room for rats, he told us, so
when a rat showed up and ran over the first man, the man would fling it to
the next man, who in turn would toss it to the next one, shouting, "Here
comes another one, boys," and so on down the line, until the last man
would hurl the rodent overboard to triumphant cheers, like a team jubilant
at scoring the winning goal.

The ship moved northward, hugging the Vietnamese coast, stopped
in Saigon for a few days, and then continued northeast toward Formosa
(Taiwan). About ten days after leaving Singapore, just after sunrise, Wim

and the others on deck sighted land. When they got closer to the shore of Formosa on that Sunday morning, they heard the silvery sounds of church bells ringing. The familiar sound, which conjured up "home" for many, electrified them. Tears sprang to the men's eyes. As they came on deck for their trip to the latrines, several abandoned their place in line to kneel on the hard wooden deck and bow their heads. Prayers floated to heaven from many who probably hadn't prayed in a long time.

When the ship docked, the guards, remembering what their job was, chased the men roughly back down into the hold, urging speed by jabbing them with the butts of their rifles. Wim and a few of the officers were allowed, however, to stay on deck to continue supervising the latrine lines, thereby witnessing the welcome sight of more fresh food being winched on board. The ship lingered in Formosa for several days to give the soldiers some shore leave.

A serious problem with which Wim and the other officers had to deal was the increasing number of prisoners falling ill. Their symptoms indicated dysentery. When he'd assembled his group of one thousand in Changi, Wim was not allowed to include any with medical expertise. The Japanese military authorities had given strict instructions that no doctors or medical orderlies were to be included in the group nor was Wim allowed to bring along any medicine.

Having no doctors and no medicine with which to treat the ill, all Wim and the other officers could think of to do was to rig up a makeshift sick bay on deck to isolate those that were definitely sick. "Dysentery broke out onboard," Wim reported. "Congestion in the hold of the ship was great. With pieces of old canvas some sort of sick bay was rigged up on deck, next to the benzene and the kitchen facilities on the aft deck (the empty foredeck not being allowed) for the urgently required isolation of the sick. For the 3 days in Saigon and the 5 days in the port of Takao (Formosa), no medicine was obtainable from shore or from other ships."

They also segregated the healthy from those suspected of being sick by reorganizing the latrine lines, with the healthy using the starboard latrines, the suspected unhealthy, the port latrines. The first to die was one of their own officers. The first lieutenant was given a proper burial at sea with as much ceremony as could be mustered. Two others of the Dutch contingent would join the lieutenant. One soldier died on board and, after their arrival, a sergeant died on the way to the hospital in Kokura, where all the serious dysentery cases were being taken.

On May 20, 1943, twenty-five days after leaving Singapore, the *Kyokku Maru* came to rest in the harbor of Moji at the northern tip of Kyushu, the southernmost of the four main islands that make up Japan. On the ship's arrival, the Japanese quarantine service removed the bodies of those who had died, quarantined about a dozen others, and declared the rest of the prisoners to be healthy enough to proceed.

Accompanied by loud yells and jabs of rifle butts, the bearded, smelly, emaciated men, many in tattered clothes, surged from the bowels of the hell ship that had brought them to this land, this country of their enemies about which they knew very little. Mt. Fuji, cherry blossoms, Madame Butterfly, geisha girls? They couldn't see any of these from where they waited dockside in Moji, Japan.

5
Klara
August 1943

"Just get rid of the fear and you'll be all right," said the voice within, my inner direction. Easy. Get rid of the fear. Just get rid of the fear.

To Camp

On August 25, 1943, Magdi Rees, a new Hungarian acquaintance, sent me a few hasty lines by messenger. Strong rumors were circulating, she wrote, that all Hungarian women would be interned shortly. I immediately went to see Trethan. There I found Magdi and the other Hungarian women still at large, all of us alarmed by the rumors. Trethan didn't know anything about our imminent internment and dismissed the news, saying that it was the usual whispering wind. We left reassured, thinking that if anyone would know, he would.

Well, he didn't.

When I arrived home, Manggoen greeted me with a perturbed face and the news that in my absence a policeman had called with a camp summons but wouldn't leave it with Manggoen. I was supposed to go fetch it myself at a police station on the other side of Bandoeng. I got back on the bike and returned to town.

This time the summons was serious. In five days the children and I had to be in camp.

There were two camps in Bandoeng: Tjihapit in town, which held the people from Bandoeng, and Karees on the outskirts of town, which held the women from plantations and the neighboring small villages. My summons was for Karees. Because all my acquaintances were in Tjihapit, I thought I would try to have my summons changed so I could be with my friends.

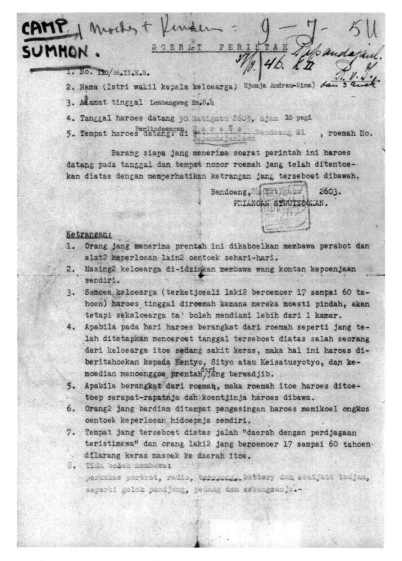

Klara's camp summons for internment in Karees, Bandoeng, 1943

I had five days to achieve this and make my preparations for camp life. Five awful days.

I lost two days in attempting to reregister for Tjihapit. Trethan said he couldn't help me. Wester, the Swedish consul, was equally unhelpful. Like a hunted rabbit, I dashed around town to different native authorities, stood in line for hours, was pushed around by clerks, was sent from office to office, until finally I lost my temper, wished them all to hell, and gave up the idea of changing camps. The only thing I managed to settle was to return to Laci the money he had sent through diplomatic channels. It had been sitting in the bank all this time, pending the outcome of my written application, which I had put in some time ago.

The Japanese bank clerk Makifa was very obliging. When I told him that the children and I were going to be interned, he was sympathetic. He advised me never to show the children that I was unhappy and never to cry in their presence. He said he had lost his father when he was quite young and the deepest impression he had of his childhood was of the tear-stained face of his mother, who cried almost every day.

As he was telling me this, a Japanese officer entered the bank and threw a glance at us. Makifa stiffened, bowed slightly to me, and left, whispering, "Have courage. I cannot talk any longer to you."

I understood. He didn't want to risk being caught chatting or, even worse, sympathizing with a European. Japanese civilians were afraid of their own military people.

I was told we were allowed to see our future quarters in order to judge what furniture we should take with us to make it habitable, so on the third morning of my precious five days, I went to visit the camp.

At the gate I showed my papers and the summons. The native guard searched my handbag and let me in. On my previous visit I had received an unpleasant impression of the camp. My impression on this occasion was no better. A general state of dilapidation prevailed: uncut grass; barefoot women and children; unkempt, tiny porches and verandahs chock full of junk; laundry hanging everywhere; charcoal fires burning; women cooking; and practically every person I saw carrying a pot or a pan.

The people at the inner-camp office, which our own women ran for internal matters, received me in a friendly way. They told me I could choose between a small room with a separate entrance or a garage, both of which were in a corner of a nearby house, at the outer edge of the camp. Searching through their records, they couldn't find my name anywhere on the lists of the women expected.

"If you don't come, nobody will know," they told me. I showed them my summons, which seemed to be correct. Again they looked through their lists, but I wasn't on them.

"We won't report you to the Japanese if you don't turn up in two days," they told me again. "If you get in trouble for not heeding the summons, just tell the Japs that you weren't on the list. It's up to you to decide whether you're coming or not. We can't advise you."

I thanked them and said I would think it over and promised to come back in the afternoon to let them know what I had decided.

Once outside the camp, the cruel, midday sun hit me full force. I rode the bike into the shade of a lone tree on the almost deserted road, got off, sat down on the dusty grass, and tried to do some logical thinking. It wasn't easy to know what decision was the right one. I was hungry and thirsty and very much inclined not to go to camp. Should I risk ignoring the summons? Who would find out that I hadn't gone to camp? And when? What would be the consequences?

"If you get in trouble by staying out, just tell the Japs . . ." resounded in my ears. Yes, "just tell the Japs." Did those ladies ever try to "just tell the Japs," I wondered. I knew of cases in which the police had come in the middle of the night to catch camp-dodgers, had bundled them into trucks, and had taken them to camp without so much as a hanky in their pocket, not to mention the beatings they received. Obviously, I couldn't risk that on the children's account.

So back I went to the police station from where an hour before I had gotten the summons. They made me wait an hour. The records were searched and my name was not found. The officials phoned here and there, until finally the police chief himself was consulted. Yes, he knew of my case. My name had been phoned through to him from headquarters after they had sent out the lists, and I did have to go to camp with the children. Apparently I was on one of their lists.

I biked back to the camp, told the women at the office that I was coming in two days, and asked their permission to have a look at the room and at the garage so I could make a choice.

The house they took me to was still empty. While nosing through the rooms, I discovered another room, not the one they had indicated, with a separate entrance, a washbasin, and a tiny porch. This is the one I want, I thought. After a little persuasive talking, I got it.

It was four in the afternoon when I started on my way home. I was so happy about our room that I had forgotten my hunger and thirst. A whole nine-by-twelve-foot room to ourselves, a washbasin, and a four-by-six-foot porch. What luxury.

The children were excited when I told them about the room. During the past few weeks, the possibility of being called to camp had looked more and more like a probability, and so I had prepared the children for an interesting adventure, a sort of prolonged picnic. Their vivid imagination coupled with my alluring description of the nice room we were going to get made them impatient and eager to go.

The next two days were spent in packing and buying our reserves. Taking along food supplies was risky. One native searcher might confiscate it all; another would leave it alone. I had to take that risk, however, and was spending our reserve cash freely. Not heeding the native prophecy that the war would not be over until 1945, I calculated six months in captivity and bought food supplies to last that long. And I was called a pessimist.

I assumed we would get enough rice in the camp, so I filled two big wooden chests with sugar, dried beans, bottles of oil, jams, honey, dried fish, dried meat, and onions. I also took a good assortment of vegetable seeds, counting on making a garden. In one of the four-foot-tall charcoal baskets, I hid our kerosene cooker. In the other charcoal basket, I put a five-gallon can of kerosene. I knew these last two items were definitely forbidden articles, but I figured the guards wouldn't dirty their hands digging around in the charcoal.

Because practically all our trunks were stolen when our house was looted, I packed what remained of the sheets, towels, clothes, kitchen utensils, and china in big baskets and in a few suitcases. As for furniture, I counted on taking along four beds with mattresses, a table with four chairs, a wardrobe, and a small cupboard. For the porch, I chose a card table and two upholstered rattan chairs. I gave away the rest of our furniture and belongings or deposited them with Mrs. Merz and at the dairy.

I also left six months worth of wages for Manggoen at the dairy, which she would be able to pick up from there every month. I was afraid that if I had given her the lump sum, she would have spent it all within a week.

I slept only a few hours each night during these hectic days. Finally the fateful morning of August 31, 1943 dawned. We were up with the sun. Manggoen made some sandwiches and a pot of meatballs. From a vendor who was passing by, we bought bananas, cucumbers, and tomatoes. The last thing we packed was the bedding. At ten o'clock the three *grobaks*, horse-drawn carts, turned up. The men loaded everything into the carts. I had ordered a *kretek*, the small, two-wheeled horse carriage, for the children.

We said goodbye to the house, the garden, and Mrs. Merz. The children climbed into the *kretek* with Manggoen. Each child had a bag to carry. Maya's was filled with light bulbs, spare plugs, and extension cords. Yvonne had two hundred eggs. Robi carried our home pharmacy.

Tearfully we gave away Bobby and her puppies and Pinkie, but we took along Mitza, the cat. She struggled desperately to jump out of the carriage, but Yvonne held her firmly. I just hoped Yvonne wouldn't become confused as to which one to hug tightly, the eggs or the cat. I took up my place at the tail of the convoy, riding my bike.

The children were excited and happy that we were finally going and that something was really "happening" this time.

It took us well over an hour to reach the camp. While driving through town, I stopped at a bakery and bought a big box of pastries and chocolate. The children hadn't had such delicacies for over a year now. Who knew when they would have them again.

We arrived at two in the afternoon. We were saying goodbye to Manggoen at the gate when the guards shouted at us to hurry up. Up to then everything seemed a slow-motion picture compared to what followed.

The two-winged, big bamboo gate was flung open and the *grobaks* and the *kretek* with the children were swallowed up, while the native policemen and a Japanese at the outer office were checking my papers. When they finished with me, I biked at full speed to catch up with our little convoy, which was well ahead already.

In a big square about four hundred yards from the gate, the men were busy unloading our belongings. I helped the children off the *kretek* and quickly led them away to our house, which was nearby. They were tired and hot from the excitement and the heat of the day. Dutifully they had held on to their respective bags, and the cat, of course. At least the bulbs, eggs, and medicine won't be confiscated, I thought. A kind neighbor brought them some water to drink. After having settled them on the floor of the porch, I rushed back to the square.

There I found bedlam. The *grobak* drivers were clamoring for their money, and some ten policemen were busy handling our belongings.

"*Boeka, boeka*," Open it, open it, they shouted. First I paid off the *grobak* men. Then I got out my keys for the cupboard, only to find I was too late. With remarkable dexterity they had forced open one lock after the other. The doors of the cupboard were torn off, hinges and all, and everything inside dumped out. The policemen shouted and laughed while I dashed from one to the other, trying to prevent things from disappearing.

In the middle of the square, under a tree, sat a Japanese at a small table, watching the scene and clearly enjoying it. The policemen fished contraband items out of our trunks and deposited the booty on his table. It consisted of all writing paper, pencils, candles, my two boxes of costly matches, all my garden tools, a handy little home tool kit, and the children's coloring crayons. This last item hurt me the most because the children loved to draw and to color.

I walked up to the Japanese official and asked for the crayons back, saying that they were for the children. "*Tidah.*" No. That was the only answer he gave me. With bitterness in my heart, I walked back to the hopeless mess. The men were through searching and were already attacking the next arrival. Only then did our luck dawn on me. The food hadn't been confiscated and the charcoal baskets hadn't been touched. This was more than I had ever hoped for. This was really good luck.

Some camp coolies turned up. For an exorbitant fee they offered to carry the furniture to our room, about one hundred yards away. By that time, Mrs. Lange, our energetic street leader, had come to help.

"Don't hire the coolies. They're out to rob you," she said. "I'll help you carry your things."

As soon as the two of us picked up the first bed, the coolies reduced their fees to normal and within ten minutes everything was in front of our porch. Mrs. Lange helped carry in the beds and mattresses, then she left.

My watch showed four o'clock. The children were still playing on the porch with Mitza. I was alone in the room, completely exhausted by then, bathed in perspiration from head to foot, and shaken by the crazy tempo of the last five days and by the fear of the unknown. I sat down on a mattress and gave way to uncontrollable sobbing. Sheer self-pity, I told myself, but I kept on crying.

These were my first and last tears in camp. I remembered Makifa, the Japanese bank clerk, who had advised me not to show the children when I felt unhappy. I bathed my face in cold water and resolved not to let myself go again. To take everything with a smile, if possible, and to create the illusion in the minds of the children that all this was just a funny adventure.

I called the children in, gave them a shower, and unpacked our food. We all sat down to eat. We had never enjoyed meatballs with tomatoes as much as we did on this occasion. When I opened the surprise box of pastries, their joy was complete.

After the meal we tossed a coin for who would sleep where. We agreed that every month we would change beds. I was sure they secretly hoped we would stay in camp for at least four months so they would each get a turn on each bed. After a game of some kind, they helped put the sheets on the beds and soon all three were asleep, Yvonne still hugging Mitza.

It was dark by this time, but I wasn't sleepy. On the contrary, I felt agitated and my nerves were taut. I sat on the porch for a long time, listening to the fading camp noises.

At nine o'clock somebody banged a piece of metal against an iron lamppost. I counted ten, eleven, twelve, and then it stopped. All lights went out. Apparently, these twelve metallic bangs were the camp taps.

I continued to sit, confused, restless. I tried to pray, but it brought no relief. I got up, went inside, listened to the children's regular breathing. I chased away some mosquitoes and returned again to the porch. "If only I had someone to talk to," I said out loud.

The house was at the edge of the camp. Our porch faced the barbed wire and bamboo fence, a distance of some ten yards. The guards thudding feet on the other side of the fence kept up a monotonous rhythm: *One, two, three, four. One, two, three, four. You, can't, get, out. You, can't, get, out.*

I went inside again, chased away some more mosquitoes, and lay down, still dressed. I dozed for a little while, got up, went back to the porch, and sat there listening to the guard's footsteps. They kept repeating the four words: *YOU CAN'T GET OUT.* I was going crazy. *I – can't – get – out.* Crazy. CRAZY!

Oh, God, help me straighten myself out.

Dawn arrived as abruptly as sunset had. The camp yawned. Some early noises broke the silence. People started moving about. I started the daily chores. As I was not used to doing all the housework, everything took twice as long. Keeping the children busy and fed was most important. All else would fall into place . . . in time.

Somehow I managed to struggle through that first day. That evening, when all was quiet and the children were asleep, I made myself a night-light. I poured some cooking oil in a saucer, placed two tiny sticks across the top of the saucer, and put a coin with a hole in the middle on top of the sticks. I fitted a thin cotton thread, which became the wick, through the hole in the coin. Now I had some light at least. Maybe with some light my thinking would be clearer.

Why was I so restless? What had gone wrong? Where was the inner balance I had managed to maintain all my life despite terrible odds during and after World War I?

I gazed into the tiny, steady flame. Suddenly it turned into a mirror. I looked straight into it and saw myself. I rubbed my eyes. I looked again. It did not change. It did not flicker. The flame was a mirror, and in the mirror I saw my soul. On the mirror written in capital letters were the words: YOU ARE AFRAID.

"Not true," I protested. "I have never been afraid."

I shivered, closed my eyes, and withdrew into myself. For how long, I cannot say.

When I opened my eyes, I knew the mirror was right. I was afraid. Afraid of what? Afraid of everything. Of losing Wim. Of the children getting sick, or dying, or being starved to death. Of losing my family in Hungary. Of losing our home and all we had. All my innermost fears came rising to the surface. I had to deal with them. But how?

"Just get rid of the fear and you'll be all right," said the voice within, my inner direction. Easy. Get rid of the fear. Just get rid of the fear.

Fear

The next night, after the children were asleep, I lit my little light-mirror and pondered for hours. I did this every night for the next three months. I argued with myself. If I was afraid of losing something, then I would have to get rid of the things that I was afraid of losing. Once there was nothing more to lose, then there wouldn't be any fear left. This was logical. Easy. The only question was how to do it. How do I lose the things I fear to lose?

First on the list was Wim. Obviously, I didn't possess Wim physically, but he was part of my soul. So then, let me cut him loose from my soul, I reasoned. As long as he was alive, he would never leave me. He would have to die for me to lose him.

The possibility of his dying in a Japanese POW camp was not remote. There were a number of ways. Being starved to death, being put in a cage out in the sun without food or water, being brutally beaten, being tortured, having his Achilles tendon severed when caught trying to escape, being beheaded, and so on.

I took each possibility separately. I went through each one mentally. I saw it happening within myself. I lived through each death emotionally. I played out this inner drama night after night, every night, for a month. By then I was exhausted, drained, numb from suffering. And Wim was dead. His death was almost a relief. Finally he wasn't suffering anymore, and I didn't have to fear losing him.

The children came next, one at a time. Crying for food, suffering from dysentery or some other nasty illness, consumed by high fever, getting beriberi, and so on. I lost them one by one, though they were clinging to my body and soul.

The day after I "gave up" the children, I accidentally looked in a mirror and was shocked to see my hair graying. Abraham's hair had probably also turned gray when he went up that hill to sacrifice his son Isaac to God.

Next on my list were my family and Wim's family. I went through all of them. And then all that we possessed: our home in Hungary, our earthly Paradise, and all our belongings. To lose these was almost child's play compared to the previous losses.

I had nothing more to lose. I was free. I was alone. There were no more bonds or emotions to tie me to anybody, to anything. I was alone in front of God.

I faced Him, naked in soul. "What next, God?" I asked. "What else do You want of me? I have given up all I had. I have given everything up. I am of no use to anybody or to anything. You might as well annihilate me."

"You are mistaken," God answered. "You belong. You are part of it all. You belong to it all."

"I don't count," I retorted. "I am such an indescribably small part of it. A nothing."

"You are wrong," God said to me. "The tiniest part has its role to play in the universe."

"One small part more or less doesn't count," I continued my side of the argument.

"Again mistaken. If all parts of everything were to think as you do, there wouldn't be an everything. No universe."

"What is my role?" I asked, but it was more like a prayer.

"Have faith in Me. Listen to My voice in your inner self. Follow it and don't worry. Don't ask questions. Just do your duty and everything will be all right."

I felt very, very small, but strangely enough, at the same time a feeling of belonging to the whole came over me. I was a tiny part, a part that had nothing to worry about and nothing else to do but perform the allotted task day by day. A great feeling of freedom, of faith, and of strength swelled in my heart. I felt I could face anything.

Fear died away.

The light-mirror in the flame had appeared every night for three months. The moment I had given everything up and fear had died, the candle flickered. The golden light of the light-mirror left the room. Only the flame remained. I sat for hours looking into the little flame. Peace descended into my soul. Peace, serenity, and acceptance. I never worried again.

Adjusting to Camp Routine

The first week in camp was spent finding a place for all our belongings, a difficult task in one small room. More important were getting acquainted with conditions and other people and setting up a daily routine. The house filled up gradually. Seeing so many women all together was strange. Counting the children, we were twenty people in five rooms, two tiny storage rooms, and a garage. Later we would be one hundred twenty-seven in a similar-size house.

A meeting was called and I was asked to take over the duties of house warden. In rotating order, we divided up the house duties, such as keeping the showers and the toilets clean and fetching the food distributions. The latter took a great deal of our time.

We were given a daily ration of one ounce of sugar, five-and-a-half ounces of uncooked rice, one two-inch-by-two-inch piece of bread, and one banana per person. In addition everybody was allowed to buy one dollar's worth of goods per month at the canteen. The Japanese deposited the money directly into the canteen.

There were many desirable things one could get for the dollar: butter, eggs, milk, jam, flour, tobacco, toothbrushes, fruit. Some squandered the dollar on tobacco, but most women were more sensible. I spent our allotment on milk, butter, and a little fruit.

We had to pay for water and electricity ourselves. Collecting this money was the house warden's job. The haves carried the have-nots. Abuse occurred, of course, with many pretending not to have any money and living off the others.

I soon learned that several gangs of smugglers inside the camp worked regularly with natives on the outside. I was ever on the alert to find out when and where some smuggled goods were to be had. Naturally, the prices were sky high, but all that mattered was to get the goods before the Japanese tracked down the smugglers or confiscated our money.

One hot afternoon, not far from our house, I saw a woman slip between the barbed wire and the six-foot high bamboo fence. It was siesta time, the camp was quiet, the children and most of the adults were asleep. From our porch I watched the woman look around furtively, kneel down, take out knife, and cut about a one-foot square piece out of the bamboo fence near a pole. She replaced the piece carefully so that no trace of its having been cut would show. She looked around again, stood up, and walked away at a leisurely pace. I was curious and wondered what on earth she was going to do with that hole. Escape, perhaps?

About two hours later, she came back and walked slowly alongside the fence, back and forth. Perhaps not a smuggler, after all. Just another one who had gone crazy.

By then I couldn't contain my curiosity any longer and followed the woman at a distance. "Three hundred eggs," she said. "Yes, three hundred," she repeated. Then silence. Again. "Twenty bottles of oil." Silence. "Fifty pounds of meat." Silence again.

The poor woman was having delusions, visions of plenty, no doubt about it. But then it dawned on me that she was giving orders to her smuggling partner on the other side of the fence, whose replies I couldn't hear. They did this ordering while walking so as not to attract attention.

At dusk she came back and resumed her walk, until contact was established with the other side. Then in a flash she removed the previously cut piece of bamboo fencing. At lightning speed, packages were pushed in from the outside and money went out. It was dark by then. She quickly returned the piece of bamboo to its place. A few associates turned up to help her carry the packages home.

I admired her skill, her daring, even her eagerness to make money. She surely made a hundred percent profit by selling the goods to us, every cent of which she richly deserved.

We established our daily routine. I got up with the sun at 6 a.m. After a shower—only cold water was available, of course—I made breakfast while the children got up. It took a few days to learn the trick of making a charcoal fire and keeping it going evenly. Because we had no matches or paper, the Vesta fire system was in use. Somebody, somewhere, always managed to keep a fire alive. The trading price was still twice the amount of black coals for the glowing coals. All the rooms had an exit to the inner courtyard where we stood, fanning the charcoal in our braziers.

Breakfast consisted of cooked rice from the previous day, reboiled in milk, with sugar sprinkled over it. This was followed by a slice of bread and butter (the bread oh so thinly buttered) and a cup of tea. I also filled the thermos with tea for the afternoon.

We brought in the bedding, which we had placed out in the sun before breakfast, and we made the beds, each our own. For five-year-old Robi, it was a big job. Then I washed the tile floor and, while the girls studied, I did the laundry. Luckily I found someone to do the sheets.

The rest of the morning we spent with lessons. Yvonne went to Mrs. Wonder, the teacher whose son Jan used to be in my little school on the Lembang road. She was the only person we knew in camp. Mrs. Wonder

143

was as hearty and as friendly as ever, but her unconventional, freedom-loving spirit suffered deeply from the monotony and oppression of camp life.

I could still handle teaching Maya and Robi in Dutch. I also started giving Yvonne some English lessons. Our only book was Walt Disney's *Snow White*.

The midday camp soup, the so-called hot meal, deteriorated so rapidly in quality that often it was no more than greenish-brown water with a spinach leaf swimming forlornly in it. I cooked rice to go with the soup, baked some dried fish or meat from our provisions, and served it with "the" banana. I redoubled my efforts to obtain smuggled food and spent several hours a day running around to get it.

A short siesta followed the midday meal. The girls spent the afternoons taking either embroidery lessons or drawing lessons. I had obtained paper, crayons, and pencils through the barter system to replace what had been confiscated when we entered camp. Instead of paying cash for the embroidery lessons, I gave English lessons in exchange.

A few months later two gifted teachers also offered a ballet class for children. The girls went twice a week to these lessons and enjoyed them very much. Later a class for adults was given as well. I joined it hoping that this might cure a cramplike stomach pain I was experiencing. Forgetting camp life for an hour a week was wonderful.

During the rest of the time, the girls played on the porch. They spent hours constructing houses out of empty matchboxes. Each girl had a doll and a bed for the doll, but no other toys. The outdoor life they had led before hadn't called for a lot of toys.

Robine's tricycle and Maya's scooter were promptly stolen from our porch. These were irreplaceable losses. I tried to minimize the loss in Robi's mind by telling her that she was getting too big for the tricycle anyway. The scooter was more difficult to "talk away." The girls were angry with the person who took them and outraged by the idea that somebody, one of our own people, would steal them. Alas, life's hard lessons had to be learned. For weeks they were on the lookout for the scooter and tricycle in the streets of the camp, then they forgot about them.

Our evening meal consisted of an egg, bread and butter, and cocoa. We were beginning to feel the lack of vegetables. My tomato plants, in the stone flower boxes on the side of the porch, were coming up nicely. We were looking forward to eating the tomatoes once the plants started producing.

I had placed the card table and the two rattan chairs on the side of the porch. With a table lamp, this made a cozy corner for the evening when acquaintances dropped by for a chat or where I could sit and read or sit and not read, after the children had gone to bed.

A new friend, Nan van Spingelen, stole our hearts. She was young, slender, blue-eyed, and always in a blue cotton dress. She reminded us of the Blue Fairy in one of Walt Disney's pictures, so we called her "Feetje" (pronounced 'FATE-chuh'), the Dutch diminutive meaning "little fairy." She gave drawing lessons to the children. As assistant street-leader she often dropped in on official business. Always cheerful and always helpful, Feetje was our sunshine in camp. On occasion she brought along two of her friends, Reintje and Johtje, both good violinists.

I had also found a chess partner, a seventy-five-year-old former Java chess champion. Through some odd ruling, about a dozen old men were assigned to this otherwise all-women's camp. He came two evenings a week. Needless to say, he always beat me when we played. With him and with two other men friends of his, I also played bridge once a week.

After several months, however, our bridge group was dissolved. I hadn't enjoyed playing with them that much since they were weak players. Shortly after the group's dissolution, one of the men died. My chess partner was also becoming alarmingly thin. The old ones and the young ones were the first to go, it seemed.

When a prisoner died she was put in a coffin made of plain wooden planks. The coffin was lifted onto a two-wheeled cart with chicken wire around it and pushed to the gate. From there natives loaded it onto a truck and took it to the cemetery. One or two of the deceased's closest relatives were allowed to accompany the body, under the supervision of a Japanese guard. The people who took care of the burial, mostly Indo-Europeans who lived in freedom, were kind to the accompanying relatives and treated them to a sandwich and some fruit after the ceremony.

When close relatives weren't available, there was never a shortage of friends volunteering to accompany the dead in hopes of receiving a sandwich. We were getting very hungry.

On one occasion a woman went to the cemetery with her mother's coffin. On the way back, sitting in the *kretek* with the Japanese guard, she asked whether she could get out to buy some bananas. The guard was kind and allowed it. After having bought the bananas, the foolish woman went into the adjoining shop to buy something else. The guard became enraged at this disobedience, got out of the carriage, dragged her out of the shop, and beat her bloody with his belt. While the guard was beating her, the driver panicked and galloped off in the *kretek*.

A week after our arrival in camp, Yvonne again developed her asthma-bronchitis. I sat up with her for several nights, holding her in my arms. A number of our own doctors ran a little hospital in a couple of houses and had set hours for consultation. For three weeks Yvonne stayed in the hospital. Her condition improved somewhat as a result of the steam inhalations she received.

We visited her daily, bringing her clean laundry, but all of us were happy when she finally came home. I kept her in bed for half the day for another week, to help her regain her strength. The change of climate from the cool Lembang hills to the oven heat of the camp, as well as the excitement of the new life, was apparently too much for her sensitive constitution. On the doctor's orders, her camp soup was canceled and she instead received a daily ration of a pint of buttermilk and some raw vegetables. Maya and Robi got a sip of buttermilk too, and everyone was satisfied.

One of the camp rules was that mothers with three children did not have to do any community work. Because I considered our children a purely personal matter, the concern of Wim and myself for which the community should in no way have to suffer, I accepted the house warden position as community work.

After a while Feetje came and asked me whether I would take over the rice distribution in our district as well. Of course I agreed to do so. From then on we played at being grocers two afternoons a week. The women would come with their receptacles to our porch. I weighed out the raw rice, five-and-a-half ounces per person per day, on the scales that I had luckily brought along with me. The children were happy to help. They felt important taking part in this grocery business.

The rice distribution, although not strenuous work, was time consuming, taking about two hours an afternoon. Transporting the heavy rice sacks to the porch from a back storage area, however, was a difficult task. Luckily I always found a charitable soul to help me push and pull the eighty-to-ninety-pound bags. Lifting them was beyond my muscle power.

Cleanliness and tidiness became a mania with me. Sheets had to go into the sun every day, the mattresses and the beds once a week. I washed the tiled floor of our room twice a day, and I was forever putting things in order. Sleeping, playing, studying, working, and—during rainy weather—cooking in one room and having it look tidy and cozy was not easy.

The first weeks' attitude of consideration and courtesy among the inmates of the camp soon wore off. Quarrels and fights erupted. Women seemed to know little about the unwritten laws and rules of communal life. Of course the conditions were trying and the circumstances exceptional, but these were the same for everyone.

For instance, once when making my daily rounds, I found one of the toilets in a questionable state of cleanliness. I called over the young woman whose weekly duty it was to keep it clean. I showed her how to clean it, using a wet rag wound tightly around the end of a stick and dipped in charcoal ashes. "If you know how to do it so well, just keep doing it," was her insolent reply. I had to count to ten to keep from exploding. My hands were itching to lift her skirt and give her a smack on her bottom, something her mother had apparently neglected to do twenty years earlier. Instead I managed to shrug my shoulders and walk away.

A similar case was that of the dirty ditch. This ditch ran in front of, and parallel with, our house. Water should have been flowing in it. Instead the ditch was clogged with refuse, empty cans, mud, weeds, and waist-high grass. Not only was it filthy, it was a perfect breeding ground for mosquitoes. I decided to clean it.

I got up an hour earlier. Between 5 and 6 a.m. I was ankle- and elbow-deep in the filthy muck, scooping out the debris and pulling out the weeds. I cut my hands and feet on pieces of glass and metal, but I was beyond the point of caring. Once it was cleaned, I asked my house companions to establish a weekly rotation for keeping the ditch clean, which meant on a daily basis picking out the refuse that passers-by threw in and pulling out the weeds and grass.

The women, however, refused to cooperate. One had a scratch on her finger and was afraid of infection. Another didn't feel well. And so the excuses went. It was exasperating. A few months later Nippon promised a good beating to the women if the ditches in camp weren't kept clean. That worked. I had no more ditch problems.

The Angel's Tree

The 25th of December is little Jesus' birthday. He'd like to invite the children of the world to his birthday party, but because there isn't enough room for all the children to sit down in heaven, he has come up with an alternate solution. He sends a Christmas tree to every child on earth to celebrate his birthday at home. His Angels fly back and forth all night on Christmas Eve, bringing a tree to every family where there is a child. In this way the children of the whole world celebrate together. The tree is beautifully decorated with lots of candles on it, lots of goodies to eat, lots of shiny ornaments, and just a few presents. This is the Angel's Tree.

Our first Christmas in captivity was alarmingly near and I was using all my ingenuity to preserve the myth, and save the Angel's face.

"Are you sure he won't forget us?" Maya asked.

"I'm sure," I answered.

"But how can he come into the camp? The Japanese won't let him."

"Oh, just leave that to him. He has wings and he can fly anywhere. Besides, he isn't afraid of the Japanese. They are afraid of him."

"Are the Angels men?" asked Yvonne.

A difficult question. I had to admit I didn't know for sure. The girls discussed the matter further.

"Will he bring a tree, Mami?" Robi asked.

"Why, naturally," I assured her. When this naturally slipped out of my mouth, it made me stop and think. After all, it wasn't quite natural that he should bring a tree in camp. Camp wasn't quite natural. In any case, I would have to be the Angel, and where on earth would I get a tree?

For weeks I had been preparing the girls' presents. Embroidered hankies made from torn sheets, tiny woolen dolls exquisitely made for them by Feetje, crocheted headbands, a cake of soap for each in exchange for onions, and the miracle of all miracles, the greatest of all surprises, a girl's bike for the three of them. Their tricycle and scooter had been stolen, but what were they compared to a real bike?

The bike looked terrible when I traded for it. I got the tires fixed, repainted the frame, and my friend Altien made a new cloth-saddle for it. When it was all done, it looked splendid, at least given the circumstances. I refrained from dropping even a hint to the children about the possibility of a bike. I wanted the surprise to be complete.

But now I had to think about the tree, and I was at a loss. Where would I get a tree?

To give myself some inspiration and stir up some ideas, I enumerated for the third time the treasures I had collected for the tree through the barter system. A dozen small candles, the fruit of some hard trading. Tinsel stars made at home when the girls were asleep. Homemade sweets from a whole pound of sugar. My last pound. I planned to wrap each sweet in a piece of colored shiny paper. I already had the paper for this, acquired, naturally, through more bartering.

That was all. Not much. The candles would be lit, however, and it would seem magical to the children. And the Angel would not lose his face either.

In front of the house where our Dutch head of camp lived were six lovely, five-foot tall tropical fir trees called *tjimaras*. I asked her if I could "borrow" one of the trees. I assured her I would replant it in her garden after Christmas, but she was hard-hearted and wouldn't part with any of them, even temporarily.

For several days I walked the camp streets looking for a Christmas tree. Finally I spotted a tall tree at the edge of the camp, in front of an abandoned, dilapidated house. It was much taller than the house and scrawny, but perhaps I would be able to climb it and cut off its top. It would make a perfect Christmas tree. Of course if I were caught, well then goodbye tree. And I would be beaten or worse.

Once I witnessed a sixty-year-old woman prisoner pick up a piece of rotten bamboo matting discarded by the Japanese while they were mending the camp fence. The woman wanted to use it for her cooking fire, which was strictly forbidden in camp. A soldier saw the woman slipping into her quarters with the bamboo and followed her. He dragged her out into the street, made her stand erect holding the piece of stolen bamboo matting, and gave her such a hard slap in the face that she lost her glasses as well as the matting. Before she had time to recover from the shock, she received a second slap, followed by many more.

When he apparently tired of beating her in this manner, he switched to hitting her with his fists. Then he unbuckled his belt and beat her with the metal end of the leather belt. By then blood was trickling down her face from her various head wounds. With the blood running into her eyes, blurring her vision, she lost her balance and fell to the ground. He hissed and readied himself to kick her with his heavy army boots. The woman knew, we all knew, that she had to get on her feet quickly or she would be kicked to death. Painfully she pulled herself up. By then she was unrecognizable. He finally stopped. As a lesson to all, he made her stand there for hours, the stolen matting in her hand.

Why was I recalling this horrible scene? Was I losing my resolve? Or was I perhaps afraid? No. I would get that treetop, I vowed, whether they caught me or not. My decision was made.

I confided my plans to my friends Feetje, Johtje, and Reintje. They encouraged me. Reintje said she would get me a saw. Feetje offered moral support, promising to go to the tree with me. We planned to meet under the tree at half past five in the morning on December 24.

The night before, Reintje appeared with a six-inch toy saw. This was all she could get. My face and my hopes fell when she produced it. But then I remembered that I had a three-inch paring knife and a great deal of determination.

Before I went to sleep, I set the alarm clock for 5 a.m. I woke a quarter of an hour earlier. It was still dark. The children were asleep. I put the saw and the knife in a canvas bag and stole out of the room barefoot.

I walked a couple of hundred yards under a dark sky. Only a few stars sparkled here and there. Then I heard the faint far-away thud of feet. I stopped and listened, straining my ears. It was unmistakably the sound of a guard's footsteps. The thumping noise was coming closer. Fear trailed its cold finger down my spine.

Strict camp regulations forbade us from leaving our rooms before sunrise. Besides the usual beating, the punishment was detention in solitary.

Where could I hide?

I searched the darkness around me. Phantoms loomed on my right. What were they? Where was I? I knew this road well, having often passed by here in the daytime. I had never noticed any dark patches before.

Then I remembered what they were: hibiscus bushes, so festive with their red blossoms during the day. With not a second to spare, I was behind them. The thudding of the guard's feet resounded in my ears, in my brain. My heart leaped into my throat. The guard passed right by me, walking slowly, meandering. His legs brushed against the branches of the hibiscus. I held my breath and pressed my hand over my heart for fear he would hear it beating.

God bless you, hibiscus bush.

I remained crouched, rooted, behind the bush. Slowly the sound of the guard's footsteps faded away. I waited a while to steady myself and then slipped onto the road again, moving low to the ground, like a panther stalking her prey. Another three or four hundred yards and I stood under the tree.

Feetje wasn't there. I couldn't wait. Every moment was precious. With a powerful leap, I grabbed hold of the lowest branch, pulled myself up, and struggled until somehow I was sitting on it.

Well done, muscles. I thanked them for not failing me. From then on the climbing was easy. The small, dead twigs scratched my face, bare legs, and arms. My hair was pulled into a tangled mess.

As I neared the top, the tree began to sway under my weight. There were six or seven more feet above me, enough for a perfect Christmas tree. The top branches were all green.

I got out the saw and started sawing a spot above my head. The trunk was relatively thin there. The saw, however, got stuck in the sappy, green wood. I rested a bit and started again. Again the saw became stuck. And it did so every time I started anew.

All the while the tree was swaying alarmingly. I was agitated and felt my strength ebbing. I tried sawing with my left hand, but that was even worse. What did they teach us in school? If at first you don't succeed, try, try again. Darn it all. I was trying and trying again.

Perhaps the paring knife would work better. I fished it out of the bag and managed to chip off two little pieces of bark. At this pace it would take until next Christmas to get that tree.

It would soon be sunrise. I was losing my grip, and my body was trembling. *Hello. Angel. This is your tree. Won't you come and help?*

As if in answer to my prayer, I heard light footsteps approaching. They stopped under the tree. Silence followed. It couldn't be a Japanese. These steps were light. Did I dare to call out?

"Feetje?" I half-whispered.

"Yes. Where are you?"

"Up in the tree."

"Can't see you."

"Never mind. Stay where you are."

I felt renewed courage at the thought of Feetje standing under the tree. After another fruitless sawing effort, only one option remained: I would have to break off the top. The branches under me formed an entangled nest. If I were to fall while struggling with the top, I would still be able to grab on to some branch before tumbling to the ground. At least so I reasoned. In any case time was pressing, and I had to do something quickly. The horizon had already turned a soft pink.

With both hands I grabbed hold of the trunk above my head at the weakened spot where I had been sawing. With a mighty swing I let both feet fly into the air, bringing my full weight onto my hands

C-r-a-a-ck. The top broke off. I was hanging on to it, and luckily it was still hanging on to the tree by its bark. I could have yodeled. After recovering my foothold, I chipped through the bark and threw the top down to Feetje.

The stars had disappeared. A purplish-dawn enveloped everything. In a few minutes the sun would be up. For a second I cast a longing glance over the housetop, over the tall barbed wire and bamboo fence, far, far away into the free world, and sighed, but there was no time to get soft about things. I climbed down. Feetje helped me carry the tree back and my neighbor hid it for me. The children were still asleep.

While I was preparing breakfast at 7 a.m., Japanese and native policemen flooded the camp. Commotion reigned. Street leaders ran around, shouting through their homemade megaphones.

"Japanese orders. All bikes have to be turned in and brought to the gate. Right away."

So this was what the Japanese had cooked up for us for Christmas. The camp became a beehive. Hundreds of women walked their bikes to the gate. Hundreds more dug ditches to bury their tires, broke spokes, smashed the pedals or the chains before delivering their bikes. Every little act of sabotage might help.

I took my bike to the gate, then ran to the hiding place of the little bike, the children's Christmas present. A guard was standing in front of the open garage door. The bike was gone. Gone. I stood there, stricken. Somehow it seemed unbelievable that this could be happening. All my efforts in vain. All my hopes of making the children happy, gone. I felt beaten.

A big lump formed in my throat. *Oh, God, help me swallow that lump, please. I don't want to cry. I don't want to cry.*

Good thing I hadn't dropped even a faint hint to the girls about the Angel bringing a bike.

Later in the day I used our last pound of flour to make a cake, some sort of a cake anyway. I cheered myself up with the thought that it was Christmas Eve and that we would have guests in the evening.

Maya was quiet and preoccupied all day. "Mami, are you sure the Angel will bring a tree?"

"Quite sure, Maya. He never forgets children."

Late in the afternoon, the three girls went over to Feetje's. I told them I would follow later.

When they were gone, I decorated the room with some of the pine branches. I planted the tree in a bucket of sand, put on the homemade trimmings and the candles, placed the presents under it, and arranged with my neighbor to light the candles at a set time. Then I went to get the children.

"Has the Angel come?" the girls asked as we started for home.

"I haven't seen him."

"What if he forgets?"

"Don't worry. The Angel never forgets," I said, as our house came into view.

"Mami, I see a light in our room," Yvonne shouted. By then the three girls were running. They stopped on the threshold of the candle-lit room. Their faces were transfigured. It was there. The Tree.

153

Feetje followed right behind us. Reintje, Johtje, and Altien joined us a minute later. As the women played their violins ever so softly, we sang the familiar words, "Silent night, holy night . . .." Feetje's lovely voice led the singing. Our music filled the room with joy and peace.

This was truly the Angel's Tree.

Camp Life, War Rumors, and Food Rations

News from the outside world about the war reached us only via the grapevine. At first we believed everything. When we analyzed the news, however, much of it seemed far-fetched. In October 1943, for instance, the news spread that Germany had capitulated. Even the optimists among us realized that such a capitulation was too soon and too sudden.

In November the air-raid alarm sounded. The sirens howled all night and our hopes skyrocketed again. We were hoping for the arrival of Allied planes. The next day the rumor circulated that Priok, the port of Batavia, had been bombed. True? Not true? Who could say?

A few days later the milk distribution was stopped, a serious blow for the children. The camp kitchen also ceased to function. Raw vegetables, sometimes some fish, or a little meat was distributed, and irregularly a bit of peanut oil or coconut oil. However small these portions were, we found cooking our own food more satisfactory than eating those horrible soups.

The Japanese were after our money. We were each allowed to keep twenty guilders (about ten American dollars) and had to hand the rest over to the Japanese. Of course, no one was foolish enough to obey such an order. The street leaders, however, told us we had better hand over some money before the Japanese became angry and took drastic actions.

At the same time another Japanese order was issued. All boys past the age of eleven were to be taken away from their mothers and placed in a boys' camp under the supervision of Dutchmen. The mothers of these boys were heartsick.

When the day came for the boys to leave, hundreds of women accompanied their sons to the gate, helping to carry their bundles and suitcases. After a short goodbye, which left the mothers sobbing, the gates were flung open. The boys climbed into the waiting trucks outside the gates. The gates were closed. We heard the boys shouting "bye-bye," as they drove alongside the camp. "Bye-bye," we shouted back from inside. The answer was a hail of stones from the guards outside. One small child inside the camp was so badly hurt that he had to be taken to the hospital. Quietly, sadly, we dispersed.

As we had the year before, we celebrated New Year's Eve by creating a life-sized old man, representing 1943, from pillows stuffed into a shirt for the body, rolled-up towels for the arms and legs, and a filled pillowcase with a charcoal-drawn face and cotton wool beard for the head, topped with a hat. In his arms we placed a doll, representing the New Year, 1944. As part of the tradition, we also melted lead and told each other's fortunes by analyzing the shapes the melted lead took after being poured into cold water. After midnight we beat up the Old Year until he fell apart, to the delight of the children, because once again he hadn't kept his word. He hadn't brought peace and he hadn't brought Wim back.

Feetje, Reintje, and Johtje celebrated the evening with us. I had no more cake to offer them because I had used the last of the flour for the Christmas cake. We enjoyed the cup of coffee that I could still give everyone. We reminded each other that it could be ever so much worse. I felt, though, that all evening we were only pretending to be cheerful and happy. We were beginning to feel the depressing effect of camp life.

Soon after the beginning of the New Year, the Japanese granted us permission to write a postcard to our husbands or closest relatives. The order said that we would be allowed to do this every three months. We winked at each other knowingly. How silly the Japanese were. Didn't they realize the war was bound to be over in three months? How we deluded ourselves with our wishful thinking.

A few days later one of our women found these postcards, which we had so carefully worded in order to say neither too much nor too little, in the wastepaper basket of the Japanese office. Nippon must have reasoned that allowing the prisoners to write, thereby giving them the joy of thinking they were communicating with their loved ones, was sufficient. They didn't need to bother actually sending the postcards.

In the middle of January, I resigned from the house warden job. Coping with the moodiness of many of my housemates took too much nervous energy. We held a meeting, but nobody wanted to take over the job. Finally we decided that every month another woman would have to do the work and be the head of the house. I continued, however, to be in charge of the rice distribution, which had been reduced to about four ounces of rice per day per person.

Because vegetable distribution had also decreased, we were ordered to create vegetable gardens. Somebody lent me a hoe (what a treasure) and every day before dawn, I hoed part of the gravel path in front of our porch, hoping that something would grow there. Later I dug up the earth alongside the barbed wire fence and planted cucumbers there. I saw them in my mind's eye, climbing up the fence. We fertilized the plants with our human manure, which I carried out in the chamber pot in the gray hour of dawn or after sunset under cover of darkness.

In another Japanese order we were told to keep the grass cut around the houses. Because our garden tools had been confiscated at the time of entry into camp, we found ourselves on all fours, cutting the grass with table knives and scissors.

Signora Pomidora and Mrs. Tomatea, our two tomato plants, were laden with green fruit. Not only our home-produced manure but also our loving and encouraging glances made them grow ever faster. Three of the tomatoes were already pink, but we didn't want to pick them before they were fully ripe. "Maybe tomorrow," the children said, looking at them with anticipation before going to bed.

First thing next morning we went to look at how pink they were. Well, they weren't pink. They were gone. Yes. Stolen. Two of them. The third one was somewhat hidden among the branches. We stood there, stricken. I was bitter and furious. We were determined to catch the thief. She would undoubtedly come back for the third tomato, which she probably hadn't seen in the dark. We would keep watch. We settled the order of watch rotation in a matter of minutes. Yvonne was to be the first to sit behind the half-closed door. She was getting settled into her position when in an alarmed voice she exclaimed, "Mami, the third tomato is gone." And so it was. What a clever thief. The whole thing seemed so comically tragic that we almost laughed.

I made a sign and hung it on one of Mrs. Tomatea's branches. The message read: THIEF, LOOK OUT! YOU ARE BEING WATCHED!

For some psychological reason this worked. In a few days we picked and enjoyed the fourth ripe tomato.

And so we reached Easter. Tradition had to be kept despite conditions. I didn't want the children to miss the thrill of the egg hunt. I had saved three of the smuggled duck eggs and colored them with crayons after boiling them, hoping they hadn't turned bad in the preceding ten days. From our scanty sugar ration, I had saved enough during the last two weeks to make nine tiny fondant eggs, each no bigger than a marble. I wrapped these candies in colored paper. The kind embroidery teacher crocheted a little bag for each child from cotton thread I had acquired through bartering. I prepared three nests, put a crocheted bag containing the duck egg and three little sugar eggs in each nest, and hid them the night before.

The next morning the children, in their eagerness, started the hunt before it was fully daylight. What a lot of fun they had finding the nests. All day long they walked around with their little bags, counting their treasures from time to time. They had to be coaxed to eat the eggs. For them it was the proverbial problem of wanting to have their cake and eat it too.

A few days after Easter, I received a letter from the Hungarian legation in Tokyo, dated October of the previous year (1943), asking why I had returned the money my brother Laci had sent me and requesting a telegram with information on how we were. I went to the camp office, obtained an interview with the Japanese commander, and after showing him the letter asked whether I could send a telegram in reply. He said he would talk it over with his superiors.

A week later I was summoned to the office. I took with me a draft of the answering telegram, which I had written in both Malay and English. A bank official awaited me in the office. He wanted to know why I had returned the money to Laci. Of course I could have said, "Why did you not give me the money?" But I thought it wiser not to provoke the man. I said something about not being able to keep or to use the money in camp.

Then I asked him to forward my telegram. That was none of his business, he said. The permission had to come from the military authorities. Thus my telegram problem was in the same stage as before.

Two weeks later I was summoned again and told that I could send it. The next day I was told the opposite. This went on three or four more times until, finally, the telegram was never sent.

Besides struggling with the telegram issue, I was also dealing with a health problem. I was experiencing cramplike stomach pains so acute I often had to lie down in the middle of doing my work. For a time I ignored them, but when they continued to increase in intensity, I went to see the doctor. She wanted me to go to the hospital for observation, but I couldn't leave the children alone. We agreed that I would stay in bed at least half the day and she would send me someone to do the laundry and wash the floor, for financial remuneration, of course.

A few days later the doctor brought a colleague to see me. The two of them poked me all over. They discovered a lump the size of an egg in my intestines, the center of the radiating pain. They said it probably had something to do with nerves and put me on a soft-rice diet.

I followed the diet for a while, but the sight of the mushy rice nauseated me and consuming it provided no improvement in my condition. When the person who was helping me with the housework left, I was no better off than I had been before I had gone to the doctor. Analyzing my condition, I noticed that the pain was most acute about three hours after eating. I experimented by cutting out a meal. The pain did not come. The cure was easy, I reasoned, all I had to do was to stop eating!

On the two following days, while going about my work as usual, I took a good dose of castor oil, ate nothing, and drank only weak, unsweetened tea. I felt weak, but I had no pain. On the third day I ate two, thin, almost transparent, slices of bread after having dried them in the sun. I continued to drink the unsweetened weak tea. I felt no pain at all, and the lump seemed smaller. I increased the slices to six or seven a day, took a few spoonfuls of vegetables, and kept drinking the unsweetened tea. I stuck to this miserable diet for six weeks, doing my work at the same time. I lost a considerable amount of weight but felt perfectly fine. Carefully I returned to eating rice, which, after all, was our staple food. The pain never returned. I was cured. (After the war a surgeon told me that scar tissue provided evidence of what had apparently been a sizable ulcer. The ulcer had almost eaten its way through the intestinal wall.)

We were in regular contact with the Tjihapit camp through the medical services. Tjihapit had more doctors, as well as a hospital equipped for operations. All serious cases, therefore, were sent over there from Karees. An eye doctor from the Tjihapit camp also came once week to Karees to see patients in our camp. Because my eyes were weakening rapidly, I went to see him.

I lined up with the other patients at 8 a.m. My turn came at 2 p.m., a long wait but not as boring as might have been expected. At nine o'clock a Japanese guard came to inspect us. Obediently, we stood up and one of the patients shouted, "*Kiotskay!*" Stand at attention! We bowed deeply. The guard asked in Malay whether there were any relatives of the doctor among the patients.

A thin older woman stepped forward. "I am the doctor's mother," she said. "Go home," said the Japanese. The old lady gathered up her knitting, bowed, and walked away.

Nobody said a word. My whole body shook with indignation and rage. Some of us had tears in our eyes. All wasted compassion. The old lady wasn't a mother for nothing. Half an hour later we found her sitting and knitting in a group of other women on the porch of the house next door. About an hour passed. She kept on knitting. The Japanese guard didn't return.

Then, at a given signal, she quickly walked over to us and slipped into the consultation room between two patients. Through the half-open curtain, we saw her sitting in the patient's chair, while her son, the doctor, fitted her with one pair of glasses after the other as the two talked quietly to each other. To play the game convincingly, she emerged from the consultation room with a prescription in her hand. She was all smiles now. She had seen and talked to her son.

Other than my most recent stomach pains and Yvonne's asthma-bronchitis shortly after our arrival in camp, we had on the whole not had any serious health concerns. Remembering how fortifying the salt baths of my childhood in Hungary were, I used our more than adequate salt rations to help keep the children healthy. I put some salt in the water in our small washtub, warmed the water up in the sun, and let the children bathe and splash in it for about an hour every day. The sun added to the salt water was like eating health with a spoon, I told the girls.

I also had one sulfur pill, the size of an aspirin. Whenever the girls had a little wound that wouldn't heal, I would scrape a bit of this tablet on it and bandage the wound. The effect was miraculous. The wound would close in a day.

According to a new order we were allowed to keep only about four dollars' worth of Dutch money. The rest had to be turned over to the Japanese. The same thing happened as at a previous similar order. A little "show money" was turned in and everybody sat tight with whatever she possessed.

We had been under the Japanese rule for many months now and we were hungry. Although we still had some money, smuggled goods were practically unobtainable. Milk and canteen goods were also no longer available. The rice ration had been reduced, as had the vegetable ration. And for the last few months we had received no oil at all.

When we entered camp I had brought along, for lighting purposes, some peanut oil in a kerosene bottle. Now that our coconut oil reserve, which we had been using for cooking, was finished, I was compelled to use this peanut oil. I heated up the tainted oil with a piece of bread in it, hoping the bread would soak up the kerosene smell. It didn't work. Rice fried in the oil tasted like swallowing a kerosene lamp.

On May 12, 1944, I received two postcards from Wim. I read them and reread them for hours. They were the first sign of life from him in nearly two years. They carried no date and no postmark, but he said he was in Japan and in good health. Why had they taken him so far away? I wondered whether to believe it. On one of the cards he wished us a merry Christmas. Did he mean Christmas 1942 or 1943? Who could tell? The cards were typewritten, but the signature on the cards was unmistakably his. They were both addressed to our home on the Lembang road, our bungalow in the *sawahs*, which meant he hadn't received any news from or about us and didn't even know that we were in camp. It was better this way.

In June another happy event was the arrival of American Red Cross packages. What a day that was. Each package, apparently originally meant for one person, was to be shared by eight people. With what care and love the contents of these packages were chosen, and how well informed the Red Cross was of the needs of prisoners. They contained everything we did not have and everything we needed so badly: canned meat, cheese, butter, powdered milk, instant coffee, sugar in cubes, raisins, chocolate, and cigarettes.

We received half a package for the four of us. The children danced around it and kept packing, unpacking, and repacking the unheard of treasures. I made a cup of milk for each of them. We divided one of the four five-cent Hershey bars among the four of us. And we each had ten raisins and three lumps of sugar. We were convinced that never before had we eaten such delicious things. And how I enjoyed smoking a Chesterfield to top off the Lucullan meal. I figured that with wise economy I could make the contents of the Red Cross package stretch over a few weeks.

Besides the contents of the package, what touched us so deeply was the connection it gave us with our people. With this gift they showed their compassion and love for us, countering the hate emanating from our Japanese captors.

To offset the joy of receiving the Red Cross packages, the Japanese introduced their version of roll call, called *tenko*. Twice a day, at 6:30 a.m. and at 5:30 p.m., we had to line up in front of our houses and await the arrival of our street leader. When she approached, the house warden shouted *"Kiotskay!"* stand at attention. We all stiffened. She followed it with *"Kiray!"* bow. We bowed at a forty-five-degree angle. The street leader in turn bowed the same way to us. Then the house warden shouted *"Nowray!"* straighten up. We stood erect again.

The first time we performed this ridiculous Punch-and-Judy show, we laughed at the absurdity of it. We got used to it in time, however. Sometimes a Japanese would pass by to inspect whether we were bowing properly and whether those who didn't appear at *tenko* were really sick and in bed.

Bowing was terribly important to the Japanese, not only during *tenko* but also when we met a Japanese anywhere in camp. Beatings were dealt out for not doing it properly. The Japanese were forever on the lookout for slackers.

One day a Japanese picked up a dozen women who hadn't bowed well enough, lined them up in front of the main office, beat them, and made them stand there under the broiling sun during the hottest part of the day, between noon and two in the afternoon, without any head covering. For twenty minutes out of the two hours, the women had to stand in the bowing position. If they fainted they were carried into the shade. Poor Mrs. Wonder was among the "culprits." She dropped in for a cup of water after her release.

Twice orders had circulated to deliver all electrical appliances to the Japanese. Nobody obeyed. After such an announcement, all equipment disappeared for a while. Then slowly the more courageous ones dug up their gadgets, with everybody else gradually following their example. It would be bad luck if an unexpected house search took place. Only the first house, however, would suffer. The news of the search, through the watchword "aspirin," which warned others when a Japanese was in the neighborhood, would spread in no time, giving the occupants of other houses time to hide their things.

One day, our house was subject to such an unexpected visit. I was the shock absorber because the Japanese came to our room first.

I had learned how to boil water on our upturned iron and always hid the iron after using it. Luckily this time was no exception.

The Japanese looked around, found my electric cord on top of the cupboard and put it in his pocket.

"Where iron?" he asked in Malay.

"No iron," I said. (No iron for you, I meant.)

He looked around again, said the room was nice and tidy, and left. Now I had an iron, but no cord for it. Within two days I managed to get another one through the barter system.

For some reason or other, the Japanese started giving us a newspaper. The four-page *Voice of Nippon*, which was written in English and printed in Batavia especially for the prisoners of war, came every two weeks. This newspaper was a joke, full of Japanese victories and heroism and accounts of the brutality of the Americans toward Japanese prisoners. But we were occasionally able to read between the lines.

They couldn't fill the whole four pages with war news, so the paper sometimes contained interesting stories. A story about the Australian pajama girl, for example, which provided a lengthy description of how brutally she had been murdered. At the end of the story, in tiny letters, were the words, "This happened ten years ago." Or, as another example, the announcement that the Japanese prime minister had given the prime minister of Manchuria a beautiful Mercedes-Benz as a birthday present. Then, again in small letters, "The car was confiscated from Europeans in Shanghai."

We couldn't enjoy the paper for long because it stopped coming as abruptly as it had started. We took it for a good sign that perhaps the tide of war was turning. We often heard the piano being played by Indo-Europeans who lived in liberty in the house across the road, beyond the barbed wire and bamboo fence. In confidence I had learned from the head of our camp that an arrangement had been made between these folks and the camp head that whenever the Allies won an important victory, the Indo-Europeans would play a certain Dutch tune.

One afternoon late in June, we heard the long-awaited tune. When it was finished, they played it again. By then the head of our camp was walking along the fence with a friend. I joined them. "Something very important has happened," they whispered.

When the tune was being repeated for the third time, I climbed up on the parapet of our porch and looked over to the house across. I couldn't see the piano player, but another woman stood on their porch, holding a bunch of marigolds above her head. We were quick to interpret this sign language. Unmistakably it meant "orange above." In Dutch, *oranje boven,* with *oranje*, orange, meaning the House of Orange, the Dutch monarchy. So the Dutch were "above." We were guessing that perhaps Holland was free. Much later we learned through the grapevine that the Allies had landed somewhere in France.

And then came a series of strange events. The first was in response to the news that Nippon was looking for bar women. Those who volunteered, so the announcement went, would be taken out of camp and placed in various bars in Bandoeng. Everybody treated the idea as a joke. We were convinced that not one person would step forward. Once more we were wrong. No fewer than twenty women presented themselves, dressed in their best dresses, and were taken to town in a truck. They were never heard from again. According to the old saying, there's a buyer for everything.

Another story circulated that three women escaped to town by creeping out through the sewer pipe. They were caught in a Chinese restaurant, brought back, and questioned. Their simple answer for why they had done it was that they were terribly hungry and wanted a good meal. After the usual beating, they were put in solitary for ten days on rice and water. The Japanese warned us that any future escapees would be punished more severely.

An even more bizarre story was that of a woman who put on her best dress and hat, packed her belongings in a small suitcase, and went to the gate. She told the guard that she had to go to the Japanese camp office, which was just outside the gate. She seemed so definite about it that the guard allowed her to pass. She entered the office building and told the surprised guard in the anteroom she had come to see her husband. After questioning her, they determined she had lost her mind. Because she was harmless, they conducted her back to camp and placed her in a house with a few others in a similar condition.

Great commotion also erupted when some Dutch men prisoners were led into the camp to do some heavy work for us. The women made the mistake of trying to talk to the men. In consequence the men were beaten up. The next time the men were brought in, we disappeared into our rooms in order not to provoke the guards. We heard that in Tjihapit, the other camp for Bandoengers, a Dutchman on heavy work duty had wanted to help a woman carry a heavy load. The Japanese guard had responded by kicking him to death in front of the woman. Was this story true? We had no way of checking.

Things were not going well for us under the heel of the Japanese. Clearly they wanted to starve us. The rice ration had been reduced again, to three and a half ounces this time. The vegetables we received were so inadequate that we went digging in the hospital garbage. We seldom saw fruit. Dysentery was spreading, as were cases of swollen legs from beriberi. Skin with nasty, dark red, itchy patches was common. More than half the women had wounds full of pus that wouldn't heal. Many had vomiting fits accompanied by fever. Some collapsed from exhaustion.

I hoped my little garden would produce more soon. So far we were getting tomatoes and a little spinach out of it. I cooked the tomato greens also, as well as the leaves of the bean plants. I tried to cook grass, but found it inedible. I extended my respect to, and admiration for, cows.

Although smuggling was practically nonexistent, with great pains I managed to acquire a bottle of oil for the equivalent of about ten dollars. It used to cost a nickel.

The children didn't complain of hunger; only Maya came more and more often to get something between meals. I was glad always to be able to give her some rice with sugar. Of course I didn't tell the children that I felt terribly hungry myself. Not that we small eaters couldn't fill our tummies. The rice was quite enough for us. I even saved some of it for a rainy day. The diet, however, was completely unbalanced, which led to horrible cravings for food of a particular kind, dreams of meat, butter, chocolate, and fruit. The children still looked well, thank heavens, but I had lost weight again.

We had been in Karees for a year. It seemed like ten.

One hopeful note was another postcard from Wim. No date on it, but the handwriting was definitely his. I carried it in my blouse during the day and put it under my pillow at night. Such undated news conveyed little and yet meant so much.

The charcoal distribution had stopped. We received wood instead. I was at a loss the first day on how to make a workable fire. Yvonne came to my rescue. Fire making was apparently in her blood. She was a genius at it. She found two bricks, stood them up lengthwise, put the pot on top of them, and placed the long stick of wood between them.

In a few days we even learned how to make charcoal. When the rice was cooked, we took the burnt but still glowing pieces of wood, doused them with cold water, and dried them in the sun. It was important to have some charcoal because we had to cook in the room during rainy weather, which would have been difficult to do with a wood fire because of the smoke and flames.

Fate had spoiled the woman in the room next to us. She still had her electrical cooker. And the head of our camp even had her fridge because she was fortunate enough to be living in the same house she had had been living in before the war. Even camp life was meted out differently to everyone.

Take, for example, the transport that had arrived a few weeks earlier, made up mostly of French, Belgian, Norwegian, and other non-Dutch Europeans. The women had been pulled out of their beds, some didn't have so much as a small suitcase with them, and one had only the nightgown she was wearing.

In cases such as these, our solidarity surpassed expectations. An immediate collection was taken up and, within ten to twelve hours, the women were supplied with the most necessary things. At the arrival of every transport, we were on the square by the hundreds, watching the native policemen splitting open the suitcases with their handy little hatchets. We stood by ready to assist the newcomers. Because there were no more coolies, we helped to carry their belongings to their living quarters.

In a wave of generosity on one such occasion, I had lent, for a few days only, our sole and precious chamber pot to a newcomer who was slightly ill. Precious, because it was the only means of transporting our night soil to the vegetable garden.

The woman recovered but refused to return the pot.

The garden, which grew in importance the hungrier we became, could not be left without manure. The solution was to "do it" in an empty five-pound lard can. Only those who have tried this maneuver know what a delicate operation that can be.

After several weeks I managed to wrest the chamber pot from the woman. The girls greeted its return with cheers.

The rice, bread, and sugar rations were again reduced. As for vegetables, every second or third day we received either a few stalks of celery, some half-rotten, yellow cabbage leaves, or one or two miserable-looking tomatoes. We heard that, undoubtedly as a result of the poor nutrition, eighty-two people from the two Bandoeng camps, Tjihapit and Karees, had died during a single week.

The street leaders received permission from the Japanese to buy additional food for us—with our own money, of course. Somehow the fact that we were not supposed to have more than four dollars' worth of cash was overlooked. Small canteens opened at street leader locations where we could get, at astronomical prices, microscopic amounts of bacon, dried wild boar meat, and sugar. One reason why the prices were so high was that those with money had to pay for those who had none or pretended to have none.

It was around this time that I took a piece of charcoal and wrote on the wall of our room, in beautiful Gothic letters:

Honger Is De Beste Saus	Hunger is the best sauce
and	
Si On N'a Pas Ce Qu'on Aime	If one doesn't have what one likes
Il Faut Aimer Ce Qu'on A	One has to like what one has

The latter was the first, rather peculiar, French lesson I gave the girls.

The children were a great help, a source of joy, and no trouble whatsoever. I spanked them only once and never again after that. The spanking occurred a few weeks after our arrival in camp, back in the late summer of 1943, when they had gone firefly hunting at dusk. I had given them permission to go but told them to be back in about an hour's time.

The hour passed. And then another half hour. By then it was totally dark outside. I began to worry and went looking for them. I didn't dare to go too far for fear they would come home from the opposite direction and, not finding me in the room, they would become worried. Back I went and waited some more.

Another half hour passed, but no children. Panic set in. Had the Japanese picked them up? I paced back and forth, peering into the darkness, listening to oncoming noises, and trying to focus on what to do.

Ten minutes later they turned up, laughing and happy, as if everything was as it should be. They showed me the jar full of fireflies they had caught.

I could have cried from joy at having them back safe. At the same time I was angry with them for not having returned on time and for having caused me such anxiety. After having made this clear to them, I lifted one skirt after the other and spanked each of their little behinds. When each child had been spanked, I emphasized that the punishment was not for catching the fireflies but for causing the worry.

The scene over, I suggested we play for a while with the fireflies, but their fun had been spoiled. I felt they resented the corporal punishment, which they weren't used to receiving.* I suppose it seemed too much like the beatings the Japanese were doling out to us.

In September it was my turn to a give a talk in French to the members of our little Alliance Française club that met once a week. I chose a pertinent subject: Are we learning something from camp life or are we allowing the miserable conditions to poison us?

I presented the ideal, twofold viewpoint: that we had learned not to be possessed by our possessions and that we had come to accept that what cards we are dealt is not as important as how we play the hand. I threw myself whole-heartedly into my presentation. When I was finished, however, I had to ask myself whether I really felt and believed all that I had said, and whether I was living up to it. The path to perfection wasn't easy.

A week later I was asked to become the president of our little club because our Russian president had become ill. I couldn't accept the honor, however, because of the extra work it involved. I could hardly carry my own load as it was.

---

*We children clearly remember getting our "revenge" for this unjustified (in our eyes) spanking by not brushing our teeth but saying we had, and, after having been sent to bed in the dark, of releasing the dozens of fireflies to light up the room.

In October I received another telegram from Laci through the Hungarian Legation in Tokyo, which read, "Please accept money." I gathered that he might think us dead if the money were to be sent back again, so I accepted it. That is, I would have accepted it, had the Japanese paid it out. I received only fifty guilders in cash and a notation on my camp card that the remaining one thousand four hundred and fifty guilders had been deposited in my name at the Yokohama Specie Bank. (After the war I learned that Laci had never sent this telegram. The Japanese had faked it in order to get their hands on the money.)

In November 1944 we received the surprising news that Karees was going to be evacuated and we would be transferred to other camps in Java.

6
Wim
May 1943

*The mine honchos, or foremen, ruled the men in the mines
in a manner varying from "frequently rough," that is, slapping,
to "regularly beastly," that is, beating, kicking, and assaulting
the men with any tool available.*

From the Frying Pan into the Fire

After the hell ship *Kyokku Maru* had disgorged the fifteen hundred prisoners onto the shores of Japan at the port of Moji on May 20, 1943, the men were split up into five smaller groups. Each group was destined for a different camp:

One group of 300 British with three British officers
One group of 200 Australians with two Australian officers
One group of 400 Dutch with four Dutch officers
A second group of 400 Dutch with four Dutch officers
One group of 200 Dutch with only one Dutch officer
    (one officer having died onboard)

Wim, Frits Wilkens, two other officers, and one group of four hundred Dutch soldiers were headed for camp Fukuoka #7* to work in the coal mines of Futase City. There the men would endure another sort of hell for the next two-and-a-half years of captivity. Until the end of 1943, this camp was under Japanese army administration. After that, the mining company

---

*Although first numbered Fukuoka #10, the camp was later renumbered Fukuoka #7 and will be referred to as such throughout this account.

took over the camp's administration until September 2, 1945, at which time it came under Wim's command. The owners of the Honko and Shinko Mining Company, for whom the prisoners would be working, had a contract with the Japanese government for the employment and exploitation of the POWs.

Fukuoka #7 was only one of well over three hundred POW camps located in Japan proper. Various companies, both in the homeland and in other countries the Japanese had conquered, used the prisoners as slave laborers. The POWs were forced to work long hours, under dangerous conditions, and with inadequate clothing, shelter, food, and equipment. The industrial giants Mitsubishi Corp., Mitsui & Co., Nippon Steel Corp., Kawasaki Industries Ltd, and Showa Denko K.K.* were among the companies who later faced a class action lawsuit for engaging in the use of prisoners as slave labor.

In what had become usual Japanese fashion, after having been hurried off the *Kyokku Maru*, Wim's group of POWs was made to wait for hours. As evening approached they were loaded onto a passenger train, only to wait some more. Their first meal on Japanese soil arrived in two wooden *bento* boxes. The first box contained rice. In the second box the prisoners found *ebbie*, little, red creepy-crawlies. The Japanese savored these sea creatures; the prisoners did not. Nevertheless, the latter learned to eat them in order to benefit from their rich protein content.

Through the night and part of the next day, the exhausted and weak men waited. Then with a squeal of metal on metal, the train lurched into motion at midday and chugged in fits and starts southwest to the city of Iizuka. The men could see nothing of the countryside because the Japanese ordered the shades pulled down. What lay beyond the train window? Were there flowering fruit trees, or mirrorlike water-flooded rice paddies bristling with sprigs of young rice plants, or newly tilled and planted fields of soybeans, or dusty industrial towns? They had no way of knowing.

After they arrived at the impressively large train station in Iizuka, Wim had the men line up in rows to form four squads. To bolster the men's spirit and make a show of bravado, Wim had them march with military precision

---

*As reported in the *Tokyo Weekender*'s cover story by Milton Combs, May 26, 2000.

from the train station. For the next three or four miles they walked along the cinder-coated streets through the slumlike areas of the coal-mining towns of Iizuka and then of Futase and on to Fukuoka #7. The local people seemed neither hostile nor friendly, just mildly curious. They may have been wondering why, if these dirty, emaciated, weak-looking prisoners were an example of the enemy, it was taking so long for their glorious Japanese military to win the war?

As the men approached their new home in the late afternoon, Wim, who was at the head of the first squad, could see smoke spewing from the four-hundred-foot-high smokestacks of the Honko and Shinko Mining Company power plant. The prisoners would be the new slave laborers for these mines.

Wim's camp, Fukuoka #7, Futase, Japan, 1943

A twelve-foot-high wooden stockade fence surrounded the camp, which covered approximately seven acres of land on the crest of an old slag and rock heap. Fastened to the top of the fence were sharp bamboo spikes angled inward to thwart any who attempted to escape. In addition an alarm system was attached to the fence. Without these measures the men might have tried to escape, but how far would a Westerner dressed in shabby military garb and not speaking Japanese have gotten among the Asian populace of rural Japan?

The prisoners were housed in wooden barracks. The main one was a large U-shaped wooden building. The minimally heated (a single five-inch pipe running through one end of each room), light frame structure had dim lighting, a concrete floor, poor ventilation, and a leaky tile roof. The beds were three-tiered bunks that lined the length of the building on the two sides. The vertical space from one bunk to its neighbor above was so tight that the men could not sit upright on their beds. They had little breathing room, with the wooden platform above pressing down on them. Covering the platforms were two-and-a-half-inch-thick straw *tatami* mats. No pillows, no sheets, just two thin cotton blankets. Later, as winter approached, the Japanese gave them overcoats, which the men used as blankets for additional warmth.

Kitchen at Fukuoka #7

The compound had a huge mess hall, large enough to seat four hundred on benches at one sitting, a large kitchen, and superior bathing facilities.

The latter consisted of two large steam-heated pools. One was for soaping oneself, at least as long as the luxury of soap was available, which wasn't long; the other, for soaking in. The soaking pool could hold about forty people, forerunner of the contemporary hot tub, although minus the curvaceous naked blondes and the martinis close at hand.

Bath house at Fukuoka #7

The men were a little disconcerted at first, not being used to communal bathing, but the steam-heated hot water was much appreciated after a twelve-hour shift of setting dynamite charges, wielding pickaxes, or scooping up and tossing coal into carts in the mines. Although the water was continuously being refreshed, it soon ran black from the coal dust washing off the men's bodies.

Latrines were located both in the main building and in a separate structure. Holes were cut into, and flush with, the floor. Underneath were receiving pits. Twice weekly men on poop duty emptied these pits. The men filled two wooden buckets to the brim with the cesspool contents. They carried the dangling buckets on a pole on their shoulders and dumped the contents on the nascent vegetable garden as fertilizer.

POWs emptying contents of cesspool pits at Fukuoka #7

At the extreme end of the main building was the sick bay, which would see instant use after the prisoners' arrival at the camp. Several of those who had barely survived the hell ship would succumb within the next few weeks and months.

One of the first to be stricken was Frits Wilkens. The Japanese doctor decided he had dysentery and prescribed purging as the treatment. The expected result ensued. With the continuous "drainage," Frits became ever weaker. Wim sounded the alarm that this treatment was disastrous. Using vivid language, he warned the Japanese command that allowing a *senior* officer, with an emphasis on the term senior, to be the first to die in the camp would be a blemish on their reputation and prestige. The Japanese were apparently disturbed enough at the possibility of such an outcome— perhaps they thought they would lose face if that happened—that they summoned a new doctor.

The new doctor decided that the basic problem was lack of vitamins, especially vitamin B. So for the next three months, as his life hung in the balance, Frits received first intravenous and then painful spinal cord injections of vitamins. Later it was determined that in fact he was suffering from an advanced case of beriberi, a heart and nerve disease caused by a deficiency of thiamine, that is, vitamin B1.

Besides the vitamin injections, Wim's nonstop badgering kept Frits from drifting through death's half-open door. For many days Wim argued with and needled Frits, telling him that so much needed to be done, that this was no time to give up, that it was Frits's job to show the Japanese what the Dutch were made of. Like the grain of sand that irritates the oyster into creating a pearl, Wim's persistent heckling irritated Frits into creating the will to live when it would have been so much easier for him to sink into black oblivion.*

Wim would use this technique on others who were also ready to throw in the towel. He succeeded with some but not with all because there were some whose illnesses were too advanced and who just didn't care anymore.

"Heigh Ho, Heigh Ho, It's Off to Work We Go"

Nine days after stepping onto Japanese soil, the prisoners, regardless of age, former occupation, or physical condition, donned the standard miners' outfit and went to work on the slagheap. This outdoor topside labor, which consisted of digging, scraping, and shoveling in and on the slagheap, lasted for about a week. During that time the Japanese were figuring out how best to organize the new labor force. The slagheap work turned out to be foreplay for the main event, work in the underground mines.

It also served to set the stage for a showdown between the Japanese command and Wim and the other Dutch officers. The Japanese insisted that all men, including the officers, join the workforce in the mines. Wim and the other officers (minus Frits Wilkens who was hovering between life and death at the time) refused to do so, as per the rules of war that officers could not be compelled to work. To break down their resolve, the Japanese

---

* Many years later, when I met Frits in Holland as an adult, he told me that he credited Wim for having talked him back from the brink of death.

locked the officers up and put them on short rations. Despite threats of dire consequences, the Dutch prisoners who manned the kitchen defied the Japanese orders and smuggled food to their officers.

Eventually the Japanese relented, at least partially. They agreed that the Dutch officers, assisted by the kitchen staff and a few orderlies, would run the camp. The rest, including the noncommissioned officers, whom the Japanese didn't consider to be officers, would be sent to work in the mines.

Both the Japanese command and the prisoners accepted Wim, who was the senior officer, as camp head. He handled all problems that occurred among the men and served as their morale booster, cheerleader, gadfly, and disciplinarian. In addition he functioned, with utmost diplomacy, as intermediary between the men and their captors, "playing" the Japanese command to ensure the best possible outcome for his men.

"We found," he wrote, "that in order to make life bearable for the men, we had to work the Japanese with small bribes and 'soft soaping,' as we had frequently been told that POWs have *no* rights, and we could have prevented becoming POWs by committing hara-kiri as all Japanese would do when losing in war."

After Frits Wilkens recovered from his long illness, he became the administrative officer. One of his first jobs was to record the weight of each of the four hundred prisoners monthly and produce eleven copies of these records each time. When Frits told the Japanese that this was an almost impossible task without a typewriter, copy paper, and carbon paper, the Japanese agreed and provided him with an ancient machine and the requested paper.

At Wim's suggestion and unbeknownst to the Japanese, Frits also kept careful secret records of the food the men received, which provided a clear picture of their weight and health as linked to their nutrition. After the war these reports were included in documents to be used at the Tokyo War Crimes Trials.

Later another one of his duties was to distribute the weekly batch of eight thousand cigarettes, with each man allowed three cigarettes a day. In the absence of calculators or adding machines and with the Japanese seemingly counting-challenged, as evidenced by the interminable counts and recounts of the men during the twice daily *tenko*, or roll call, the number of cigarettes Frits was to distribute varied weekly. Sometimes the count was over. Sometimes it was under.

One of the two other officers was in charge of "catering," that is, dealing with the delivery of food supplies, the kitchen staff, and the preparation and distribution of food. The remaining officer handled any detail not associated with the men working in the mine. For example, this officer assigned men labeled as the "walking sick" to empty the cesspools or to work on a nearby farm, planting sweet potatoes and other vegetables.

The Japanese rejected Wim's contention that the noncommissioned officers were officers. The NCOs were, therefore, forced to work in the mines with the rest of the men, but at least in the higher position of gang bosses. As such they had more authority than the other workers. They were often able to protect their fellow prisoners from the brutality of the Japanese civilian mine hands by intervening at crucial times, sometimes even being backed up by the Japanese sergeants.

One additional person Wim managed to save from mine work was Pieter Braber. Braber was a scientist from a research lab in West Java. But more importantly for Wim, he was also a linguist. While a POW in the various camps in Java, Braber had spent his time studying Japanese and was fluent by the time he reached Futase. He became the camp's official interpreter, a godsend since he excelled not only in translating the words of the Japanese orders but also in adding helpful comments. He was adept at deducing the intentions of the orders from the way they were given and thus managed to provide hints to Wim and the other officers on how they should react. And so, with roles established and functions assigned, the machine of camp life with its interconnected parts creaked into motion.

Several months after arriving at the camp, the men were inexplicably allowed to send brief postcards to their families. Wim sent one to Klara saying he was in Japan and in good health and another one to Phien, his cousin in Holland. His card to Phien arrived in Holland on December 15, 1943:

Dear Phien,

At last a sign of life for the folks at home. Since a few months I'm in a POW camp in Japan. In perfect health, so don't worry about me. The last news I had from Klara and the children, a

year ago, was quite favorable under the circumstances, and I
have good reason to believe and trust that she is managing all
right. I'm longing for more recent news from her as well as from
you, p.t.o for address. Please advise Gabor in Aracs, or Magda at
the legation accordingly.

Best wishes, love
Wim

Work in the coal mines was nonstop, proceeding around the clock.
The mine workers were divided into two shifts, with each shift on for
twelve hours and off for twelve hours. Two hours of "off" hours were
spent hiking to and from the mines. *Tenko* twice a day took another hour.
Additional time was needed for eating and for bathing to wash off the coal
dust and grime. This schedule left about six to seven hours for sleeping.
The night shift was slightly better off, because they didn't have to take part
in the evening *tenko*.

Besides the twelve-hour workday, the Japanese instituted a ten-day
work "week." The prisoners were allowed only three free days a month to
attend to personal matters, such as washing their clothes or spending time
in some sort of recreation.

Rules regarding recreation time, however, varied from one Japanese
commander to the next. Of the six Japanese commanders who headed the
camp during the two-and-a-half years the POWs were there, the first few
restricted recreation even on the three rest days a month. Not until the last
commander, Captain Sakai, who was assigned to the camp in February
1945, were the men allowed to spend their free day, starting at 10 a.m., doing what they liked, including making music, attending religious services,
playing chess or cards (with cards supplied by the YMCA), or reading.

A miniscule library, consisting of a few, very few, Dutch books and
a YMCA-supplied set of English books, was available. The non-English
speakers, however, suffered from the scarcity of Dutch books.

Another factor hindering recreation was the lack of a recreation area.
The unheated dining room, the only inside area available, was usable only
between meals or after the evening meal. On workdays, therefore, effectively no area was available.

Outside recreation was initially possible in the square formed by the legs of the U-shaped main building, until the area was transformed into a vegetable garden in early 1945. Another possibility was the yard in front of the main building, but the Japanese offices, guardhouse, and guard living quarters bordered this area, so the prisoners avoided it. The POWs didn't relish the idea of kicking around a soccer ball, even if they had had the energy, while their Japanese tormentors looked on like Roman spectators at a gladiatorial match. Recreation, therefore, was virtually nonexistent because neither working hours nor regulations, except during the last six months of their imprisonment, allowed for it.

Mine work was hard and dangerous. As part of their minimal training, the workers learned the Japanese words for *mine, danger, coal basket, hoe, pickax*. They didn't need instruction to learn the terms for *take a rest* and *stop work*.

The men trudged to the mines dressed in their mine uniforms of thin blouselike tops, cotton shorts, rubber-soled shoes (which were later replaced by rice straw sandals that often didn't last more than one work shift), and black miner's caps made of rubberized cotton with a fiber bracket to hold a lamp.

The two main mines were Honko and Shinko. Honko was a thirty-eight-hundred-foot-deep vertical shaft mine. Caged lifts transported the new, apprehensive miners two by two straight down to the working area in the bowels of the earth. The lamps on their miner's caps bobbed up and down, casting circles of light on the walls of the pit as they descended.

In the assembly area below, the Japanese divided the men into work gangs and sent them off, through the tangle of tunnels resembling the tentacles of a convention of octopi, to their work location. They were assigned either to construction work or production work. Construction work meant extending the laterals, laying more tracks, and shoring up the roof and walls. Those doing production work blasted out the coal, scooped or hoed it up into baskets, and loaded it into carts or onto conveyors. Many of the men had probably never so much as dug a hole in a garden or hung a picture, but now they were handling heavy pneumatic drills to drill holes for dynamite charges, swinging pickaxes, repairing or replacing overhead timbers, or placing new supports.

Shinko, the second main mine, was an old, inclined shaft mine located a few miles beyond the Honko mine and on the other side of the slagheap mountain. Earlier closed because it was unproductive, the Shinko mine had been reopened to meet the urgent war effort needs. The miners working the Shinko mine assembled in work gangs at the entrance, then walked down the steps located at the side of the forty-five-degree-incline shaft that extended some two hundred yards into the mine.

In neither Honko nor Shinko nor in the four additional smaller mines in which the Dutch and later the American POWs were forced to work were adequate safety measures taken to protect the workers from cave-ins, falling rocks, faulty equipment, or flooding. The smaller mines were especially vulnerable to cave-ins and wet conditions, with the greatest number of fatal pneumonia cases stemming from these mines. The prisoners lived in constant fear of the danger of cave-ins and falling rocks in the dank, dark, poorly ventilated mine tunnels.

F. E. van Rummelen, a Dutch mining engineer in civilian life, made suggestions for increasing the safety of the mines and lessening the danger of cave-ins by, among other things, strengthening the mine supports. The Japanese ignored this advice because acting on it would have required a greater supply of wooden poles, which they were loathe to provide.

The Japanese were also enamored with the *speedo* idea. Several days of the month were designated *speedo* days, when workers were made to work extra hours. The one advantage was that at the end of a long *speedo* day, the workers were given a ball of rice, a boiled yam, or a potato as a reward for the extra effort, a little like a dog receiving a doggie treat after it has successfully responded to a roll-over or give-me-a-paw command.

The resulting increased production from this extra effort would help to end the war sooner, or so the prisoners were told. Instead of having the desired result, on *speedo* days and on every other day of the month as well, the workers did what they could to hinder production.

As Don Versaw* reported, "When possible and we could get away with it, we filled the car bottoms with rock, covering the tops with coal. We stole and buried dynamite, a precious wartime commodity. We ruined

---

* From his *Mikado no Kyaku (Guest of the Emperor): The Recollections of Marine Corporal Donald L. Versaw as a Japanese Prisoner of War During World War II,* 1998.

drills by driving them into glass-hard basalt. We derailed loaded cars running at high speed so they would tear up the track and tunnel supports."

Every bit of sabotage inflicted damage that would require time and material to fix and thereby delay production. In the end the net effect was probably negligible, but it gratified the men to feel they had at least done something to impede the enemy.

Death Stalks the Camp

As Frits Wilkens lay near death, others joined him in sick bay. The number of sick increased rapidly. At the end of May, fifty-one of the original four hundred men were ill; by June the number had risen to eighty-one, nearly a quarter of the men. The majority of the early cases suffered from dysentery. Later, pneumonia became the number one disease.

Sick bay at Fukuoka #7

A Japanese army doctor dropped in occasionally to prescribe Epsom salts and put the sick on a diet of only rice water. A sadistic duo, Sergeant Nagano and Private Sakai, who were ostensibly medical orderlies, assisted the doctor. The two delighted in tormenting their sick charges. Private Sakai took the lead during these so-called sick calls, tyrannizing the men with the help of a stick.

"After a few weeks," Wim reported, "the sick and convalescent skeletons were compelled to attend and do gymnastics and physical exercises outdoors in the square. When, at the crazy orders, I tried to intervene, they threatened to cut off the supply of the few medicines that were made available and to have no further consideration for future sick cases."

According to the post-war sworn testimony of Corporal Claude Wilmoth, taken in 1946*, it was the policy of the Japanese officials to allow only a certain percentage of sick soldiers to be excused from work details. Wilmoth stated:

> In December 1944 I saw the Japanese compel an American Army sergeant who was sick with pneumonia to march to a coal mine, which was about 1-1/2 miles away, and work. The American Army doctor . . . protested to the Japanese doctor in the camp, but his protests had no effect. The American Army sergeant was taken away at four o'clock in the afternoon and brought back to the camp at one o'clock the next morning. He was unconscious and was being carried on a litter by four of the American soldiers in his work detail. He was placed in the camp hospital and died at five o'clock that morning.

To prove they were really ill, the men showing up at sick call were required to bring along a stool sample. Blood in the stool was a clear indication that they weren't faking their illness. With many of the men willing to go the extra mile to get out of mine work, a brisk trade in excrement developed. Turds became a valuable commodity and were exchanged for cigarettes or food.

Later another unusual trade developed. To improve health conditions, the Japanese decreed that the prisoners had to catch a certain number of flies a week. The enterprising among them caught more than their quota, sliced the flies in half with a razor blade to increase their catch, and sold them to their fellow POWs for cigarettes or a mouthful of rice.

---

* This and subsequent information on Japanese beatings of and brutality toward POWs at Fukuoka camp #7 come from testimonies and affidavits available at National Archives and Records Administration, UD 1180, Record Group 331, Box 922, Folder #12 FU-8, Location 290.

Infirmary at Fukuoka #7

Some of the sick suffered from dysentery, others from pneumonia, still others from accidents in the mines. From June through August 1943, ten men died of dysentery-enteritis. From December through the following April thirty-six died from pneumonia. Additionally, one died from acute internal inflammation and two died in mine accidents. Later other deaths followed, the majority from pneumonia. By September 1945 fifty-one of the original four hundred Dutch POWs had died.

Wim ascribed the high death toll to general undernourishment dating back to their time at Changi in Singapore and continuing on in Fukuoka #7, with the food provided insufficient and lacking in protein and fat content. He also cited the working conditions and long hours, with mine workers required to work twelve to fourteen hours a day in the damp, unhealthy, coal dust–filled mines.

Other factors included a lack of proper medicines, particularly one of the sulfa drugs universally acknowledged at that time as indispensable for fighting pneumonia, and inadequate clothing and unheated buildings. Most POWs from the Dutch East Indies had never been exposed to cold climates and had little resistance to pneumonia and bronchial infections.

Other contributing factors included low morale and lack of physical resistance as the result of all the above factors, chiefly during the cold winter months. Also part of the equation were inadequate hours of sleep, inadequate medical care, and brutal beatings inflicted on the men.

Sometimes men who had been pronounced too sick to work were beaten for being sick and being unable to work! To rectify these conditions, Wim made the following futile appeal to the Japanese command:

> The increasing number of men clearly showing signs of weakening (losing weight) and unable to stand up to the hard labor is mainly due, I believe, to the lack of fats; whereas some are just too old and were marked for light duties only. I wish, therefore, to make an urgent appeal to you as camp commander as well as to the company (who perhaps did not know that some of the men were not meant for working the mines) to have special consideration.

> The main trouble is a certain, and some cases a considerable, degree of undernourishment, which is obvious from the appearance of these men. It is perhaps still possible to prevent these men from becoming entirely useless as mine workers by increasing their present rations and by enabling them to recover from their present sickness in outdoor farm work for the next few months.

Wim's plea was disregarded.

With the Grim Reaper making frequent visits to the camp, the medical orderlies had their hands full trying to cope with the dead as well as the sick. Thus the Dutch officers were assigned sick bay duty to assist in the laying out of the dead. As a total novice, Frits described his frightening experience on his first night on deathwatch.

Half a dozen men were lined up at death's door. One of them, a large man still physically strong, seemed unlikely to be the first to knock on that final, black door. As the night progressed, however, he became restless. Frits had all he could do to wrestle the man back into bed. After a tremendous struggle, the man collapsed and lay still. Frits, his heart racing, ran for the doctor, who declared the patient dead and ordered Frits to help the orderly lay him out.

Frits and the orderly carried the heavy man to the mortuary. To ensure that the corpse was still pliable when they placed it in the coffin, the orderly hurried the laying out process. Because the Japanese were smaller than the Dutch, the coffins, too, were smaller, so Frits and the orderly had to jam the large body in and quickly nail down the coffin lid because "it looked as if he would spring out at any moment."

To give the dead a proper send-off, the officers took turns conducting the cremation ceremony. Besides the officer, the Japanese allowed four men to accompany each coffin. Two men pulled a two-wheeled formal funeral cart carrying the coffin, which was covered in a black shroud. The other two men followed the cart. When there was more than one coffin, a farm cart carried the additional coffins, each coffin again accompanied by four men.

The funeral procession proceeded slowly through the center of Futase on the two-mile trek to the crematorium. As the cortege passed by, the Japanese inhabitants stopped and showed their respect by bowing. At the crematorium the guards withdrew so the prisoners could perform the ceremony undisturbed. The bearers lined up the coffins in front of the ovens. Four bearers stood around each coffin. As the crematorium attendants pushed the coffin in, the officer leading the ceremony would utter a brief prayer and call the men to attention, then all would give a final salute.

While the remains were being cremated, a process that took about forty-five minutes, the prisoners retreated to the waiting room and were served tea. The officer went to the cemetery "shop" and bought urns and boxes in which to place the urns. After the cremation was completed, they collected some ashes from the head, middle, and foot area from each of the cremated remains and placed them in the urns. The men then sang the Dutch national anthem, "Het Wilhelmus," placed the urns in the boxes, and covered them with the black shrouds. With the officer in the lead, one man carrying each boxed urn, and the rest of the men lined up in twos behind them, the column made the solemn return journey back to the camp.

Because of the frequent funeral trips through the town, the men became familiar with the layout of Futase and with the location of the pharmacies. When possible, one of the men in the rear of the column would break away (not too difficult to do since the Japanese guards always walked at the front of the column) and slip into a pharmacy to buy whatever sulfa drugs were available. Surprisingly, it was the Japanese doctor who had hinted to the prisoners that they should try to buy this medicine, as it was the best antidote to combat pneumonia at that time.

Once back in camp, they placed the boxed urns in an open cupboard in the officers' room. Meanwhile Wim, as meticulous as ever, had Frits record all the information known about the deceased, including name, rank, home address, history of his illness, as well as a list of his personal possessions, such as wedding or other rings, pen, watch, photos, correspondence, and the like. Wim safeguarded these possessions in the hope of being able to return them to the man's family after the war.

In the summer of 1944, at about the time that two hundred American POWs arrived to join the Dutch, the Japanese made several improvements to conditions at the camp. Work in the mines was reduced from a twelve-to-fourteen-hour day to a ten-to-twelve-hour day, some of the older and walking-sick men were acknowledged to be unfit for mine work and were allowed to do agricultural work instead, medical treatment was improved, and the living quarters and the sick bay were expanded, resulting in less crowding. Thanks to these changes, the stream of deaths slowed to a trickle during the remaining year and a half of the men's incarceration.

"Christmas Js A-coming . . ."

As the winter of 1943 neared, Wim approached the Japanese commander. He pointed out that the prisoners were unequipped to handle the plunging temperatures in their tropical uniforms. The Japanese commander assured Wim that measures would be taken when it got cold enough, which, according to them, was not until mid-November, no matter the temperature recorded by the outdoor thermometer.

At the end of October, the Japanese delivered a huge pile of winter uniforms. Although the clothing was washed, it didn't smell Downy fresh. The men, however, had learned to deal with lice, fleas, and the odors emanating from the bodies of their fellow soap-deprived, sweaty mine workers, and they would deal with this as well. Operation Winter Clothing took place the next free day, with the prisoners acting like children playing dress-up as they dove into the piles and tried to find a uniform that fit them reasonably well.

The winter underwear, which consisted of long-sleeved undershirts and long johns, presented more of a problem. Made of some cottony material, most were in bad repair. The long johns had no buttons or elastic waist-bands but instead sported ribbons attached to each side. They were all size Large, which meant that the small-framed Indonesians had to wrap the ribbons around their slight middles, thus blocking off the fly opening. These rags had to be turned in at the end of the winter of 1943-1944, only to be reissued the following winter.

In addition the prisoners got overcoats from old Japanese army stocks and from supplies that must have been a consignment meant for Koreans, who were much larger than the Japanese. These greatcoats dwarfed the slight Indonesians, but nobody minded. The coats were warm and a welcome addition as bed covers because the authorities provided no winter blankets in the uninsulated barracks. The following winter, the coats issued came from British and Australian war loot stocks.

The prisoners were not allowed to wear their winter uniforms in the mines. The mining company was responsible for providing the men with their mine clothing. These outfits were to be worn both winter and summer since the temperature in the mines varied little throughout the year. The shorts and shirts were made either of poor quality flimsy material resembling poor grade silk or of thin material used for flour sacks.

As time passed, exchanging worn-out clothing became increasingly difficult, and the quality continued to deteriorate. Especially poor was the footwear. Rubber-soled shoes gave way to shoes made of rice straw, which barely stayed intact through a single ten-hour shift in the mines and caused foot problems for many. Other Japanese issues included a single towel and, extremely irregularly, tooth powder, soap, and toilet paper.

In early December a rumor that Christmas parcels had arrived from the Red Cross heartened the men. The kitchen staff confirmed the rumor, having seen stacks of boxes in the storage building. Shortly thereafter the Japanese distributed forty boxes, with their contents to be divided among the almost four hundred remaining men. Divvying up a can of beef among ten men was a tricky task.

As the distribution was underway, the ever-vigilant kitchen crew reported that a truck loaded with boxes had driven out of the camp. Clearly, the Japanese were helping themselves to the rest of the Red Cross shipment. On the heels of this news, the Japanese commander entered the officers' quarters with a receipt needing Wim's signature. The receipt stated that the POWs had received three hundred eighty boxes. No, Wim countered, they had received forty, not three hundred eighty, boxes. He refused to sign. The commander left and later sent a message that either Wim would have to sign or take the consequences. Wim again refused to sign.

The next day the commander, accompanied by his sadistic sergeant, burst into the room yelling, "On your feet." With spittle flying, he shouted that if the officers didn't sign, they would be punished. Once more Wim refused. Then, with no warning, the two Japanese swung wildly at the officers. The enraged commander vented his fury on Wim and Frits, while the sergeant attacked the other two officers. The officers did their best to brace themselves and stay upright as the Japanese inflicted dozens of full-fisted blows left and right to their heads. Other than the noise of the crunching blows, no one said a word. One of the other officers almost fell down, but fortunately righted himself. If he had fallen, he would have undoubtedly been severely kicked.

Because of the suddenness of the attack, Frits hadn't had a chance to remove his glasses, which were the first casualty. They went flying across the floor and were stepped on in the course of the melee. The commander and the sergeant were sweating copiously by the end of the beating. Then, like the clouds parting to reveal a cheerful sun after a brief, intense summer hailstorm, the commander's rage vanished and his face softened. He told his sergeant to pick up the broken glasses and take them to the optician to be repaired. The two left the room.

"We sat down on our *tatami*," Frits wrote,"rubbing our very sore jaws and wondering what next? Nothing all day, but late at night we were enjoying a cup of tea before going to bed (we had refrained from eating that day, the operation was too painful), when the commander came in, carrying a new pair of glasses and was most concerned that they fit properly. Then he sat down and asked could he also have some tea and started chatting (he spoke English fairly well), as if nothing had happened. The parcels and the receipts were never mentioned again."

A few days later, emboldened by this incomprehensible switch from raw anger to conciliatory behavior, Wim and the others decided to approach the commander and ask whether something could be done to celebrate Christmas. Braber volunteered to be the one to sound him out.

To everyone's great surprise, the commander agreed enthusiastically. "Yes. Yes. Very important day," he told Braber. "Me Christian too." His largesse knew no bounds. Not only would the prisoners have the day off, they would receive a special meal, even a Christmas tree. He himself would contribute bottles of sake so that each man could drink some Christmas cheer.

The Christmas committee swung into full gear. With a Christmas tree and some additional greenery, an old piano, and a few drums provided by the Japanese, the men decorated the dining room and set up the band. The special meal turned out to be double rations of rice and tofu. After the men had eaten, Wim addressed them with a heartfelt, Christmas speech.

Wim giving Christmas speech at Fukuoka #7, 1943

In it he drew a contrast between the theoretical Christmas and the Christmas in practice. By Christmas in theory he meant the pre-war Christmas of "peace on earth," of religious observances, of joyful celebration in the bosom of one's family. Stacked up against that ideal was the Christmas in practice, the Christmas of war and deprivation, work, and brutality they were currently experiencing. He urged the men to extract from the ideal Christmas its essence of goodwill among men and to create a sense of solidarity with, and to foster harmony among, their fellow companions in distress.

"We are all so different," he added, "—old and young, Indonesians and Dutch, professionals and shopkeepers—but we are all in the same boat. Even if there is no peace on earth, there can and shall at least be peace in our boat and that, therefore, is our Christmas in practice."

Although Wim was himself not a church-going religious man, he had a strong moral core and an optimistic nature. He tried to infuse his men with the same spirit. He wound up his Christmas address with the following:

No wonder that our morale and spirit are depleted when we are materially and physically exhausted and our bodies are visibly weaker. Still, we should try to keep our spiritual compass steady or bring it back on track if it unexpectedly needs adjusting.

- The *religious person* does it by finding his inner strength in faith and exhibiting it in his attitude and his deeds.

- The incorrigible *optimist* has so much imagination that he stays upbeat even after his castles in the air have been shot down.

- The *cynic* is a poseur because he pretends to be a pessimist.

- And the true *pessimist*—well, he doesn't exist and if there is anyone who still claims to be one, let him come see me and I will set him straight.

I call to your mind the following saying: *Chacun pour soi et dieu pour nous tous.* Everyone for himself and God for us all—but not in material things! Remember God helps us over the bridge.

Geduld was steeds "een schone zaak"   Patience was always
                                                                   an attractive trait

In 't vredig dagelyksch bestaan	During daily life in freedom
Maar reken het gerust de eerste taak	But consider it easily the primary task
In de krygsgevangene baan	In the job of the prisoner of war

After Wim's address came the Christmas cheer, gift of the commander: twenty bottles of sake. Frits, as expert "sharer-outer," located the cap of a medicine bottle as a measuring device and poured out nearly four hundred equal shots. Naturally, the Japanese firewater barely wet the bottoms of the ridiculously large kitchen teacups, but no matter, it was hugely welcome.

Frits doling out sake at Fukuoka #7, Christmas 1943

The "cheer" and the music made the party special, with the prisoners singing the old Christmas songs. The Indonesians among them, some of whom had held on to their guitars, entertained the others with songs from Bali and Java. In order not to miss the festivities, the Japanese had plunked themselves down in front of the band and swayed along appreciatively to the music. After a while they had the grace to leave, telling the prisoners to pack it in in half an hour and reminding them that Christmas or no Christmas, *tenko* was at the usual time.

The Christmas spirit continued for a short time after the Christmas celebration, with the prisoners allowed to send brief postcards to their families. Wim sent one to Klara telling her he was in good health and wishing her a merry Christmas. He also sent one to his cousin Phien in Holland, which she received on April 20, 1944:

Dear Phien,

Are again allowed letter to relatives. Therefore please tell folks that I'm still in good health and spirits. Also try advise Klara accordingly via Laci and Gabor at their respective addresses. Best wishes X-mas and New Year. Keeping patience and good faith in speedy reunion.

W. Andrau

Why the commander had so readily agreed to allow the prisoners their celebration became clear when the prisoners heard he was leaving and would be replaced by a new commander in January. The old tyrant wanted to leave a good impression, as though his Christmas generosity could wipe away the brutality he had inflicted on the prisoners in the previous months.

On the first of January a new commander took over. He was an older man and, like the previous commander, he was a lieutenant, at variance with the proper military custom dictating that his rank should have been the same as Wim's, that of captain. He was immediately recognized as having worked in Bandoeng as a photographer, a popular cover for Japanese spies before the war. He was also known to be fluent in Dutch, which made Braber's task as translator much trickier.

Up to this time a strict no smoking policy had been in effect in the camp. Because all the buildings were made of wood, the Japanese were apprehensive of the risk of fire. The new commander, trying perhaps to start off on a good foot, reversed the policy and even provided a ration of three cigarettes a day per man. Smoking time and place, however, were strictly regulated. Smoking was allowed for only half an hour after the evening meal and then only within spitting distance of urns filled with water. As the men clustered around the urns, smoking and talking, the commander strolled around the room, eavesdropping on their conversations. Because everyone knew he spoke Dutch, it's doubtful he harvested any useful information.

One Good Slap Deserves Another

In the beating they had received at the fists of the departing commander, Wim and the officers had gotten off lightly compared to the brutality continually inflicted on their fellow prisoners. The daily threat of receiving a beating was the norm, resulting in high levels of stress and tension in the camp.

The Japanese held the POWs in contempt for having surrendered rather than either committing suicide or fighting to the death. Many of their soldiers, for example, had chosen death over capture when they fought unsuccessfully to defend Okinawa against the invading Americans.

Perhaps as a result of this contempt, both the Japanese guards (some of whom were disabled retired soldiers pressed back into service) and the civilian mine employees (who managed the work crews) felt justified in meting out brutal beatings for any offense and with any weapon at hand. Wim reported that the mine *honchos*, or foremen, ruled the men in the mines in a manner varying from "frequently rough," that is, slapping, to "regularly beastly," that is, beating, kicking, and assaulting the men with any tool available.

Slapping, punching, kicking, hitting with a crowbar, a wooden stick, the flat of a saber, the butt of a rifle, a bamboo cane, an axe handle—the Japanese used all these methods. Corporal Claude Wilmoth* stated that a Japanese civilian guard beat him with an eight-inch-long metal socket wrench until he blacked out. Wilmoth never learned the reason for the beating.

---

* From his testimony available at National Archives and Records Administration, UD 1180, Record Group 331, Box 922, Folder #12 FU-8, Location 290.

Wilmoth reported that in another incident in August 1945, Japanese civilian guards forced twenty-five American soldiers who were working at a nearby coal mine to pair off and beat each other, with the guard beating the odd man. The mass beating lasted for about fifteen minutes. The reason for the beating? Some twine had been misplaced and the guards claimed the Americans had stolen it.

Not resisting, not uttering a protest, and coming to attention after each blow were the quickest ways to halt or at least shorten the beating. The men also learned that trying to help a buddy who was being beaten was a huge mistake and increased the length and severity of the beating for both prisoners.

The men never knew when, for what offense, or with what weapon they would be struck. They were beaten for being sick, for being weak and unable to work, for peeing in their pants when being beaten, for not bowing low enough or bowing too low (both an insult to the emperor), for not working fast enough, or for no clear reason.

Don Versaw* writes of one such beating. He and his bunkmate were caught taking a last puff on their cigarettes after the bell had sounded for the end of smoking time. The Japanese first sergeant, still limping from his China war wound, burst in on them.

> With a raised right and left, he knocked us both to the floor. I jumped back to my feet before he could kick me, preferring to take another blow I could roll with to being kicked. Eddie may have been struck harder and didn't get up. He was kicked with a series of blows and beaten again with a stick the size of a riding crop. It took some heat off me, but I stood there with fists clenched, wishing I could help him up. Defending him would have sealed my fate and his too, I expect. There is nothing so easily riled to uncontrollable anger as a wounded Japanese First Sergeant.

Sometimes the beating was so cruel and damaging that the victim, flogged into insensibility, required hospitalization.

---

*From his *Mikado no Kyaku (Guest of the Emperor): The Recollections of Marine Corporal Donald L. Versaw as a Japanese Prisoner of War During World War II*, 1998.

Wim kept a record of the guards' names with the descriptive nicknames the prisoners gave them, such as Cobra, Yellow Dog, Gorilla, Blackjack, Village Idiot, as well as their level of brutality. Some of this information was later sent to the Tokyo War Crimes Tribunal, with a few of the worst offenders being given prison sentences for inhumane treatment of prisoners.

One guard, whom the Americans nicknamed "Bull-Neck," used his fists frequently. In one incident he struck an American private a dozen blows for smoking at an unauthorized hour and then forced the soldier to kneel on the floor with a broom handle placed directly behind his knees in such a way as to cause great discomfort. He was kept in this position for approximately forty-five minutes.

Although practically every Japanese in camp at one time or another took a turn at beating prisoners, some, such as the medical orderly Sugi Horibumi, seemed to be exceptionally cruel. Sugi's duties were concerned with medical administrative matters not with discipline, but he relished catching prisoners in the slightest infraction, for example, not bowing quickly enough or smoking during unauthorized times, and would beat them with his fists. If they fell down, he would kick them in the testicles and the ribs until in some cases they were knocked unconscious.

The first lieutenant Japanese camp commander also seemed to enjoy inflicting pain on the POWs, especially in the form of mass punishment of the prisoners. He would frequently force the undernourished prisoners to stand outdoors in cold weather for as long as an hour without any outside garments on and with only rubber shoes on stockingless feet.

According to Makoto Kimura*, a Japanese guard, other forms of punishment included standing at attention for one hour, saluting steadily for thirty minutes, being struck by guards with the palm of the hand or fists eight to ten times, being slapped, kicked, and hit with fists for about five minutes. When asked whether guards were given orders to beat prisoners, Kimura replied, "No. The guards took it upon themselves to beat the POWs to instill discipline."

---

* From his testimony available at National Archives and Records Administration, UD 1180, Record Group 331, Box 922, Folder #12 FU-8, Location 290.

When asked whether any of the guards were known as *joto-nai*, (meaning "no good"), Kunio Shimoyama,* a Japanese civilian, testified that there were three persons in particular who weren't well spoken of. When the war ended, he added, a Dutch captain (i.e., Wim) had told him that "these three men better get out of sight since he couldn't be responsible for the things which the released POWs would do to them."

For serious offenses, such as stealing camp food supplies, the offender would first be beaten and then thrown into the punishment cage. The *aeso* was a six-sided wooden cage made of pine boughs, with one side being the entryway. The *aeso's* dimensions, about three to four feet in height, depth, and width, made it difficult if not impossible for a tall or even a medium-sized man to lie down or sit comfortably, which was likely the intention. To add to the discomfort, the floor was made of cylindrical poles. The *aeso* was located inside another room that served as the stockade, or detention center.

Makoto Kimura† testified in 1946 that the men who were put into solitary confinement were fed according to the seriousness of the crime. For the worst offenders, the least amount of food given them was a third of a slice of bread per day and all the water they wanted. In one case this punishment lasted twenty days.

As rations were steadily reduced, hunger drove more and more of the men to steal from their fellow prisoners. Wim and the other officers first tried strictly monitoring the dining room to prevent double dipping, sneaking in with the next shift for a second meal. When that source of extra food was cut off, the thieves focused their attention on the barracks. A bit of rice or a pickle from their evening meal that some men saved to eat later in their bunk became an irresistible target for the thieves. Room thefts increased, with the thieves stealing not only food but also clothing and cigarettes.

Wim tried curbing their privileges, but because there were so few privileges to begin with, this disciplinary measure was ineffective. The

---

* From his testimony available at National Archives and Records Administration, UD 1180, Record Group 331, Box 922, Folder #12 FU-8, Location 290.

† From his testimony available at National Archives and Records Administration, UD 1180, Record Group 331, Box 922, Folder #12 FU-8, Location 290.

room heads were consulted. They suggested corporal punishment, with the culprits forced to run the gauntlet of their roommates. That worked for a while but not for long.

Next the room elders suggested reporting the problem to the Japanese, who threw the guilty men into the stockades for a day or two. The thieves just laughed and continued their criminal ways when they were released. Finally, Wim hit upon what turned out to be the most effective punishment technique to date: ostracism. Even the criminal element, it seemed, didn't like having the rest of the community turn their backs on them.

The other measure Wim took was to try to improve the living conditions as much as possible by appealing to the Japanese at every turn. He knew that desperate situations make people do desperate things. Conversely, improved conditions help to stabilize people and to generate goodwill. Therefore, by soft-soaping the commander and massaging his ego, Wim could help to improve the conditions and the morale of his fellow prisoners. To that end he sent the new commander the following list of suggestions:

Suggestions to make this camp more enjoyable:

1. Failing the receipt so far of any news, letter, postcard, or other sign of life from our families since April 1942, it would be a great comfort to all men and it would most certainly greatly improve the good spirit of all if the Japanese headquarters could issue a formal statement regarding the position, life, and condition of living of our wives and children.

2. Strict adherence to the official working times during workdays (that is, no more than 12 hours away from the camp), in order to allow the men a reasonable amount of leisure at home and to enable them to take their bath, wash their clothes, eat their meal at home, smoke their cigarette before *tenko*, and read some before going to bed.

3. On Sunday complete rest. If there are any formalities, hold them during the early morning hours on Sunday in order to enable the men of the night shift, who have come home on Sunday morning, to have at least some hours of sleep in the afternoon.

4. When the temperature is such that one can make use of the dining hall for recreation, it would be greatly appreciated if the evening hours on Sunday could be spent there with music, cabaret songs, etc.

5. Adhering to the regular army issue of articles: soap, toothpaste and toothbrush, towels.

6. Give the men the opportunity to spend their money on such articles as vitamin tablets, tea, spices, sweets, tobacco, etc. Also issue such articles to the non-smokers.

7. Extension of the bathroom, increasing the capacity of the reservoir and consequently increasing the water supply and pressure since experience shows that the water pressure is inadequate for filling the reservoir at the clothes washing place while taps are running.

8. Issue of Red Cross articles at least once a week, preferably on Sundays.

Futase City Camp
18 Feb. 1944
W. Andrau

No appreciable changes resulted from this memo.

*There we had to bow, and bow, and bow again, endlessly.
Midnight came. The Japanese soldiers roared at us. Sonei gave
threatening speeches. We were kept bowing until two in the morning.*

The Journey

We received two weeks' notice that we would be moved from Karees. Great commotion erupted. The unrest grew daily. People ran back and forth trying to find out where the Japanese were taking us. Nobody knew, not even the street leaders. Orders concerning packing, groups that were to travel together, and dates of departure for these groups were given on one day, only to be changed on the next.

One thing was definite: we would each be allowed only one suitcase weighing no more than forty pounds and one knapsack, if we were able to carry them both. Children were allowed twenty pounds each. We were permitted one mattress for every two people. Thus the four of us were allowed two mattresses. Around one of these I sewed our kapok quilts. Trucks would transport these separately from us. We weren't allowed to take any food reserves with us and were permitted only one cooking pot per family.

People were packing, unpacking, repacking. Everyone was sewing knapsacks and hip-bags, stitching names on everything, and sewing valuables inside their mattresses, only to take them out again for fear they would be confiscated, mattress and all.

I was no exception. I decided to save Wim's riding breeches, the only piece of his clothing I had in my possession. I slipped them into the kapok of the mattress. I hid a pound of sugar, which I had been saving almost grain by grain, and some tea in tiny sacks in between our clothing.

I also had two cherished silver trays, Djokja handiwork, specially made to order. The edges of both trays boasted a two-inch embossed and perforated flower border. Every flower was different and true to nature. I sewed the trays into pillowcases, put them at the bottom of the suitcase, and hoped for the best. I gave them up mentally because a search seemed inevitable, but why not chance it?

Then Robi came down with a fever. It was not malaria but a once-a-year, recurring high fever we called Pladjoe fever in Sumatra and Bandoeng fever here in Java. It usually lasted between three and six days. It took another six days for her to recuperate fully.

About ten days after the first news of the move, the Japanese ordered nine hundred women to assemble on the big square for a rehearsal. The women stood in the hot sun with their bulging knapsacks. Everyone wanted to take along as much as possible, of course. Straps broke, bottles burst, children cried, women fainted, and the Japanese inspected and shouted. Then they sent everybody home.

Next morning, before dawn, their mattresses were loaded onto trucks, and at noon the women themselves lined up again. Shortly thereafter, they filed out through the big gate. The sick ones were put on trucks.

Robi was better after three days, but then Maya and I came down with the fever. Luckily, Maya's wasn't severe, but I was really sick this time. My temperature was a steady 104° and I couldn't eat anything. I was in pain all over. Even my hair hurt. An impossible situation. I had to finish the packing. I would get up for five or ten minutes at a time, only to collapse on my bed again. Feetje and a few charitable souls dropped in from time to time to help, but they were busy with their own packing. Yvonne and Robi took care of themselves and of Maya.

The day before our departure, my temperature was still 104°. Fortunately, Maya's had gone down and she felt a little better. With the doctor no longer available, Feetje sent a kindhearted, hunch-backed nurse to me. The nurse gave me a shot to reduce the fever and even went to the camp office to try and have our departure postponed, to no avail. We received orders to leave with our own group of women, sick or not. Because Maya and I would have to ride in the sick transport, ever-helpful Feetje offered to look after Yvonne and Robi.

Early in the morning one of the mattresses was taken away. Later Yvonne and Robi left with Feetje and Altien, their hip-bags bulging and each carrying her doll. Yvonne also carried our red enamel kettle filled with water for the journey. She had thought of this excellent idea herself. When I saw them leave, my heart filled with anxiety.

At noon two nurses came for the sick. I got up but could hardly stand. I had never before felt so rotten. This was the seventh day of the fever. The nurses helped Maya and me to a garage. They brought over our mattress with the two quilts sewn on them. We lay there for hours with the other sick women and children. Nobody spoke. A few people moaned from time to time.

When our turn came we climbed into the waiting truck by ourselves and were driven to the train. We sick had to ride in a fourth-class carriage that had wooden benches along the sides and two back-to-back rows of benches in the middle. Our mattresses were placed on top of the backs of the middle benches and hung down on the two sides.

The carriage was overheated, having stood in the sun the whole day. Touching the wooden benches almost burned our fingers. As the carriage filled with the sick, the heat and the stench from the dysentery patients were almost unbearable. The sick groaned and released clouds of foul, putrid gas, accompanied by soft burbling sounds. The nurse who was supposed to be taking care of us was nowhere to be seen.

Maya asked for water. I had the thermos and the chamber pot in the knapsack, which had been put high up on the baggage rack. I had to gather all my will power and strength to accomplish the simple act of stepping down from the high-perched mattress, climbing over another sick woman, and reaching up for the thermos in the rack.

The train remained standing. Was it late or early? We had lost all sense of time. After the sun had disappeared, our nurse returned. Five Japanese soldiers, making a lot of noise, stomped into our carriage. They looked on as the dysentery patients were cleaned and the pots emptied.

Then, with a tremendous jerk, the carriage started to move. Just in time I caught Maya from rolling off the mattress. The sick kept moaning.

Maya asked for more water. One of the Japanese offered each patient a piece of sponge cake, which seemed such a puzzling humane impulse. In a similar strange gesture, I heard of guards giving the street leaders bunches of flowers on Easter Sunday, after having slapped them a couple of hours earlier. Maya devoured her cake. I gave her my piece as well. Poor kid. When would she eat a piece of sponge cake again?

We still didn't know where we were going. All night long we rolled, stopped, and rolled again. You could have cut the fetid air with a knife.

With a jerk we stopped again. The dark enfolded us. The soldiers exited. Shouts came from all sides. A beam of light flashed into our carriage and a voice roared, "Get out!" in Malay.

A Chinese doctor in the next carriage, who was in charge of the sick transport, tried to explain to the soldier that we were all ill and could not walk. The Japanese nearly slapped him and roared again to get out. Silence followed. In the darkness we fished out some clothing from the knapsacks and put sandals on our feet. Maya hugged her doll.

We got out of the train, which was stopped in a field, and settled on the wet grass. I hugged Maya and covered her with my coat while also holding onto the knapsack to keep it from disappearing in the dark, which was a distinct possibility with so many people running around like crazies. In the flashlight beams we saw the mass of women and children swarming in confusion near the standing train. We were shivering now, but inhaling the fresh night air after the suffocating odors of the carriage was a relief.

Shouts and roars surrounded us. Somebody passed by and said we were in Batavia. We were herded to a nearby truck. Nurses helped us climb up with our belongings. I was seated on the floor of the truck and had Maya on my lap, a woman on my shoulders, and another woman on my outstretched legs.

We drove off and were soon riding through house-lined streets. We kept moving for about a half hour. When we climbed down from the truck, we found ourselves on a small square teeming with our people. In the darkness we couldn't see what was going on. We were ordered to stand here, stand there, and again over here. In rows of ten, then by pairs, then again in fives. Accompanied by roars, the soldiers drove us forward, as though we were no better than cattle.

A few *heihos*, native soldiers, were seated in front of a big bamboo gate. Each row of five women had to stand at attention in front of these soldiers and bow deeply. Once more. Then a third time.

One of the soldiers slapped a woman in the row in front of us and made her stand next to the *heiho's* chair. We didn't know why. Maya's hand tightened around mine. I gave her a reassuring squeeze. I wondered whether I would get slapped because my nightgown was showing.

After the bowing we were told to proceed through the gate, into Tjideng camp. Into hell, although we didn't know that as yet. The sky was coloring on the horizon. Soon the sun would be up and another day would begin.

Tjideng Camp

[Tjideng camp was a civilian internment camp set up by the Japanese in a suburb of Batavia in 1942. The estimated population of the camp, which consisted of European (mostly Dutch) women and children, ballooned by the end of the war to 10,500, as more and more women and children were crammed into fewer and fewer houses. Lt. Kenichi Sonei, the camp's commander from April 1944 to June 1945, was notorious for his cruelty, especially at full-moon times. Savage beatings, kickings, and head shavings were common for even minor infractions. Inadequate nutrition, lack of medicines, incredible overcrowding, nonexistent sanitation facilities, all contributed to the camp's high death rate. After the war Sonei was tried as a war criminal for crimes committed under his regime and was executed on September 2, 1946.]

Inside the gate at Tjideng camp, nurses met us with orders to take us to the hospital. My fever had disappeared completely. Was it the shock of the move or the injection I had received from the kind, hunch-backed nurse? Whatever the cause, I felt normal, only terribly weak and shaky on my legs. I had no intention of going to the hospital. On the contrary, I wanted to hurry and find Yvonne and Robine. Maya still felt feverish, so I walked with her to the children's hospital, where she was put to bed.

The nurse who accompanied us wouldn't let me go in search of my girls. She insisted I go to the hospital. First I made sure, however, that the nurse would fetch my mattress. I carried the knapsack myself. An unusual attire: a nightgown, a coat, and a knapsack on my back.

In the hospital, which was an ordinary house transformed for nursing purposes, I was put to bed and given some horrible mush to eat, the first food I had had in days. I was burning with impatience to get out and find the children. At about eleven in the morning, the doctor examined me. My temperature was normal, so I asked him to let me go. He insisted I stay. I was consumed with worry. I couldn't understand why Feetje or Altien hadn't come to see me. Later a nurse told me that the women who were not in the sick transport were still standing in the street, bowing to the Japanese soldiers and *heihos*. It was three o'clock by then.

At last, toward five o'clock, Feetje came. She told me they had been lined up in the street and made to stand and bow in the hot sun from the moment they had entered the camp, around daybreak, until three o'clock in the afternoon. Without food or water. This was the welcome by the commander of Tjideng. While the prisoners stood and bowed, soldiers searched the suitcases and knapsacks lying in the dust of the road.

Houses in Tjideng camp, 1945
(credit: Image bank WW2 – Netherlands Institute for War Documentation)

Lieutenant Kenichi Sonei, the dreaded camp commander, gave the women thundering speeches in Japanese, which an interpreter translated into Malay. The speeches contained warnings and threats to be obedient otherwise things would go badly for us. As if they weren't going badly enough already. His wish, he said, was to see us all dead.

Exhausted women fainted by the dozens while he raged on and on. In the row directly in front of Yvonne, a five-year-old girl died in the arms of her mother. Feetje told me that nineteen people had died during the journey from Bandoeng.

This Sonei sounded like a beast.

The nurses agreed that he was awful. He was a woman-hater, a European-hater, a sadist, and a madman. He went completely berserk at full-moon times, perpetrating incredible horrors. At the last full moon, the nurse told us, Sonei ordered a roll call in the evening and kept the women bowing until midnight.

Feetje told me that we, the Andraus, were being housed with Altien Hommes and her five-year-old daughter, Marjolein.

Next morning, after a lot of begging on my part, the doctor discharged me. With the knapsack on my back, the mattress in a roll on my head, I left. I was amazed once again, in a quite impersonal way, what the body can endure under the command of the will.

First I went to see Maya, who had slept well but still had some fever. Then home. The word "home" can mean different things to different people. In this case, home was a small, dark storeroom in the former servants' quarters of the house. A *kaki lima*, a long corridor open on one side, led to the main part of the house. Along this corridor was a series of rooms: one biggish room, three small storerooms, a tiny kitchen, a toilet, and a shower. Twenty-one of us were billeted in that corridor area. Our home, one of the storerooms, had no door, only an opening in the wall and two tiny, high windows overlooking the corridor. A sliding door in one of the room's sidewalls opened and closed onto the toilet. Most of the children and some of the women using this toilet suffered from diarrhea. All the consequent noises and odors came through the badly fitting sliding doors to our quarters. This was our new home.

A five-foot-wide, muddy grass strip, bordered by a high wall, ran along the open side of the corridor. In the middle of this grass strip, in front of our doorless room, was a septic tank, filled to the brim. From it, a brownish, disgusting-looking liquid seeped through the top cover, making little gurgling noises. An overpowering stench emanated from it. The odors of the toilet and the murmuring juices of the septic tank were to be our inseparable companions.

When I arrived I found Altien, Marjolein, Yvonne, and Robine in the middle of all our belongings, still numb and too tired from the journey and the previous day's bowing to do anything. We attacked the mattresses first, only to find that the Andrau family had only one mattress, the one I had carried from the hospital on my head. Altien told me they couldn't find the other mattress. Our own people had probably stolen it after it had been dumped on the street along with the other mattresses being transported. A disaster, but what was the use of moaning about it? How lucky that I had sewn the two kapok quilts to the mattress we still possessed. The quilts would make beds for two children and the third would sleep with me on the mattress. Altien had her mattress to share with Marjolein.

In the corner of the room, we lined up our enamel mugs and bowls and called it the "dining room." We had no furniture whatsoever.

While we were settling in, the call came to fetch the soup. Second disaster: Altien had not brought her cooking pot with her. We went with ours to fetch enough soup for all of us, but our pot turned out to be too small and the precious soup spilled on the way. We were told that at noon and in the evening we would get vegetable soup. Bread would do for breakfast.

In the midst of the confusion, we decided that we needed a cup of tea. To make tea we would need a fire, and for fire we would need some wood. The children went out to hunt, while I looked around for two bricks with which to make a fireplace, the way Yvonne had taught me in Karees.

Yvonne, breathless, returned in ten minutes. "Mami, quick. We found a long bamboo. It's nobody's. Robi is guarding it." I ran as fast as my legs would carry me. In triumph we brought the bamboo to our room, chopped it into pieces with a table knife and the blunt head of a hoe, and for a few days our cup of tea was assured. We had left our electric iron, on which we used to boil the water for tea, behind in Karees with the rest of our belongings.

After this first foraging expedition, we were ever on the lookout for combustible material, especially because the Japanese stopped the distribution of the camp soup after three days. We were given charcoal with which to do our own cooking, but a three days' ration was just sufficient to cook one bowl of rice.

One night Altien and I spirited away two two-by-four posts the Japanese had discarded when they repaired the fence. We hid them under our mattresses and chopped them up bit by bit with the head of the blunt hoe. We felt every stroke up to our shoulders. Our hands were full of blisters by the time we finished the job.

Later I "earned" a writing desk by helping some women move, on Japanese orders, from one part of the camp to another. The women had come from Batavia and had been able to bring some furniture along with them. Now they had to leave most pieces behind. I got the desk. It would have been almost impossible to make firewood from it by using only the hoe head and the table knife. Fortunately I got hold of a three-foot-long iron pipe. With it I hit and hit the beautiful, carved, hardwood desk until it gave way. I felt like a murderer.

We cooked on the cement floor of the corridor. Because we didn't have even a wooden plank on which to cut the vegetables, I cleaned a patch of the corridor floor thoroughly and we chopped our vegetables there. Our kitchen knife had been confiscated at the time of entry, but we still had a couple of table knives.

The women and children passing from their rooms along the corridor to the toilet and back had to step over our "kitchen," and, alas, sometimes they kicked over the pot or landed with their feet in the vegetables.

We had been expecting the Tjideng women to take up a collection among themselves and supply us, the newcomers, with the most necessary furniture, as we had done for the have-nots in Karees. Nothing of the kind happened here. The old Tjidengers, who had come from Batavia with furniture and all their precious belongings, slept in their comfortable beds, had chairs, tables, and whatnots, and seemed not to care about anyone else. Someone suggested I go from house to house and ask for the basics. So I went begging.

On the front lawn of a house, I saw four good-looking rattan chairs. I explained our situation to the owner standing nearby and asked for one of the chairs.

"Sorry, I can't give any away because we like to sit out on the lawn in the evening," the woman said.

"Don't you have any other chairs in your room to sit on?"

"Of course, but it would be too much trouble to get them out every night."

This hard-heartedness shocked me. She hadn't learned a thing yet, I thought. I continued on my begging quest.

Two houses farther I caught sight of a small plank lying in the grass. It would make a perfect cutting board. I went to the house and asked for it, explaining that we were a new batch of prisoners without any kitchen utensils or furniture and that we had to cut our vegetables on the cement floor.

"No. I can't give that away," the woman said. "You can never tell what it might be useful for one day."

This was too much to swallow. Although living on the floor was tiring and our backs ached from lack of support, I gave up trying to melt stone hearts and never went begging again.

About a week later the wife of one of Wim's friends gave us a kitchen chair. She was from Batavia and had brought a lot of her furniture into camp with her. The chair served us as a table.

On the third day after our arrival, we were called out of bed at eleven at night. "*Tenko*," roll call, the street leaders shouted through their megaphones. "No lights allowed. Be there in five minutes."

In the dark we put on our sandals and a coat or a dressing gown over our pajamas. We obediently followed the somber crowd. Here and there children were crying.

The Japanese guards lined us up and marched us out of the gate to the square. There we had to bow, and bow, and bow again, endlessly. Midnight came. The Japanese soldiers roared at us. Sonei gave threatening speeches. We were kept bowing until two in the morning. Besides the apparent humiliation and discomfort, what was the aim of this exercise? Maybe only to awaken fear in us.

St. Nicholas day arrived again. Poor kids, no Sinterklaas on a wheelbarrow, no Zwarte Piet, black Pete, nothing at all. The wife of a pastor, mother of five, gathered the thirteen children of the house in her room to read them stories and sing songs so they would forget that Sinterklaas wasn't coming this year.

For an American child, Santa Claus not showing up is unimaginable. For a Dutch child, a no-show Sinterklaas is similarly inconceivable. I felt that the children's magical world would collapse if nothing happened.

With a piece of charcoal and Altien's help, I blackened my face and hands, borrowed a red housecoat from one of the neighbors, and in five minutes I was Zwarte Piet, the Saint's black servant who brings the sweets. Yes, the sweets. If he has any.

The sweets. I had a hard fight with myself. I had tucked away a few emergency sweets. Nine pieces in all, none bigger than a marble. Three for each of my girls. But what about the other ten children? Did I have to distribute the sweets to them all? Hadn't I painfully saved them for my children? Why hadn't the other mothers done the same for their children? The inner debate continued.

"A nice and generous thought," said my inner voice. "Can't you make them all happy?"

"Nine sweets, thirteen children. Am I a magician, inner voice?"

"*Vol verwachting klopt ons hart,*" our hearts are beating with anticipation, the children sang.

"Beating with anticipation, beating with anticipation," the words echoed in my heart. "Oh, God, can't you perform just a little miracle? Can't you send me just a few sweets?"

I quickly cut out four tiny squares of colored paper and filled them with my Christmas sugar savings. Now I had thirteen sweets. Holding these treasures in one hand and a twig broom in the other, I entered the room where the children were singing. I'll never forget those faces.

Zwarte Piet, Zwarte Piet," they shouted. The tiny ones crept closer to their mothers.

I told them that Sinterklaas didn't feel well that night, but he had heard their nice singing and sent me to bring them the sweets. At the word "sweets," their eyes became bigger. I pushed a sweet into every outstretched hand and disappeared as quickly as I had come before the bigger ones discovered my identity.

The Sinterklaas spirit apparently moved some hearts. We were given a tiny table and a baby-changing table without drawers or a door. With these we felt terribly rich.

Two other events cheered us up. Maya had come back from the hospital looking well and had been able to join the other children for the Sinterklaas event. And Nippon allowed the camp management to buy extra food for us with the money they had confiscated from us in Karees. A handful of beans, a piece of soap, and some tea, coffee, or sugar were allowed once a week. The quantities were miniscule and the soap was like sandstone but something was so much better than nothing.

Then Altien got diphtheria and had to be quarantined for six weeks. Now I had four children on my hands. Marjolein was a sweet, gentle girl, but stubborn, a difficult eater, and in spite of her five years, still had to be helped on the potty. Yvonne, Maya, and Robine did this sometimes, but they definitely didn't like the job.

Christmas had come. Before leaving Karees, I had managed to buy a small, folding, artificial Christmas tree. I had also bought a small, well-made wooden dollhouse for the children. Like the bike the year before, the house never reached the children. I had to leave it behind in Karees. I had the tree, however, and a few fondants, made with sugar saved up since Sinterklaas. I also cut three long candles into twelve pieces to fit into the tiny holders on the tree. I had made more headbands and embroidered hankies as presents.

When the children returned from their walk late in the afternoon on December 24, the tree in its candle-lit beauty awaited them. The news of the tree traveled fast. Within a few minutes some twenty children had gathered around it. We sang Christmas carols, and my girls went to sleep hugging their presents.

When all was quiet, Feetje appeared. We sat on the cement floor of the corridor with a cup of coffee and a horribly bad cigarette, recalling past glorious Christmases. We hummed a few carols, to which the gurgling septic tank lent the accompaniment.

The neighborly cheer didn't last. Two nights later two of Altien's thin blankets and my only good blouse were stolen from our clothesline. I saw the woman and ran after her, but she was a clever thief and disappeared over the high garden fence.

One night, in my sleep, I stretched out my arm along the cement floor. I woke up feeling that my hand was in water. All was dark. I sat up, patted the floor, and, indeed, I was splashing in a little pool next to the mattress. I turned on the light and saw a yellowish liquid seeping out from under the sliding door that led to the toilet. I went in to investigate and saw that the toilet bowl was plugged and the overflow had found its way into our room. My hand had been splashing in urine.

Another night I woke up to the unpleasant feeling that some small body was walking over me. I sat up and tried to make out what it was. It looked like a black cat as it jumped up against the mosquito netting stretched over our doorway. I turned on the light. An enormous rat, apparently bewildered, ran from mattress to mattress. Marjolein was screaming by then as the rat ran over her face. Everyone jumped up. The chase was on. We threw pillows at him, which didn't accomplish anything. He escaped when I lifted up the mosquito netting.

The rat returned night after night, entering other rooms as well. The whole house was on alert. Two nights in succession I sat in the corridor for hours, holding my broom at the ready. Once I managed to duck him under the water in the front gutter. I thought that was the end of him, but he must have been a good diver, because the next day he was back.

For nearly three weeks the struggle continued until we finally got hold of a rattrap. I heard a "click" during one night's vigil. We found the rat sitting inside the trap the next morning. He filled the entire trap, his long tail sticking out between the wires.

We celebrated New Year's Eve as in the past. We seated the Old Year on our only chair. In his arms was the little New Year, who carried on his arm a small basket filled with New Year's resolutions on tiny rolls of paper. We each drew one. Great was the laughter when I drew one that read: "I shall be obedient without arguing." We melted tin soldiers I had acquired through trading and poured the molten lead as usual. We saw a swan, a vine stock, and a bird with an olive branch in the "pourings." This time, the signs, we agreed, were unmistakable: the New Year would bring peace.

Also as before, we beat up the Old Year. Then we settled cozily on the floor and I told the children about the different cakes Nagymama, grandmother, would make for them next Christmas in Aracs, our country home in Hungary. I told them again the story of our goodbye from her. How she had walked to the edge of the property and had waved from the top of the hill for as long as we could see each other. Before the distance swallowed her up, we had shouted, "We will be back in eight months." That was four years ago. We talked about Grootvader and Grootmoeder, grandfather and grandmother, Wim's parents, who used to spend the summer with us in Aracs.

"Grootvader always chewed on his tongue," Yvonne said. She had a good memory. We remembered Uncle Gabor, my brother, who had the barber come to the Budapest apartment to cut Yvonne's hair, and Uncle Laci, my other brother, who brought a suitcase full of toys from London. Maya remembered the suitcase of toys. We talked about Rezi, the cook, and Mari and Matyas, who looked after the property and lived in a separate house at the edge of our little forest. And we thought of sweet, cheerful Lizi, who cleaned the rooms and with whom roaming in the forest was always an adventure.

I told them about the big house with the magnificent view over Lake Balaton. About the hundreds of almond trees that looked like giant bridal bouquets when in blossom. About the cherry, apricot, peach, plum, green-gage, apple, pear, and nut trees that were all awaiting us. About the vintage feast when all were allowed to drink as much as they wanted of the sweet grape juice flowing freely from the press.

We talked about the last vintage when the children had been allowed to stay up around the bonfire, listening to Mari, Rezi, and Lizi singing those bittersweet Hungarian folksongs. And we recalled how the gypsies began to play and we had laughed and cried long into the night. We talked about the cow and the baby cow and the pony they would get when we returned to Aracs.

The girls asked again about the cakes. What kind and how many would there be? I gave a vivid description of each cake, and it was almost as good as eating them.

We prayed for Daddy, for all our loved ones, and for peace to come. Full of hope and trust we entered 1945.

8
Wim
July 1944

*The Red Cross packages were evidence that the world beyond the high,
sharp-bamboo-spiked fence had not forgotten them.*

Meeting the Swedish Consul General

At the beginning of July 1944, Wim heard that an inspection by the Red
Cross was imminent and that "high officers" would accompany the Red
Cross representative. This was a golden opportunity, he felt, to present a
list of their complaints, including the poor food, the suffocatingly cramped
three-tiered bunks, the many cases of cruelty, the treatment of the sick, the
lack of medicines.

No one knew whether the Red Cross had any power to effect changes.
Presenting such a list could backfire and result in a worsening of their situation. Therefore, to ensure the men were onboard with this proposed risky
action, Wim insisted they be sounded out and if necessary a vote be taken.
The outcome was heartening. The POWs gave Wim an overwhelming vote
of confidence to proceed with the presentation of the complaints.

On the appointed day Wim and Frits Wilkens were ordered to present
themselves at the commander's office. Although they each still had an intact Dutch uniform, they dressed in scruffy Japanese uniforms to emphasize
their status as prisoners. At one side of a long table in the commander's
office sat an array of Japanese officers, including two full colonels, as well
as a solitary European civilian. Wim and Frits sat down across from them,
next to, unexpectedly, the camp commander. Was the latter also in the dock?

One of the colonels opened the proceedings with a few remarks and introduced the European civilian. To Wim and Frits's surprise, the man was not a Red Cross representative but the Swedish consul general in Tokyo, Sweden being the "protecting power" for the Dutch prisoners. The consul explained his role. He would present whatever news he had about conditions in Holland, would receive any "specific questions" from Wim to be transmitted to Holland, and would listen to any comments they wanted to add to the proceedings.

In his heavily Swedish-accented English, the consul described the situation in Europe. His information was not particularly revealing because at the time the prisoners were still receiving a daily copy of the *Nippon Times*. This English-language newspaper was surprisingly informative about the European war theater, especially events on the Russian front.

Then the Swede asked for any "specific questions." Wim explained that they were unprepared for this situation and thus had not canvassed the men. The consul nodded and suggested to the Japanese colonel that they proceed directly to the final part of the business, that is, any comments Wim wanted to add to the proceedings. The colonel indicated his assent.

Wim whipped out his list, which he'd transcribed into a statement. He said he'd jotted down a few things, would he be allowed to use his *aide-mémoire?* Consternation among the Japanese. After conferring with his team, the senior colonel said that if the prisoner captain needed such an aid, they would allow him to use it.

Bunks in barracks at Fukuoka #7

214

Wim, thinking it wise to start with a fairly innocuous point, brought up the matter of the suffocatingly confining three-tiered bunks. By the time Wim got to more serious matters, such as the brutal treatment of the prisoners at the hands of the Japanese, the English-speaking Japanese captain raised the alarm. The senior Japanese colonel, realizing what was going on, made a grab for Wim's paper. He wasn't quick enough. The more agile Swede snatched the paper from Wim and aimed a harangue in quick-fire Japanese at the colonel.

A long silence followed. The colonel signaled to the English-speaking Japanese captain. The captain stood and said, "This meeting is now closed. Thank you."

They all stood. The Swedish consul winked at Wim and patted his breast pocket into which he'd secreted Wim's notes. "Don't worry," he said. "I will read these and act if I can."

Wim and Frits were politely ushered out. For a few hours, that was it. Then late that evening they along with Braber were summoned to the commander's office. The commander gave them a long, angry lecture, which Braber translated faithfully, knowing he shouldn't mess up on that. The upshot of the lecture, Frits recounted, was that they "had behaved disgracefully, not as proper soldiers at all and should be taught a lesson in discipline—he [the commander] had been far too lenient—and from now on they'd better mind their p's and q's and respect the least detail of his instructions."

A rough time followed, with more punishment and more severe punishment for even the smallest infraction of the rules. The men bore the brunt of the stricter regime and waited apprehensively for an improvement in their situation. They didn't have to wait long. As Wim wrote:

> The treatment of the POWs in the mines was one of the points raised by me in our first contact we officers were allowed to have with the Swedish delegate, Mr. Gawell, on July 6th 1944 in the presence of the Japanese camp commander and a whole flock of Japanese authorities. The latter . . . listened intently and occasionally objected to the revelations made regarding Japanese behavior and treatment. However, the result was that from that day on all cases of brutality and maltreatment of the civilian foremen and workmen could be and were regularly reported by me to the camp commander, Lt. Joshizugu (20th June 1944 – 12th Feb. 1945) as well as to Captain Sakai (12th Feb. 1945 until Japan's capitulation). They

. . . took due notice of these complaints and I believe took certain steps to try and prevent further occurrences. Copies of these numerous reports are no longer available.

As a matter of fact, camp guards were frequently sent out to investigate such matters from the Japanese side and to punish the Japanese civilian mine workers. The Japanese loved to slap each other but slapping POWs who are defenseless remained still more attractive, which was the reason that it continued throughout the years in prison life. A certain restraint on the part of both guards and mine workers, however, was felt under the above-mentioned camp commanders.

About a month after the meeting with the Swedish consul general, an army of carpenters arrived and built a new barracks. They also took out the top bunk of the three-tiered bunks in the old barracks and raised the middle tier. Almost literally, the prisoners could breathe more easily. Other measures were taken as well, especially with regard to the maltreatment of prisoners and to health concerns. There was no way of knowing whether these changes were attributable to the risky complaint list Wim gave to the Swedish consul or to other circumstances. But no matter, the improved conditions made life in the camp a bit more tolerable.

The new barracks turned out to be meant for a new batch of POWs. About two hundred American soldiers led by two officers arrived at the camp at the beginning of August 1944. Several of this bedraggled group of Americans were survivors from the six-month-long siege of Corregidor in the Philippines, the island that General Douglas MacArthur had abandoned in 1942 after uttering the famous words, "I shall return." Others were survivors of the infamous Bataan Death March. All had been shuffled from camp to camp throughout the Philippines before being packed into the hold of a hell ship. The *Nissyo Maru* had narrowly missed being torpedoed by American submarines before depositing its human cargo in Moji, the same port where Wim's group had arrived the previous year.

As Don Versaw, one of the two hundred American newcomers, noted in his account, "none of the present inmates came forth to greet us" except for the Dutchman Pieter Braber, who "was speaking what seemed to be fluent Japanese and acted as both a camp official and an interpreter."

216

Instead of being an intentional slight, the Japanese had, in all likelihood, dictated this unfriendly welcome.

At first the two groups, separated by their different cultural backgrounds and by the language barrier, eyed each other with mistrust. To help create harmony Wim again felt it necessary to speak to his men on the importance of "playing nice" and getting along with each other in the unusual circumstance in which the prisoners found themselves. He addressed* head-on the stereotypes each had of the other.

> Americans might say that the Dutch are crazy, work too hard, are docile, are slaves. The Dutch might say that Americans are lazy, obstinate, not alert, careless. The Indonesians might say that whites lack spirit and imagination. But let's not generalize. These characteristics appear in all three groups. The importance is to try to remain cooperative even under these extraordinary circumstances of living in a forced integrated society where no one is completely normal physically and is impatient, crabby, jealous, and inwardly rebellious.

> If we all had rest, good or at least adequate nutrition, sleep, pleasant occupation, and good friends, we would laugh about the annoying and irritating traits we discovered or maintained we had discovered in others. Let's forget about it and let's laugh at our own flaws and shortcomings.

In the rest of the address, he again appealed to the men's better nature and then branched out from the theme of getting along with the Americans to one emphasizing the importance of staying positive so they could all return to Java as pillars of strength in their families and in their country and not as helpless wrecks.

Whether his address had any direct influence or not, as time went by and Americans, Dutch, and Indonesians worked side by side in the mines, washed the coal dust off next to each other in the same bath water, and ate side by side in the mess hall, individual friendships did develop. The two American doctors who arrived with the group were especially helpful in bridging the gap, thanks to their medical expertise. They patched up

---

* Excerpt translated from Wim's Dutch address to the men.

grateful Dutch and Indonesian as well as American POWs who had been injured.

Although the number of deaths, especially from pneumonia, had slowed, the increase in the number of mine workers meant a rise in mine accidents. Cave-ins and other accidents resulting in lost fingers, broken arms and legs, and other injuries mounted. Dr. Barshop's exceptional skill as a surgeon meant that limbs were saved and repaired and bloody lacerations stitched up, whereas before his arrival the victim would likely have been crippled, if, indeed, he survived the injury at all.

Frits recalled an occasion when a victim was brought in with a completely crushed hand. "Barshop managed to save most of it," Frits wrote. "He had to sacrifice two fingers, but somehow or other he managed to sew up the rest, and many months later that deformed hand was quite serviceable again—and all that without anesthetic. Of course early on in the operation, the man fainted. 'I counted on that,' Barshop said. 'It's the only way out.'"

In some cases breaking a bone was considered, literally, a "lucky break" because it meant a release from mine work. As Don Versaw wrote, "Some prisoners were so desperate to avoid going to the mines that they gave away their food rations to brutes who would break their bones for them."

Rice and Chickens

From the arrival of Wim's group in 1943 until the beginning of 1944, the Japanese military ran the camp, which meant that a Japanese soldier was in control of the camp kitchen and of the POW kitchen crew. To forestall the uncertainty and arbitrariness of this Japanese control over the food rations and concomitant corruption and stealing by the Japanese, Wim formulated a request that the administration of the POW kitchen and the preparation and distribution of the food be placed under the supervision of the Dutch officers.

He stated that this had been the usual practice in all the other camps. Having been imprisoned in four previous camps, he spoke from experience. Becoming increasingly adept at soft-soaping and selling his request by citing its advantages to his captors, Wim added that shifting the responsibility to the POWs themselves "cannot be but convenient for the Japanese army."

He continued by suggesting that once a day, preferably in the presence of and under the constant supervision of the Japanese camp commander and another officer, rations for the whole day be handed out and turned over to the Dutch POW kitchen. Wim, verbally bowing and scraping in order to avoid the danger of looking as though he were overstepping his bounds, wrote:

> Would it be possible to effect a separation between the POW kitchen and the Japanese Army kitchen in order to avoid a possible mix-up in ration preparation of the three POW meals per day in the Dutch fashion? For instance:
>
> > Breakfast – rice porridge
> > Lunch – bread or bento box with some vegetables and miso
> > Dinner – fish, vegetables plus rice, oil
>
> All would be under the daily and constant supervision of the Dutch officers, who would also be responsible for keeping the kitchen in good order, clean, and subject to inspection at any time by the Japanese camp commander. Consequently, the Japanese kitchen man's presence would no longer be required after he handed out the daily rations.

Wim was successful with this request. The suggested change smoothed out the kitchen routine. In January 1944 the Japanese military handed the daily running of the camp over to the civilian mining company. With the company's acquiescence, the Dutch officer Lieutenant Fasse continued to be in charge of ration drawing and kitchen affairs.

Although the Dutch officers repeatedly asked for information on what quantities of base food the POWs were supposed to receive, this information was never forthcoming. Consequently all figures mentioned by Frits Wilkens in his "Report on Food Conditions in Fukuoka Camp No. 7"* are based on weights of the food the POWs actually received, in so far as Wim

---

* Frits Wilkens prepared the report for use at the postwar Tokyo Trials. The report is available at National Archives and Records Administration, UD 1180, Record Group 331, Box 922, Folder #12 FU-8, Location 290.

and the others were able to check on these. Some were estimates and others were the figures given by the Japanese.

As in all other camps, rice, usually highly polished, was the staple food. Occasionally substitutes were given. Sometimes the substitute was rubbery steamed bread. Because it contained no leavening—neither yeast nor baking powder—and no eggs, the bread was extremely dense. It seemed to be made from just flour and water.

At other times the prisoners were given barley, maize, or kafir (a grain sorghum) instead of rice. Toward the end the rice substitute was soybeans, either in the form of beans or flaked. Although the soybeans were linked to digestive problems, causing the majority of the prisoners to suffer from diarrhea, the men gobbled them down anyway because they were filling.

The quantity of rice or rice substitute a prisoner received depended on his position in the work-food pecking order. The rationale sounds a little like the saying "from each according to his ability, to each according to his need." In other words, the more you sweat, the more food you get. Workers performing light duties, which included sick bay patients, inside workers, officers, and farm workers, received five hundred grams (about seventeen and a half ounces, or a little over two measuring cups) of base food daily, whereas topside mine workers received six hundred and fifty grams, and deep mine workers received seven hundred and thirty to eight hundred grams.

In June 1945, when the outcome of the war looked increasingly bleak for the Japanese, the rice ration was cut twice in rapid succession, the first time by ten percent, the second time by an additional five percent. Also, on the three days of rest per month, days the workers were not required to work, food was cut to two two-hundred-gram meals per day for all the prisoners, barely enough to survive on.

Other food supplies the prisoners received included fresh fish and the occasional bit of meat, although by 1945 these had disappeared. During the last few months of the war, the POWs occasionally and only haphazardly received dried or salted fish. These issues never lasted more than a few days. The supply of vegetables also decreased. By the summer of 1945, fresh vegetables were becoming a faint memory.

Irregularly, the POWs received two soybean products: miso, a fermented soybean paste, and tofu,* or bean curd, made from soybean milk to which a coagulant had been added. The former was especially appreciated because of its saltiness, which added flavor to the plain boiled rice.

And fruit? No one could remember what a banana or an orange tasted like. As Frits wrote, regarding the issuing of fruit, the number did not "amount to more than a dozen issues of one or two tangerines or an apple per man in all the twenty-seven months" of their stay in Japan.

In the middle of the summer of 1944, the camp received a huge box from the Red Cross containing a variety of seeds. It was still early enough to plant and, with the Japanese commander's support (he seemed to be just an old farmer at heart), the prisoners dug up a patch of earth and planted a vegetable garden. The old lieutenant was so enthusiastic, no doubt picturing a lush Garden of Eden of fresh vegetables for his own table, that he donated a bag of seed potatoes to the endeavor. The spuds caused a tug-of-war with the guards, who wanted them for their dinner. The two sides negotiated a compromise. The prisoners would cut out one or two eyes from each potato and the rest of the potato would go into the guards' cooking pot.

Every few days a rotating crew of the walking sick emptied the cesspits and spread the contents over the new garden as fertilizer. The results were astounding. In no time, a jungle of green sprouted and grew. Unfortunately, the potatoes had ample foliage but few tubers. The end result was only a small bag of potatoes. And as for the rest of the garden, the guards promptly stole whatever vegetables were produced.

Shortly after planting the seeds, the prisoners received another surprise gift from the Red Cross: a box containing a hundred, live, day-old chicks. The old lieutenant was so delighted (perhaps in his pre-military life he had come from farmer stock and missed being surrounded by the smells and sounds of a barnyard) that he at first kept the chicks in his office, during which time a quarter of them died. He blamed the prisoners, of course.

---

* Today tofu is a well-known food, especially among vegetarians, but during the war it was largely unknown by the general populace in the Western world.

Wim was instructed to build an enclosure for them outside, but after a few weeks, the lieutenant ruled that the prisoners' husbandry was useless, mainly because the birds hadn't produced any eggs as yet. He decided that the young chickens would be transferred to the nearby farm in order to be "educated." Predictably, many were thus schooled in the art of becoming the main ingredient in chicken à la king.

Wim (left) and other POWs with chickens, Fukuoka #7

To the prisoners' surprise, however, after about two months some three dozen of the now almost full-grown chickens were returned to the potato patch and ordered to eat the potato foliage. The birds were reluctant to do as instructed and shied away from the cesspit-fertilized greens.

The Japanese in charge was not amused. And what does a displeased Japanese soldier do? He beats you. Since Frits was in charge of the chickens at the time, he was subjected to the usual punishment. The beating was milder than usual, thanks perhaps to the visit of the Swedish consul earlier that year when Wim had cited cases of extreme brutality on the part of the guards.

The sadistic sergeant then took it out on the chickens. The cockerels, being the ringleaders, were removed and met their end in the guards' cooking pots. The remaining hens, maybe from fright at what might be in store for them, started popping out eggs left and right. Soon the eggs were so plentiful that on some days every patient in sick bay received an egg.

Another Christmas

As the weather turned colder, the prisoners braced themselves for the coming rigors of another winter. The Dutch prisoners knew what to expect, this being their second winter in Futase. The Americans were less prepared. They were used to the warmth of the Philippines. The color of their skin had only recently turned from a tropical dark tan to coal-mine pallor.

Christmas came again. Although this time the festivities didn't include a band, extensive decorations, or a tree, the prisoners did get the day off and a good meal. Each also received an American Red Cross package. As in the previous year, Wim gave a Christmas address, again emphasizing the positive: that they were still alive, that they had made it through another year in captivity, and that joy was still possible even in difficult circumstances. Also, he reminded them, the Red Cross packages were evidence that the world beyond the high, sharp-bamboo-spiked fence had not forgotten them.

To keep the Japanese sweet and ensure their continued "generosity," Wim wrote them a thank-you memo after the holiday. He laid it on so thick it's a wonder the Japanese didn't see through to what lay behind Wim's sycophantic flattery:

> I am glad to have the opportunity to express my thoughts and feelings by writing some words of appreciation and gratitude to the Japanese Camp Commander and the civilian authorities of the mining company connected with this POW camp for the way and the means provided to us to celebrate our Christmas 1944 in a most enjoyable manner.

> Because of the happenings on this holy day (25th Dec.), all men remained home, with no work being required at all for anyone. Religious services were held in the morning hours. An American Red Cross package was issued to each man, but besides that, there had been placed at our disposal the ingredients for preparing three quite abundant and rich meals: flour and sugar for bread, and rice, vegetables, one whole pig, and oil for an excellent fried rice dish.

During the evening entertainment of music and songs by the men, a further issue of cakes, tangerines, and sake was made.

All these delightful extras had obviously been obtained thanks to the thoughtfulness and exertion on the part of the Japanese authorities and our camp commander in order to ensure our material well-being on this commemorative day. Altogether a most enjoyable day spent in relative luxury and freedom in this camp and which will have greatly improved the morale and refreshed the spirit of the men to continue their life and work as POWs till universal peace will reign again in the world.

Unlike under the previous camp commander the year before, this time all the American Red Cross boxes were distributed, with each box containing about thirteen-thousand-calories-worth of delectables, such as butter, cheese, chocolate, and Spam, plus ten packs of cigarettes. It had two remarkable effects. The monthly weight levels of the prisoners shot up and trading among the men was reinvigorated, with "prices" of the different treasures quickly becoming established.

With some of the packages containing butter and others cheese, the men had to decide how much a small can of butter was worth compared to a similar size can of cheese. How an ounce of Spam stacked up to a bowl of rice. How many cigarettes you would need to score a quarter bar of soap. Who or what determined that twenty Chesterfields were equal to nineteen Camels, which were equal to eighteen Lucky Strikes? The determiner, of course, was the economic principle of supply and demand.

A negative effect of the influx of these riches was the inevitable increase in thefts. Stealing became an even greater problem than it had been before, so Wim and the other officers had to again apply strict disciplinary measures to clamp down on the culprits.

As the year 1944 exhaled its last breath, Wim took a moment to reflect not only on the problems he had had to deal with on a daily basis as CO of the camp and on what he had accomplished in improving the conditions for his men over the last year, but also to wonder how Klara and the children were faring. Were they still living in the bungalow in the *sawahs?* Was it difficult for Klara to keep food on the table, now that she could no longer depend on any income from him? Were the children and she all right and healthy? He didn't know.

Although Wim had been allowed to send a few postcards to Klara, he had no way of knowing whether or not she had received them. He had received no news from her since April 1942 and didn't know what was happening in Indonesia under the Japanese occupation. It was Wim's nature, however, to be optimistic. He repeatedly stated that he had been born on a Sunday, which to him meant that luck was always on his side. So he raised his cup in a salute to the arrival of 1945 as he looked up at the moon, the same moon Klara could see hundreds of miles away, and sent his love and positive thoughts to her in far-off Java.

9

Klara

January 1945

Have your fingertips or your knees ever been hungry? ... Have you ever been prepared to cut slices off your shrunken buttocks to feed your starving children? This is starvation.

Tenko

As in Karees, *tenko*, roll call, was held twice a day in Tjideng. But unlike in Karees, in Tjideng it was taken seriously. Young girls with megaphones or big bells went around morning and evening ordering all ten thousand of us to gather on the main artery of the camp. In rows fifteen-deep, we were lined up, the street leaders at the head of each group of five hundred. When the Japanese guard appeared, the street leaders called out "*Kiotskay!*" stand at attention, "*Kiray!*" bow, and "*Nowray!*" straighten up.

Each *tenko* was different. Some were long. Some were short. Sometimes we would have to bow five or six times, then stand at attention for hours. Other times we had to bow for hours. It all depended on the guard.

The 1945 New Year's morning *tenko* started with the announcement that the buying of all extra food with the money that had been confiscated in Karees would stop immediately. The reason: our greeting of the Japanese soldiers and the *heihos* was, in general, unsatisfactory.

Later in the day Sonei made the rounds of the camp and found two children smiling while bowing to him. The children found this bowing ridiculous, of course. Sonei went after their mothers and beat them up with a heavy stick. The women had to be taken to the hospital to be sewn up and bandaged, after which they were kept in prison for ten days. In prison they

227

received only rice and water and slept on the bare floor. We came to dread *tenko* because we were never sure how long we would be kept there, what new rules might be ordered, and what punishment could be meted out.

Long after we were freed, I continued to have nightmares about *tenko*. "*Kiotskay!*" would come the street leader's shrill call in my nightmare. The order sounded far, so very far away, but still imperative. I automatically stiffened to attention, and as usual the word caused jitters in my stomach. Somewhere deep within my mind, I didn't understand why there should be a roll call. *Tenko* was in the past, so many years ago, in the Japanese prison camp.

I kept trying to figure it out as I lined up with the other women and children in my dream *tenko*. All ten thousand of us. All white Europeans. All of us emaciated, bedraggled, tired, sad, and hungry.

What an effort it cost us to straighten up to attention. Getting those limp muscles, stretched out like old rubber bands, to do their work and hold the body erect was exhausting. Hardly a body after all these years. Skeletonlike frames, loosely covered with dry skin, rough and scaly like the neck of an ancient tortoise. That was what hunger had done to us former beauty queens.

The fortunate ones wore rubber boots, toes peeking out in front. Some still clung to old, tattered evening shoes, pitiful reminders of parties, music, dancing, and loving cheeks pressed one against the other. Most of us wore homemade flip-flops, scavenged pieces of textile culled from the dump heap, diligently stitched for hours until the patchwork slippers took shape. The patience and ingenuity of women.

The string that held the flip-flops together was the fruit of bartering in the invisible camp market, a miraculous bazaar thriving in the midst of squalor and privation. A pair of panties for half a banana. A bra for a piece of coconut. A bra garnered less than panties because who was lucky enough to have anything left to put in one? Only one thing was never bartered away. Rice. Our staple. Life itself.

The "parade leader," no longer one of us, performed her antics, calling us to attention, marching in front of us, lifting her legs high in the air, goose-stepping in order not to crush the dangling sole of her shoe, held on by only two stitches. What a sorry sight.

From the corner of my eye, I saw the Japanese soldier slosh-sloshing slowly along the endless fifteen-deep rows of women, who stiffened to attention like so many tin soldiers, and just as thin. The little fat one, the one we called "the Pig," was coming. He was small, long-armed, flabby-looking, puffy-faced. His turned-out shirt collar, almost like a *Schillerkragen*, was immaculately white. His long sword dangled loosely at his side and sometimes got caught between his legs. We were forever hoping he would fall and lose, not his sword, but his face. Alas, it never happened.

Children in Tjideng went barefoot
(credit: Image bank WW2—Netherlands Institute for War Documentation)

He was the bad one, who for no apparent reason would make us stand and bow for hours in the sweltering tropical heat. A faint smile on a woman's face was a good enough excuse to add another half hour to the nightly *tenko*. The bowing was prescribed, exact, rigid. Bow from the hip, forty-five degrees forward, face down, arms held tightly to the sides. Motionless, of course. This was the position the Pig would keep us in during the roll call. Sometimes for only five to ten minutes. Most of the time, longer. Once he ordered a special *tenko* during which we were kept bent like jack-knives from six until after eleven in the evening.

Because the Japanese guard came only at intervals to inspect us, we crouched or sat on our heels from time to time to relieve our piercing back-aches from the prolonged bowing. The pain started in your lower back and traveled up the spine to your neck. Your arms, pressed to your sides, began to weigh a ton each, until finally the shoulder muscles let go and your arms dangled. After a while your head, full of blood, felt twice its size. "It will burst, it will burst," the buzzing noise kept sounding in your ears, until your eyelids provided relief. They shut out this horrible world and you gently fell to the ground. You counted yourself lucky if the Japanese guard wasn't around. Showing disrespect like that was worth a few kicks.

The children . . . the children simply collapsed and fell asleep on the ground while the faraway stars shone in the deep violet-blue tropical sky.

For us mothers to see the children suffer from this whole camp experience was the greatest heartache of all. We felt helpless, spiritually crucified. The only relief we could give them was keeping their minds busy with stories, games, and lessons. How responsive and noble they were, never complaining, never even mentioning how hungry they were.

"Kiray! Kiray! Kiray!" The order to bow came at me from all sides of the black, hollow nothing that surrounded me. As I bent forward, a terrible fear gripped me. I became panicky and trembled all over. I started shrieking: "I can't take it. I don't want a *tenko*. I won't do it." Like someone possessed, I straightened up and started a crazy, blind dash away, away from the *tenko*, only to crash into something and collapse.

Then I would wake up. This dream was the recurring nightmare of the dark reality of the prison camp. For how many years would it go on? Wasn't it enough that I had lived through it? Did I have to live through it again, night after night? What was the purpose? What had been the purpose then? Did it prove anything? Did it make the world a better place? The universe provided no answer.

Life in Hell

The deluge started with a flash of lightning in the middle of the night, followed by an earsplitting crash of thunder. The rain came down in torrents. It didn't drum on the roof, but hammered, as if the clouds were throwing rocks. It poured into our doorless room, on the mattress that Robi and I were sharing. We woke up with a start and, in spite of the strict order of no lights at night, we put the light on and moved the mattress.

Maya noticed that in the corner to which we had moved the mattress, water was running down the wall, making a big puddle under the baby table. "Quick, quick," Altien and I shouted to each other. "Get the bucket and rags." Shouting was necessary because the beating rain and the thunder made a hell of a racket. By the time we got down on all fours to mop up the puddle, it was three times the size. We discovered two more rivulets on the opposite wall. It looked as if we were in for a swim, bedding and all.

We picked up the mattress Marjolein was on and carried it along the dark corridor in a whirlpool of wind and rain to the big room of the minister's wife and her five children. Trying not to put her on top of anyone else, we reached out with our hands in the dark, feeling our way, and deposited the mattress and Marjolein as best we could. We explained to the minister's wife what was happening, apologized, and ran back to our room.

Yvonne, Maya, and Robine had piled up the remaining mattress in the only dry corner, the quilts on top of it. The game was to keep this corner dry.

By then more than half of the room was flooded and water was streaming down the walls. The ceiling started to leak, showering us with water from above while we worked feverishly to sop up the water on the floor with the rags. At this point we were so thoroughly soaked, it didn't matter from where the water was coming. All that mattered now was the children's corner and the mattress and quilts.

When we had emptied the twenty-fifth bucket of water, we realized we couldn't keep pace with the incoming water and took to using brooms. Sweep, sweep, sweep. The water turned into our enemy. Then the light went out. Our misery was compounded. Until I found the matchbox with our three emergency matches and lit our single three-inch candle, the world seemed hopelessly black and wet.

The children were betting on the game and gave us shouts of warning when a sneaky little stream would approach the mattress and quilts. We swept the water nonstop from one until three-thirty in the morning, at which time the storm abated. The heavy drops kept falling from the ceiling for another hour or so.

All our clothing on top of the baby table and we ourselves were drenched. With chattering teeth and wet fingers, we smoked a cigarette. We had won the game. The corner was saved and the children, the mattress, and the quilts were dry.

During the next two weeks, we had three more nights such as this one. The walls were moldy from the water, and everything felt and smelled damp. Robi's bowel discharges were full of blood. She was apparently heading for dysentery. What to do? Years previously I had heard that the natives cured dysentery with a banana diet. In Europe they did it with an apple diet. Instead of taking her to the doctor, I decided to try the banana diet. I kept her in bed. Yvonne, Maya, and I gave her our banana ration. For two days she didn't get anything to eat but those four bananas a day. Miraculously, she got better and the blood disappeared.

Then I went to the street leader and told her that our situation was really untenable. She sympathized and promised to help.

A week later, a week without storms, thank God, we were allowed to move into the front room of another house whose occupants had been taken to the hospital. Goodbye seeping toilet juices, moldy walls, and gurgling septic tank.

The sunny, nine-by-twelve-foot front room we were given had a separate entrance from a tiny porch. The ceiling leaked in only three places. Our new home also had a four-by-six-foot grassy patch of a yard in front of it and two white oleander bushes. It seemed like heaven to us. As in Karees, we once again looked out onto a double bamboo and barbed wire fence, but beyond the fence we could see trains chugging by on a high embankment. To watch them pass by a few times a day gave the children never-ending enjoyment.

Much of living took place outdoors in Tjideng
(credit: Image bank WW2—Netherlands Institute for War Documentation)

At 5 a.m one morning, megaphones roused us for *tenko*. It was still completely dark. After the usual *kiotskay*, *kiray*, *nowray*, we were told to go back to our rooms, leave all our suitcases and bags open, leave behind any and all money that we might still possess, and reassemble for *tenko* at seven o'clock, taking along what food we had left from the previous day. Our quarters would be searched, mainly for money.

We did as we were told, but everybody took her money along in a handbag, pocket, or on her body. I slipped our remaining two hundred and fifty guilders in my bra and put twenty-five silver guilders in a tiny linen bag under the oleander bush in front of our room.

Once back at *tenko*, we waited and were rearranged in rows of four, five, ten, and fifteen. Then the ten thousand of us were driven out of the gate, accompanied by the soldiers' wild shouts. We were made to march around the camp between the two bamboo fences. Like a giant serpent we curled out of the camp. A few hundred yards from the gate, right after a sharp bend, was a little square, behind which was a row of empty houses, evacuated some time ago. We were heading for those houses.

Until we came around the bend, we didn't know the surprise that awaited us. A body search. Sonei had decided he wanted all our money.

All the women were being searched and some of them were being beaten. In panic, women emptied money out of pockets or bags into the roadside ditch. Banknotes swirled around like autumn leaves. The ditches on both sides filled up with piles of good Dutch guilders, tens of thousands of them. Our street leaders did the actual hands-on searches. Two Japanese soldiers flanked each street leader and watched the procedure closely. Women caught with money on them were beaten on the spot.

Like the others, my first impulse was to toss my cash, but I didn't decide to do so quickly enough, and then it was too late, the Japanese soldier would have seen me. One more row of four and then it was our turn. The hands of the street leader moved like lightning as she searched the woman in front of me. My gaze traveled from her hands up to her face and I almost whooped with joy. The street leader doing the search was our beloved Feetje. She was so dazed by the speed of the work and her nerves were so strained by the Japanese guards watching on both sides of her that she never once looked up at the face of the person she was searching. She likely didn't want to know who it was.

When she dived into my pockets, I whispered to her, ever so faintly, "It's in my bra." A fleeting glance was her answer. Now, with redoubled vigor, she turned everything she could lay her hands on inside out. Pockets, sandals, pot of rice, matchboxes filled with pebbles for the children to play with. She almost overdid it, nearly pulling my shorts off. The guards became impatient. "That's enough. The next one," they shouted. And I walked off with my money.

Well done, Feetje, I thought. *You will get my cup of coffee tonight— with sugar!* Three spoonfuls of sugar, the equivalent of about one-and-a-half measuring teaspoons, was our daily ration and the most prized thing we could offer one another.

The search over, we crossed the square and were marched into the empty houses. We were ordered to lie down on the cement floor, three to four hundred women per house. We dozed until 3 p.m., after having consumed the boiled rice we had brought with us.

As we were marched back, women on all sides whispered the ominous words, "another body search." Some of the women who were lucky enough to have gotten through with their money, now became frightened and threw their money away. I held on to mine, trusting in luck. And I was right. There was no second search.

When we got back to our room, we were surprised to find a small suitcase full of plated silverware resting on the floor. The initials of the Royal Dutch Navy were on the spoons and forks. I asked everyone in the house about it. No one claimed it. A Japanese soldier must have confiscated it from some other house and left it here by mistake. My two Djokja silver trays sewn in the pillowcases, which had escaped confiscation when we entered Tjideng, were still at the bottom of my suitcase, and the small linen bag with the silver guilders was still under the oleander bush. Lucky? I should say so.

After the search episode, we returned to our daily struggle to survive. We needed more vegetables in our diet. So, using a table knife, Altien and I cut the grass on the little stretch of lawn in front of our room. With a borrowed hoe, we dug up a strip of grass for a vegetable garden. After bartering for the seeds, we sowed spinach, Chinese cabbage, hot small peppers called *tjabe rawit*, and *katjang ketjipir*, a peculiar, fuzzy green bean. We remembered with gratitude Signora Pomidora and Mrs. Tomatea, who together bore us over three hundred tomatoes in Karees. We didn't plant any tomatoes here, however, because we didn't have enough soil to spare and because they would most likely have been stolen.

We also found a tiny papaya tree suffocating in the tall grass. We cleared the ground around it, although we hoped that by the time it would be big enough to bear fruit in six to eight months, we would be free.

Before long I was able to serve a plate of mixed vegetable leaves at every meal. I cut the greens into strips and salted them. I hoped that their vitamin content would save us from beriberi, which was the great killer among us. Despite the extra vegetables, Altien was losing strength rapidly. She was soon unable to help with the garden work.

I often traded leaves and gave away as many of them as I could spare. Despite this, we awoke one morning to find that someone had stolen all the spinach leaves and had cut off the top of the papaya tree. I felt bitter about such behavior, especially considering that everyone could have made a little garden for herself.

The Japanese needed socks, and we knitted them. A year earlier in Karees, I had declared that I would knit for the devil himself before I'd knit for the Japanese. But we received ten little pieces of candy for a pair of socks, which meant three candies for each girl and one for an emergency. Sugar was like medicine for them. So I knitted.

The camp office distributed needles and cotton thread, which was weighed before and after. The cotton was so thin that it had to be doubled. Even then, it often broke. Unfortunately, the needles were also thin. Only one thing was easy about it. The socks didn't need heels.

The first pair took me ten days, but I gradually increased my speed and was able to knit a sock a day. It took me four and a half hours of steady knitting. Not to go gaga from the monotonous, straightforward knitting, I amused myself by counting the stitches in different languages: Malay, Hungarian, English, French, German, Dutch, and Italian. Too bad I didn't know more languages. Soon clever Yvonne developed into a good knitter helper, and we made the socks together. Even Robi, the ever-ready-to-help seven-year-old, became a co-knitter.

The approaching Easter gave me a headache. What could I do to make it special for the children? There were no eggs to color, no sugar, no flour, nor any other ingredients to make even the semblance of a cake.

Just about then the book *The Tale of Peter Rabbit* fell into my hands and triggered an inspired idea. Instead of laying eggs, the Rabbit family itself—Peter, the naughty little rabbit, and his siblings, Flopsy, Mopsy, and Cottontail—would come to the children this year.

When I discussed this idea with Feetje, she mentioned that years earlier she had designed and made toys in Holland. When I asked her for help, she said she would do it with pleasure.

In a few days the designs were ready to be cut out of cloth and stuffed with cotton. I traded vegetable leaves for cotton material, some in solid blue and some in red-and-white checks. Altien helped with the sewing.

Two of the costumes had blue trousers with checkered jackets. The other two had the reverse, checkered trousers with blue jackets. I cut an opening in our mattress and pulled out enough kapok to stuff the rabbits.

Standing erect, with their big ears pinkish inside, one flopping and the other stiff, their embroidered big eyes, their sharp-looking neckties, their stump of a tail (except for Cottontail, who had a fuzzy one), they were about the best-looking toy rabbits I had ever seen. I embroidered their names on the lapels of their jackets: *Peter, Flopsy, Mopsy, Cottontail.*

The day before Easter we read the Rabbit family story again. I told the girls that sometimes rabbits visit human children around Easter time. In any case we would go nest hunting the following day. Next morning before *tenko*, the four of them, Marjolein included, were on the hunt.

What joy they had when each found a nest with a few tiny sweets in it (from sock knitting) and the rabbit that had laid them. For days they didn't part with those rabbits for a minute, hugging them at night as well. They were hugging their dreams come true.

A little after Easter I was summoned to Sonei's office. Having no idea what it was about, my heart beating fast, I bowed to him. He said something in Japanese, to which I answered in English that I didn't understand. Then he switched to Malay and told me to go into the next room. There, a bank official told me to make out a receipt for the one thousand four hundred fifty guilders I had received in Karees from my brother Laci through the Hungarian Legation in Tokyo. Of course they had handed over only fifty guilders to me at the time.

I made out a receipt stating that the money had been deposited in my name at the Yokohama Specie Bank.

"No good," said the man. "You should say that you received the money."

"No good," I said. "It isn't true. I didn't receive the money and I cannot make a false statement."

He tore up the receipt I had written and dictated another one, the way he wanted it to read. I hesitated signing it. The liaison woman who worked in the Japanese camp office and who had come with me whispered in my ear, "Sonei is rolling his eyes in the next room. If you don't sign now he will beat you and make you sign."

I knew I had no choice. With a hand trembling from impotent anger, I signed. Then the bank man whispered, "Make out another note and sign it also. We will send it to the Hungarian Legation in Tokyo. They will forward it to your brother in Lisbon. He will know that you are alive."

For a moment the warmth of human contact flooded my heart. I thanked him, bowed, and left, not suspecting that it was all a lie. The receipt never reached my brother Laci.

Shortly after that incident, at nine in the evening, we were summoned to *tenko*. I pulled the children out of their sleep, slipped the three sweets I had been saving for Maya's birthday into their mouths, and off we went.

Nobody knew why or what the *tenko* was for. Sonei himself received our bowing and gave a thunderous speech in Japanese. He bellowed and rolled his eyes. The interpreter translated his message into Malay. He, Sonei, knew that we still had a lot of money hidden and that this money must reach him. It was not ours anymore. It was Nippon's. If we didn't obey, he would withdraw our food, even the food for the sick in the hospital. He concluded his speech with the words, "I wish to see you all dead."

Same to you, Sonei. Same to you.

"*Kiray!*" shouted the street leaders. We bowed.

Silence followed. When they removed the floodlights from the platform where Sonei had been standing while he bellowed at us, the night turned dark again. We shivered despite the heat. What hatred in that man.

The cicadas, frightened into silence by Sonei's bellowing, resumed their singing. Bright stars hung in the deep, violet-blue firmament, winking at us as we stood and bowed, and bowed and stood.

The children were wonderful. The single sweet I had given them had long since melted in their mouths, and no second one followed it, but they didn't complain. They looked at the stars and took this night torture like grown-ups.

We bowed and stood until midnight, when we were finally dismissed.

On April 16 the air raid alarm sounded. Excited soldiers ran back and forth in the camp. We were ordered to stay indoors. We listened with delight to the exploding bombs and the antiaircraft "tak-tak." The activity couldn't have been taking place far away. Perhaps Priok, the port of Batavia? Maybe the Americans were really coming? Maybe Sonei was so angry because the war was not going well for them? Who knew?

Thou Shalt Not Steal

Mothers with three or more children, who had previously been excused from community work, were now required to do it. A few times I was assigned work in the vegetable garden where food was grown for the sick in the hospital. I was also ordered to clean vegetables in the hospital kitchen. The vegetables were invariably carrots, scraped and cut into small pieces.

About one hundred women did this work. That many carrots left the kitchen in the panties or pockets of these women for "the children at home" was a well-known and accepted fact.

The night before I was to start this work, I saw myself furtively putting one of these carrots into my mouth. I imagined hearing the dry crackly sound of the carrot between my teeth.

"But why furtively?" I asked myself. "Everybody takes carrots and everyone knows that everybody does it."

That everybody knew it and everybody did it was a given. Yet despite this open secret, the carrots were not consumed openly. No carrot-eating parties took place.

"In that case, it's stealing," said my good friend, inner voice.

A long argument started between us.

"Do you think I am different from the others? They all eat the carrots. Why shouldn't I?" I asked.

"Because you shouldn't steal," said the voice, unperturbed.

"I am doing what the others do. I am not stealing."

"Don't kid yourself."

"All right, have it your way, inner voice. I won't eat any carrots, but I'll slip three of them in my pocket for the children."

"And this won't be stealing?"

"No, it won't. This will be saving my children from starvation."

"Have you ever heard of anybody being saved from starvation by one or two carrots a week?" retorted the voice.

"But it's a mother's duty to do all she can for her children," I shouted back without moving my lips.

"Yes, all she can, but not to take away carrots from the poor sick."

"The poor sick. Indeed they are poor. But don't pretend, inner voice, that you don't know as well as I that eighty percent of those poor sick don't need carrots anymore. All they need is to hear St. Peter's key turning and the Big Gate opening. That leaves plenty of carrots for the remaining twenty percent, even if I take home three for Yvonne, Maya, and Robi."

"Then why not take six? Where is the limit? Who sets the rules? Today a carrot, tomorrow some tomatoes, maybe taken from some garden? Do you remember the tomatoes stolen from your garden? Did you like it?"

"I told you that you shouldn't steal, but let us suppose you do," the voice continued. "You come home with three carrots. You pop them in the mouths of your children. What if they ask, 'Mami, where did you get these?' What will you say?"

"I will say . . . I . . ."

"Would you lie on top of stealing?"

"Of course not. Of course not," I protested. "I would tell them that I had pinched them."

"Yes, pinching sounds better than stealing. Can you hear the children say, 'Our mother is pinching carrots. We thought she would never pinch anything from anybody'? Don't you think those few carrots will do more harm to their souls than good to their bodies?"

"You might be right, inner voice, but why should I do things differently or think differently from other people?"

"What the others do and think is none of your business. This thing is between you and me. I repeat the simple and ancient law: Thou Shalt Not Steal."

The argument between us went on for half the night. But because my argumentative powers, together with my memory, suffered often from "fadings," I had difficulty at times to concoct intelligible and logical answers to my friend, inner voice. In addition I couldn't always hear what the voice was saying because I was becoming a bit deaf.

I slept for only an hour or two. When I opened my eyes toward morning, I saw a strange sight in front of me. A big hook had been hammered into a wooden pole and a frail, emaciated, little person was hanging up a large cardboard sign. In big letters, the sign said:

THOU SHALT NOT STEAL

I was that frail, little person.

"That's good enough, inner voice," I said. "The argument is finished. Thank you."

I declined the carrot-cleaning job and took night duty instead. Twice a week, from midnight to 2 a.m., another woman and I filled kitchen drums with water and guarded them against theft. From a deep cement basin, one that we literally had to bend down double to reach, we would scoop between a hundred to a hundred and twenty buckets of water each and carry them to the drums, some fifteen yards away. Because of the weight of the loads and because our legs were not what they used to be, we often slipped and fell on the wet, muddy floor. This work, however, seemed better to me than that darn carrot temptation.

Hell Becomes More Crowded

New transports continued to arrive from other camps and were squeezed in among us. I made the acquaintance of Mien Morra, a distant cousin of Wim's. Following a bad beating from a Japanese, Mien had been in the hospital in Tjihapit camp in Bandoeng for nearly six months. When she arrived in Tjideng, she was put in the hospital for a few weeks. After she was discharged, she came to live in our house, in a small back room shared with another woman and her child.

Mien's health was poor. Sometimes she lay in bed for days at a time. The children and I would fetch hot water from the camp kitchen to make her tea. I washed her sheets. One time, when she couldn't swallow the tasteless camp soup, I had a hard fight with myself. Should I give her a portion of the few spoonfuls of Quaker Oats I had kept for the children as a last resort in case of illness, or should I give it to Mien? The outcome was inevitable. Mien was ill now. The children were not. Mien got the oats.

We liked Mien with her stately figure, beautiful gray hair, gentle manner, and sense of humor. She was so miserable in the back room that we invited her to come and live with us. So, one more in our nine-by-twelve-foot room. Now we were seven. When we spread out the quilts and mattresses at night, only a six-inch path of floor space remained for us to walk on. In the morning we rolled up the quilts and used them as a divan. We were really crowded now and hoped no newcomers would be forced on us.

We met old friends among the newcomers: Ada Westra with her two children from Lembang, Eva van der Weerd with her son Jantje, Mrs. Ujlaki, the Hungarian doctor's wife, and her daughter. We openly marveled at seeing each other alive. They looked better than we Tjidengers, but of course we had been in this hell for some time.

Overcrowding in Tjideng
(credit: Image bank WW2—Netherlands Institute for War Documentation)

Then a wonderful event came to cheer us up, the arrival of American Red Cross packages. We were delirious with joy. Nobody talked about or expressed interest in anything except what she had eaten and how it had tasted. Many became ill after consuming a little canned meat, a cup of real coffee, and a piece of chocolate. Our bodies couldn't cope with such rich food anymore.

To kill our joy Sonei ordered the evacuation of thirty houses within six hours. The people living in those houses had to be crammed in among the rest of us. The result was almost unbearable. We were one hundred and twenty-seven people in our one-story house. Eleven in the garage, six in the bathroom, five in the former kitchen, and so on. The open corridors were full of people on mattresses. Privacy was nonexistent. With almost everybody suffering from diarrhea, the situation was anything but funny.

Functioning toilets and working bathroom faucets were a thing of the past. For months we had been carrying our chamber pots to a sewer-head about a hundred yards away. In time even this distance seemed too far for the tired women, and they emptied everything into the shallow gutter running alongside the houses. A few women were in charge of supervising the cleaning of these gutters. Every morning one of them would appear with a long pole, a scraper attached to its end, and call out loudly, "Ladies, the Shit Express."

To maintain a standard of privacy during this bodily function, I arranged a little corner for us. Between the two oleander bushes and the side of the house I hung an old tablecloth on a bamboo stick. This curtain formed a private "room," in the middle of which was "the pot." We didn't empty it into the gutter, instead we still walked the hundred yards to the sewer-head. The sight of the big, green flies buzzing around and the thousands of fat, white maggots swarming on top of the lumpy, brown slosh was enough to turn a person's stomach. Our stomachs, however, were empty, so there was no fear of turning them.

Once when I was carrying the pot, I met a Japanese guard. Strict orders decreed that we had to put down whatever we were carrying when we greeted a Japanese. I ought to have put the pot down. Well, I was so tired, hungry, hot, and generally sick of it all that I became recalcitrant. I bowed with the pot held high in the air in front of me.

If he slaps me, I thought, I'll pour the contents over his head. I peeked at the guard from under my eyelashes. He was one of those rare ones who had a sense of humor. He smiled at my ridiculous pose and continued on his way.

On April 22, 1945, I received a Red Cross letter. Twenty-five words, including the signature—Laci. He let me know that Mami, Gabor, and he were well and that Aracs, our property in Hungary, was flourishing.

The news of this letter traveled fast, and crowds of women came to ask about it and to look at it in wonder. From where was it sent? When was it mailed? We couldn't make out a thing from the illegible stamp it bore. Was it dispatched a month, a year, two years ago? Who could tell? Still, it was a message from the outside world. We were not forgotten.

I walked with the letter through the camp streets, oblivious of everything. My feet carried me to the communal garden where vegetables were grown for the hospital, and there I sat down among the sweet potatoes, studying the twenty-five words and dreaming of the future. We would have a glorious celebration in Aracs when and if we got out alive. We would charter buses to transport our friends from Budapest. We would hire a gypsy band for three days, as in the good old days. We would feast. We would engage a private tutor for the children and keep them in Aracs for a whole year to let them enjoy liberty and nature.

I had gotten so used to losing everything that having a house and property and servants to look after them seemed a strange thought. At least we would not have to start from scratch, as we had had to do after World War I. What an effort it had been without my father, who had died in 1916. My mother, two brothers, and I struggled to earn enough to survive, to maintain a certain social level, and to complete our college studies at the same time. Now, after this war, we would go back to Aracs, to our paradise.

These thoughts stirred up the deeply buried homesickness I had stored in the deep-freeze compartment of my soul. I got up and swiftly walked back to our room, reburying these unwelcome feelings under the crust of our hard, relentless, monotonous life.

We thought things couldn't get worse. We were wrong. Rations were cut. We were now receiving only two ounces of cooked rice, one tablespoonful of *kangkong*, a water plant resembling spinach, eight-and-one-half ounces of bread, one-seventh of an ounce of sugar, and the same of salt. The bread was like hard rubber.

We longed for earlier times when we had received a banana or some other fruit once a day, a coconut for four people once a week, and water buffalo intestines every ten days or so. The latter were simply horrible things to eat, almost more horrible to look at, and even worse to clean.

The bowels—yellow-white curling serpents—were still filled with whatever the buffalo had eaten a day or two before it was killed. Mien lent us a pair of dentist's scissors to cut them open and clean out the contents. Up to that point in my life, I had never fainted, but I thought the moment had come when I cut open the intestines for the first time and the dead-bowel odors hit my nose. Because the intestines had some nutritional value and because our present diet was leading to starvation, I made the children eat them, despite Maya's tears.

We had also almost used up our last candle, as well as our last jar of borvaseline. We used the latter to fry the rubbery, hard, thinly sliced pieces of bread.

The doctors sent a warning to Sonei, declining all responsibility for the death rate. If conditions did not improve, they said, two-thirds of the prisoners would die within the next three months. Two-thirds. More than six thousand people.

We had between three and eleven deaths a day, with an average of seven a day. Seven women were the coffin makers. Because wooden planks were no longer available, the coffins were made of bamboo rods and matting. If the person died before 2 p.m., the body was taken to the cemetery the same day. If after 2 p.m., the body was kept in the so-called dead room, which also housed a harmonium. A hymn was played before the coffin was loaded onto a truck. Sonei or one of the Japanese officers placed a bunch of flowers on the truck and saluted. Then the driver drove the truck to the camp entrance. Relatives were no longer allowed to accompany the body beyond the gate.

We became hardened at hearing that this one or that one had died. Pity, we said, but she is certainly better off now. Tomorrow it might be our turn.

We racked our brains with the problem of how and where to get more food. Digging in the camp kitchen garbage was forbidden, but we noticed that the two-wheeled garbage cart was pulled to the gate around the same time every evening. There it waited between five and twenty minutes for the Japanese guard to pull it out through the gate.

About a dozen of us followed the cart like hungry hyenas. When it was left unattended, we stormed it. Nervously we dug around in the sticky refuse, with the soft fermenting muck reaching up to our elbows, in order to retrieve a two-inch-long *kangkong* stem or the top of a carrot so thin it was almost transparent. We kept a sharp eye on the gate for the appearance of the guard. When we heard the gate chain rattle, we jumped off and ran for it. None of us wanted to be beaten.

On one occasion a cheerful, young Arab woman and I were the only diggers. Somehow we didn't pay enough attention to the balance of this giant, chicken-wired wheelbarrow and it tumbled over, muck and all, burying us underneath.

Although we were afraid of being caught, our bellies shook with laughter. We worked feverishly to get the muck back in the cart. Luckily the guard was late that day and nothing happened to us, except that we were covered with fermenting, sloshy, stinky garbage.

I took the garbage plunder home, washed it a few times, chopped it up, and cooked it. This might sound easy except that we had no brazier because we had had to turn it in to the Japanese, we had no wood or charcoal, we had no matches, and making a fire was strictly forbidden.

We decided to disregard our own limitations and the Japanese orders. Mien objected to our endeavor. She was afraid that if we were caught, the Japanese would cut off our hair in punishment. They would, of course, but I told Mien that I would take all the responsibility. If we got caught, I would tell the Japanese that she had objected to my breaking the rules. Altien had no objections.

Out of an empty five-pound lard can, I fashioned a brazier. I turned the lid upside down, bent the edge up a bit, punched holes in it, and fitted it into the can. On the lower part of the can's side, I cut a ventilation hole. The brazier was now ready.

At night the scavengers, Yvonne, Maya, and Robi, went looking or, more accurately, feeling in the dark for charcoal. When the cooks in the camp kitchen had finished cooking, they threw out the glowing wood coals and poured cold water over them, which made a sort of charcoal. Sometimes the girls burned their fingers searching for these coals. Chestnut- or walnut-sized pieces were considered a lucky find. The next day we dried the charcoal in the sun.

Hitting a sharp piece of steel against a flint stone produced the spark for the almost divine fire. The spark had to fall on a little ball of cottonlike tree marrow, which we held with our thumb pressed against the flint. Of course, the spark did not necessarily fall where it was meant to fall. If we were lucky, we got the tree marrow glowing after a few hits, but usually it took more, many more, strikes. Striking the flint stone three hundred or more times before achieving success was not unusual. The striking noise made the sound of "tzik, tzik," so we baptized the fire-making tool the *tziki-tziki.*

Everyone in camp knew this sound. Because fire making was prohibited and because we feared spies, we took precautions to cover up the sound. Mien or the children would sit on the porch and sing while we worked at fire making in the room.

Once we got the little wood cotton glowing, we placed tiny pieces of paper, which we had rubbed into a fine fluff, against it and blew. We readied the candle to catch the flame from the fluffy paper. We held the lit candle underneath a few pieces of charcoal that had been placed on a piece of wire netting. As soon as the charcoals started to glow, we blew on them until they were red hot. When one person became dizzy from blowing, another person would relieve her.

We placed these glowing pieces among the charcoal pieces on the brazier and followed up with more blowing. When the whole brazier was glowing, we put on the pot with the cleaned, chopped garbage vegetables, pushed it behind the door, and hung a towel in front of it. Even people entering the room wouldn't notice that we were "cooking."

The whole procedure took about an hour. In the course of time, we developed special *tziki-tziki* muscles. Taking the risk seemed worthwhile. Besides the plate of fresh greens from the garden, our cooking gave the seven of us a few spoonfuls of cooked vegetables to eat with the rice. Sometimes, when I had it, I put some curry powder, traded for fresh greens, in the cooked vegetables. Strange how quickly prices became fixed: eleven leaves of fresh greens netted half a teaspoon of curry powder.

Endless Torment

Every day I arose at five o'clock, while it was still dark. I took a "shower," half a bucketful of water, on the lawn in front of the room. Then I usually finished knitting the sock I had started the day before, or did a bit of mending, or worked on some other odd job. At six o'clock everyone got up, and by six-thirty we were standing at attention for *tenko*. If we were lucky, *tenko* lasted no more than twenty to thirty minutes. Punishment in the way of endless bowing was usually meted out at the evening *tenko*.

Back in the room we rolled up the quilts, washed the floor, and had our breakfast. The children had rice with sugar. I gave them half of my daily rice portion and for my breakfast I soaked a few pieces of bread in water and sprinkled salt and a chopped hot pepper over them. Sometimes I let this soaked bread ferment in water overnight. It turned sour then and had a little more taste.

Living on top of one another in Tjideng
(credit: Image bank WW2—Netherlands Institute for War Documentation)

The morning was taken up with lessons for the children, given partly by me and partly by Mrs. Wonder, and with knitting, garbage digging, cooking, laundry, and the house food distribution.

A week after we had moved into our new front room, a group of women asked me to become the house head. But because they already had a warden, Mrs. Wilde, I declined. After some insistence on their part, however, I accepted the responsibility of becoming Mrs. Wilde's assistant. She had her hands full, especially with the food distribution. Sometimes we stood for two hours a day, weighing out tenths of ounces of sugar, counting almost every grain of rice, and measuring papayas in millimeters, when we were still given papayas.

A score of women, always the same ones who mistrusted everything and everybody, would stand over us, watching. One of them, a special nuisance, would grab my hand when I was cutting a papaya, for instance, and shout, "It isn't fair. There's half a millimeter more in this portion than in that one." Endless patience and sometimes sternness were needed to keep this woman in her place.

A few minutes after she went home with her food, we often heard shouting and crying coming from the open porch where they lived. Like hungry wolves, she and her four children fought over the food, exchanging kicks and blows. They had sunk to the level of wild animals. Near starvation seemed to have affected their mental balance.

Getting the women to take turns fetching the cooked rice in big pails also became difficult, especially towards the end. They were tired, they said. But who wasn't tired? They wanted to save their strength, they said. So did we all. They didn't care, they said. What could you say to that?

After the midday meal we had an hour's siesta in the ovenlike heat, with the sun beating full strength on the room. A shower behind the curtain put up at the side of the house came next. No more than half a bucket for each of us because water was hard to get. Occasionally Mien let me use her cake of good soap and a razor. I felt like a *grande dame* after such a treat.

The afternoon was taken up with more studying, Bible stories, knitting, and games with the children. Clubs, like Girl Scouts and dancing, were no longer allowed. Besides, no one had the energy for such activities even if they had been permitted. Two afternoons a week I gave French lessons to Yvonne and another little girl, and twice a week I gave a geography lesson to a little group of children.

Teaching was altogether forbidden by the Japanese, so we had to be careful, particularly with the geography lesson, because we were supposed to have turned over all maps and atlases. When this order came I tore out five pages from my atlas—the five continents—and thumbtacked them to the underside of the top of the baby table. I removed the pages from this hiding place only for the lesson, during which time Mien or Altien sat on the porch on lookout duty.

From time to time the children and I practiced hiding exercises so they wouldn't panic in the face of real danger. Each child had a given place for hiding her pencil and paper. I was responsible for the only book we had and the maps. Each child had a toy ready to grab. We agreed on what song we would sing. If in the middle of the lesson I said the word "aspirin," the meta-morphosis from lesson to game had to be completed within ten to twenty seconds. At the beginning the children scuffled and giggled. They found this new game a lot of fun. Soon, however, they learned to control themselves, although I suspected they preferred the hiding game to the geography lesson.

At teatime we had a very thin slice of bread and one banana for the four of us, when we were still given bananas.

The evening *tenko* was at half past five. Supper consisted of bread soaked in water with either a bit of sugar or just salt and hot pepper. Then I washed the floor again, spread the quilts, and prepared for the night. I usu-ally told the children an evening story: a fairy tale, an Aesops or Lafontaine fable, or something from Greek mythology. Sometimes we just sang songs. Before I began the story, we snipped off a day from the narrow strip of pa-per we called our Hope Calendar. "When this strip comes to an end, we will be free," I told the children, praying that I would not have to make another one. This one would end with the last day of June, and it was already April.

Altien, weak, usually went to bed at the same time as the children. Mien and I would sit on the porch, talking and knitting. Or I would study Italian or write in my diary. Evening was also the time for smoking. When we no longer had any American Red Cross cigarettes, we got a bit of to-bacco from Feetje. Usually, however, we rolled used, dried tea leaves in cornhusks for our cigarette of the day.

On some evenings Mien would go visiting friends. With Altien and the children in bed, I would be alone on the porch, doing my studying or writing. The electric bulb, with a dark paper shade around it, was attached to the back of the chair, which served as a table. Two little wooden crates served as chairs. This seating area was located on the three-by-six-foot open porch, which was encircled by a two-foot-high cement wall. Darkness and silence surrounded me.

I was studying the irregular Italian verbs one evening when, right behind my ear, a deep male voice said, "*Bekin apa?*"

I hadn't heard anyone approaching and almost overturned the crate I was sitting on from shock and fright. I rose and bowed to the Japanese guard.

"*Bekin apa?*" What are you doing? he asked again.

I explained that I was learning Italian. He grunted, hissed, and almost smiled. Without another word, he left. Good thing I hadn't been writing in my diary.

And thus one monotonous day after the other passed, sometimes with more courage and hope on our part, sometimes with less.

People said Germany had capitulated. Wishful thinking or true? Who could say? Two events, though, raised our suspicion that things were not going well for the Japanese: The *Nippon Times*, the prisoners' English-language newspaper, was stopped and punishment at *tenko* became more frequent.

As our captors jammed more and more people into the camp, the water supply became ever scarcer, until the faucets were hardly dripping. We stood in line near the main tap, waiting our turn to fill our buckets. This waiting wasted hours of our precious time, upsetting our daily routine, so I decided to get our water supply at night. Unfortunately, as the dry season advanced, our house's outside faucet also ran dry. Thus began the hunt for water.

At 2 a.m. I left with two buckets and a pot and walked three hundred to five hundred yards to find an outside faucet at some other house that was still dripping. With the pot I filled the buckets (they were too big to fit in the cement basin around the tap) and returned with them to fill our big pail and to water the vegetable garden. I had to make the trip four or five times. I put the last bucketful of the night foraging in a corner as drinking water. I covered the bucket with a cloth and hung a mug nearby for scooping.

During moonlit nights the way was well lit, but on moonless nights I often returned with bleeding feet from bumping into or stepping on things I couldn't see in the dark. At 4 a.m. I went to sleep, only to get up an hour later and begin a new day. Altien and Mien helped at times when the tap in our house was still working, but they were both too weak for the nightly excursions.

We greeted the occasional downpour with joy. We would frolic in the rain, the children in panties and I in a bathing suit. The big pail got filled, the garden got watered, and I didn't need to go foraging for water. What a treat.

The soap distribution had also stopped. I washed the clothes and sheets in sun-warmed water and spread them on the grass to bleach. We possessed only one toothbrush for the four of us and no toothpaste.

I felt as though fate was cheating me. Our Hope Calendar was running out and the war's end seemed nowhere in sight. How could I explain this fact to the children when I had assured them we would be free and Daddy would be home by the time we clipped off the last day?

I had to admit my miscalculation and make a new Hope Calendar, this time for three months. The children were pleased to again have something to cut off every day. I chose to make a three-month calendar because the situation in camp was deteriorating so rapidly that either the war or we would be over by then.

One morning at *tenko*, a woman standing behind me remarked, "I see you've started it too."

"Started what?" I asked.

"The hunger eczema."

"Me?"

"Those red-brown patches on your calves, shoulders, and arms, the peeling skin. What are they then?"

"Oh, those? They're nothing," I said. "Just from the sun."

Well, they weren't from the sun, and I knew it. They had been itching and burning for some time, but I tried to ignore them because I knew it was the beginning of the end. We were skeletons.

I asked the doctor whether she could perhaps help me with some vitamin or liver pills. I told her that I wouldn't mind dying, if it weren't for the children. She had nothing, she said. Sonei had ordered the burial of the medicine that had come with the last American Red Cross package. And he had insisted it be done in his presence.

Laughingly, she said, "Only good food can help you. I have those patches myself. You can live another four months once they've started."

So, only another four months, I thought. Many things could happen in four months. The war could even come to an end. It was now May 1945.

The idea of leaving the children made me cry on the inside. Who would take care of them if I were gone? What would happen to them? On the other hand, how lovely it would be to lie down, become weaker and weaker, and slumber away into eternity. An eternity with no *tenko*, no bowing, no nightly water hunt, no digging in the garbage, and no more hunger. I felt so completely spent, so immeasurably tired. Four months seemed like such a long time yet to go.

I walked home slowly. I didn't want to arrive with a disturbed look on my face. I sat down in the dusty shade of a tree. *Oh, God, you know I don't mind dying. I am ready for it, but please let me live. Help me to want to live and fight on,* I prayed. *With Your help I could live even longer than four months, I'm sure. I cannot leave the children alone.*

At the beginning of June, fantastic news circulated. Sonei was being relieved of his position. He became so drunk when he received the order to leave, according to the scuttlebut, that he smashed all the furniture in his room. He was supposed to depart in ten days. The whole camp was feverish with anticipation.

At ten the morning after Sonei's reported drinking bout, an order flashed throughout the camp via the megaphone-carrying women. No food would be distributed for three days because some women hadn't greeted Sonei properly.

Sonei himself rode around the camp on the loaded bread truck to show that there was bread. Then he rode out again with the bread. He ordered the working gang, girls between the ages of eighteen and twenty, to dig a ditch outside the gate, throw the bread into the ditch, and cover it with dirt. Then Sonei went to the camp kitchen and the half-cooked rice followed the bread into the ditch. It too was buried.

Everyone was stunned. Was such wickedness possible? Why not take a machine gun and mow us down? Why this slow torture?

Feelings ran both high and low. The response varied from shrugged shoulders to rage, fear, apathy, and even hope. The eternal optimists encouraged the others. "The Japanese must have lost some big battle somewhere and the end of the war is near," they said. "Sonei's fury will die down by the afternoon and we'll get some food."

I expected a revolt, but instead a strange silence fell over the camp. No one in the street. No noise anywhere.

At noon I was able to feed the children with rice left over from the day before. I also had twenty thin, very thin, sun-dried slices of bread that I had saved slice by slice and day by day, for an emergency. The emergency had arrived. We soaked half the bread in water for the evening meal. Altien and Mien had theirs, too.

After the evening story and prayer, when all was quiet in the room, I went to the garden to chew on some leaves because I had not partaken of the children's scanty meal. The night was dark, with not a soul anywhere. Suddenly I heard a whispered voice.

"*Mevrouw*," madam.

I searched the darkness but couldn't detect anyone. Hunger hallucinations, I concluded.

Then, again, distinctly, "*Mevrouw*, tomorrow . . . .."

Could it be the sentry on the other side of the fence? Talking to them was most severely punished. Was he trying to provoke me? In a panic I crawled back on all fours to the room.

Mien and I tried to figure it out. What had the sentry meant? One thing was certain. It must have been a *heiho*, a native guard, because he spoke in Dutch.

The next day arrived with still no food. Sonei was sticking to his three days.

I put my very last iron reserves, a mug of raw rice saved ages ago when we were still allowed to cook for ourselves, in the pot on the brazier behind the door. The rice was for the children. The grown-ups received only the daily plate of chopped leaves and a cigarette. By cigarette I mean, of course, tea leaves in cornhusks.

In the afternoon we were playing a ball game on the grass when Maya came running over.

"Mami, bread," she said excitedly. She handed me about half a pound of real bread.

"Where did you find it?"

"It fell from heaven."

"Don't be silly, Maya. Where did you get it?"

"Really, Mami, it fell from the sky. Somebody must have thrown it from somewhere."

We examined the chunk of fresh bread. A miracle?

"Let's eat it," everyone shouted.

"Now wait a minute. Somebody might have lost it." I wasn't sure about it being a miracle. On the other hand, who on earth could possibly have a piece of fresh real bread?

"We will set it here, on the wooden crate, and wait half an hour. If by then nobody claims it, we will eat it."

The children didn't protest and we continued the game. A most trying game it was, especially near the end of the half hour. More eyes were on the bread than on the ball. I kept checking the time.

"Three more minutes. One more minute." *Oh, God,* I thought, *please don't let anyone come for it.*

"Ten seconds. One second."

Everyone cheered. We carried the bread inside. With the *tziki-tziki* we lit the candle, disinfected the treasure over the flame, cut it into seven pieces, and gobbled it up.

This bread was much better than the rubbery bread we were used to. It was, of course, the sentry's bread. Yesterday he'd wanted to alert me when he whispered, "*Mevrouw*, tomorrow . . .." He was telling us not to despair, he would throw us his portion today. What a heroic gesture. If he'd been caught, Sonei would have had him shot.

I turned toward the tall, silent bamboo wall and made a gesture of thank you. Was the sentry behind it? Could he see me? He had probably been watching us for the past months through some little peephole in the bamboo matting.

At six o'clock that evening, wild shouts aroused the camp from its torpor: "Bread is coming." And so it was.

Rumors circulated that his own subordinates had denounced Sonei to higher-ups for starving us. The rumor might have been true because the next day, the third day of our forced starvation, we received boiled rice.

In the evening, sitting on the wooden crates on our calloused behinds, or rather what was left of them, we pondered the unusual happenings of the last few days and of the strange ways of the human heart.

Hunger

Have your fingertips or your knees ever been hungry? Have you ever had a constant ache in your stomach, an ache that worsens if you eat a little food? Do you know what it feels like when your body consumes itself? When you are driven crazy thinking and dreaming of food, of seeing savory dishes in your mind's eye? Have you ever been prepared to cut slices off your shrunken buttocks to feed your starving children?

This is starvation.

Starvation is not reached in a few days of not eating. It takes months to get there. It's a slow process with different stages.

In the first stage you can fill your stomach, but with a wrong, one-sided diet. Its symptoms are continuous craving for food of a certain kind, endless dreams of wonderful meals, irritability, impatience, headaches, loss of weight, and wounds that don't heal.

Frequent quarrels, another symptom of this stage, end in abrupt reconciliation without any apparent reason. Broomstick fights turn into flaming friendships and exaggerated self-sacrifice.

In the second stage you want to fill your stomach with anything, but this anything is not available. The symptoms are extreme tiredness and a constant hunger that causes a wrenching pain in your stomach, which only worsens when you eat.

This sensation of hunger is not localized to the stomach. It spreads from head to toe, all over your body. You begin to eat up your own body. Your weight drops until you are emaciated, eaten up. Your temples cave in, your cheeks are hollow, and your eyes seem much larger, gazing glassily from their deep caverns. Hair loses its luster and falls out. Teeth become loose and fall out easily. Eyesight weakens. Hearing often becomes blunted, with temporary deafness sometimes setting in. Saliva is insufficient and frothy. Gait is uncertain.

At this stage the *beau sexe* is anything but beautiful. Wearing a brooch helps to indicate which side is your front because your breasts have disappeared. So have your behind and menstruation.

The skin is dry and peeling. Wounds don't heal, becoming deep ulcers, full of pus. The hunger eczema manifests itself either as painful red patches on feet and lower limbs, often causing them to cramp, or as red-brown patches on arms, breast, and calves. Cheeks and lower legs swell up. If you push your finger into the puffed-up spot, it leaves an indentation for five or ten minutes.

The mental and psychological reaction in this second stage is depression, melancholy, hysteria, unfounded accusations, stealing, mania for collecting anything, writing cooking recipes, talking about nothing except food, and partial loss of memory.

I witnessed pathetic scenes enacted by second-stage sufferers. A mother was leading around her six-year-old skeleton of a boy with his hands tied behind his back.

"Look, everybody, here is a thief," the mother screamed, pointing to her own son, her eyes rolling, her face distorted.

She was on the verge of going mad. What was the starving child's "crime"? Taking a spoonful of sugar from the family ration.

Two other women, who were taking care of their hospitalized friend's children, were punishing one of them, a girl of three. One was holding the child's head completely submerged in a pail of water, while the other one was beating the little creature from behind.

In camp the general policy was not to interfere with anybody's doing that didn't concern you. However, at the sight of the treatment this poor little girl was being subjected to, everything that was human and motherly in me rose up in such indignation and fury that I threw myself at the women. My strength quadrupled. I pushed the smaller one away and jumped at the tall one, shaking her so hard by her shoulders that her eyes nearly popped out of her head. I was beyond myself. I shouted so loudly that people started to gather, but it helped. The women came to their senses and burst into tears.

They should be forgiven. They didn't know what they were doing. In the meantime, however, the little girl could have drowned. And the cause of it all? The girl had wet her bed several times. That was her "crime." Ninety percent of the children were unable to control their internal muscles because of malnutrition. These were only two of the many scenes I witnessed.

The third stage of starvation is a short one. No more hunger and no desire to eat. Symptoms include complete exhaustion, apathy, swelling from toes to abdomen, and no desire to live. With rare exceptions, sufferers in this category died within three days to three weeks.

Collecting and copying recipes and talking about food were curious manias. By exciting the imagination, they gave a certain satisfaction to the body. Some did it for only a few hours a day, others spent all their free time doing it.

When I realized how far this could go, I asked my friends not to talk about food when we were together. Forced conversations were the result. No one cared whether Marco Polo stayed at the court of Kublai Khan for fifteen years or for twenty years. Or whether Beethoven composed the "Appassionata" before or after the "*Mondschein* Sonata." Or whether the Simplon Tunnel was longer than the St. Gotthard. What interested us whether, how, and when we would get more food, and what we would eat when this miserable prison life was over.

I pretended to be immune to the recipe fever. "I'm only interested in the exotic Malay dishes," I reassured myself, with little conviction. The only difference between most of the other women and me was that I knew I was becoming dotty, whereas they didn't. Fortunately, I was so busy during the day that I had little time to indulge in the recipe game. And the evening hours on the porch were mostly taken up with writing in my diary, chatting with Mien, who was, I believe, quite immune from the craze, and studying Italian. I asked myself why I was doing the latter. Perhaps to ask St. Peter in Italian to let me in at the Gate?

Little Marjolein swelled up so much that she had to be taken to the hospital. For weeks Mien and I had tried all sorts of tricks to make her swallow some food. Altien was also declining and would not last much longer without medical help, or so it seemed to me.

A sixty-five-year-old French woman in our house shared a tiny back room with my garbage-digging Arab companion. Because only the Arab woman, Mien, and I spoke French, I often went over to her in the evening for a few minutes' chat. The two of us did some theoretical cooking, and each time she talked about Nice, her hometown.

One night I found her unresponsive to my forced cheerfulness. She wouldn't even help me "cook" the *plat du jour*. "They will starve us to death," she kept repeating.

I tried to reason with her that if she kept this thought in her mind, she would starve. Whereas if she imagined the food we were getting was sufficient, then it would be sufficient. She didn't respond, just waved me away.

The next day she swelled up. Within three days her legs were like those of an elephant and her toes, swollen to a bursting point, spread out like fans made of short sausages. She was taken to the hospital. I visited her there two days later, as a nurse brought her a fried egg.

She doesn't want the egg because she has been starved and is dying. And now she doesn't care anymore. I was talking to myself. *The hospital is trying to feed the ones who are dying. What's the use? If that egg had come a little earlier, it might have done her some good, but now it's too late.* I was now talking as if to an audience or perhaps a judge. *But I am here, and I am starving too. I want that egg. I want it so badly.* I had to swallow twice to get the overflow of saliva and my tears down.

The nurse reappeared, looked at the sick woman, and took the plate away. Now the egg was gone. I kissed the sleeping, dying woman and left. Three days later I went to see her coffin being loaded on the truck.

Shortly after, two other women from our house died. And then one morning I found Altien so weak and the expression on her face so changed that I ran to the hospital and told the doctor to come fetch her. Within a couple of hours, she was in the hospital. Just in time, I learned later. The doctor slowly built up Altien's strength with injections. Her heart had almost failed in her skeleton body.

Mien and I were still holding on. Mien was a bit swollen. I had my brown patches. My arms were sticks with tortoiselike skin hanging loosely from them. When we went to *tenko*, we still put on a suspicion of lipstick. Mine had lasted two years. The gesture made us feel better and meant we were still fighters. In no way, though, did it make our faces, death masks with red lips, pretty.

What a sight we were, with everything concave that should have been convex. And some of us in such fancy outfits. More patches than original cloth on shirts and shorts. Our footgear varied from high-heeled evening sandals to rubber-and-planks fastened with string. The children and I were amused by the street leader who had to lift her foot and make a sweeping movement forward to carry the loosely hanging sole of her shoe along with the rest of it.

Our memory was also becoming more and more deficient. For ten days I had been trying to recall my cousin's name and the name of the street my mother lived on. "Give me an egg and I'll remember" became a favorite saying.

My best friends and ever-helpful companions, Yvonne, Maya, and Robi, suffered perhaps less from hunger than we grown-ups, mainly because they were less conscious of what was happening. They looked skinny and had practically stopped growing, but they were healthy and always cheerful. I never heard them say they were hungry or utter a word of complaint. Yvonne, however, had slightly swollen legs.

Talking about food was taboo for them too. I realized, however, that this might cause some psychological problems, so we agreed that on Saturday nights, instead of my telling them a bedtime story, they would order a meal. Each time a different one would start the ordering, while the other two would listen with great anticipation.

"Well, Yvonne, you are first today. What will you order today?"

"A fried chicken, please."

"A big chicken or a small one?"

"A big chicken."

"Any gravy with it?"

"Yes, lots of gravy."

"And what do you want to eat with it, Yvonne?"

"Rice. Lots of rice."

"Anything afterwards, for dessert?"

"Yes. A cake."

"A small cake or a big one?

"A big cake."

"Made with nuts or with chocolate?"

"Chocolate."

"Should it be a two-layer cake or a three-layer one?"

"Could it be four layers?"

"Certainly, we can order a four-layer one."

"Would you like to order anything else?"

"No, thank you, Mami. My tummy is full now."

"It's your turn now, Maya. What would you like to order?"

"A chicken."

"Fried or roasted?"

"Fried, please."

"A big one or a small one?"

"A big one."

The ordering would go on in this manner, with all three choosing the same things because they no longer remembered what other foods existed. As these imaginary dinners unfolded, their eyes became brighter and their cheeks rosier. By the time all three had finished their mental banquets, they looked better, even a little fatter, and they felt happier. I was convinced these "meals" had a physical as well as a psychological effect on them.

I promised them a cake for each birthday they had spent or would still have to spend in captivity. At this point I owed each of them three cakes on her next birthday. Yvonne suggested that it wouldn't be too bad if we stayed in camp a little longer. Then they would get four cakes each on their first birthday in freedom.

They looked forward eagerly to the Saturday "ordering." They were not "talking food," they were ordering a real, theoretical meal.

St. Bartholomew's Night

On the morning of June 25, 1945, a nervous excitement broke out in camp. From a word heard here and there from passersby, we learned that smuggled food was coming in through the fence. The explanation for this unprecedented occurrence, so people said, was that Sonei, who was on his way out, didn't care what was happening anymore. Women stormed the fence at several places where natives were enticing them with goods from the outside.

The grapevine was not correct this time. Sonei himself went to check on what was happening at the fence. He caught one of the smugglers, dragged her by her hair to the middle of the main street of the camp, beat her head until it bled, and then cut her hair off. This brutality turned out to be the opening scene of the awful day and night that we later called St. Bartholomew's Night.

Sonei managed to catch more smugglers, and by five in the afternoon he had cut off the hair of some twenty women. He wanted, however, to catch all who had dared to barter for food with natives on the other side of the fence.

The girl gang was ordered to repair the damaged fence. Sonei, in his rage, pushed their faces in the muddy holes they were digging for the new fence posts. He did this while kicking and beating them from behind.

The evening *tenko* lasted two hours, after which the street leaders were told, at a meeting, that all smugglers had to be brought forward or their (that is, the street leaders') hair would be cut off. With megaphones the street leaders went around camp, asking the culprits to give themselves up. Some women came forward, confessed, were beaten, had their hair cut off, and were made to stand in front of the Japanese office where the smugglers who had been beaten earlier had been standing since noon.

Sonei wasn't satisfied. He wanted them all.

At midnight, another *tenko* was ordered. We were kept there until three in the morning. No more smugglers gave themselves up. We were, finally, sent back. Then the street leaders were ordered to go to the Japanese office. There all of them were beaten with sticks and then ordered to kneel while natives shaved their heads.

Sonei's mad fury died down around six in the morning, at which time all the women were sent home. An hour later, at seven o'clock, *tenko* was ordered again. The shorn street leaders appeared in chic little turbans. Pinned to the turbans were locks of their cut-off hair, coquettishly curling on their foreheads. They were cheerful and smiling, as if nothing had happened. Wonderful women.

Feetje, who had also been beaten, later told us that after the morning *tenko* following the night of horror, Sonei's right-hand man officially apologized to the street leaders for his superior's behavior. He said that none of them could prevent it and added that when Sonei had finished with the women, he beat up his own staff, from the least important *heiho* to the highest-ranking Japanese officer.

Later we heard that this smuggling episode had been a prearranged trap between our much-hated camp commander and natives from the outside.

Two days later we had another midnight *tenko* that lasted several hours. This *tenko* was the last of its kind. We never saw Sonei again.

10
Wim
January 1945

If not all the Japanese guards, at least the Japanese camp commander must have been aware that the tide of Japanese military supremacy had turned from flood to ebb.

Signs of Change

Early in January 1945 the old camp commander called Wim and Frits into his office and announced that he was leaving. The Dutch officers were understandably apprehensive. From past experience they knew that when change came, it was usually not for the better. They had gotten used to the old lieutenant and had grown to appreciate him. He had been fair to them, at least as far as he could be, given the circumstances. What would come next?

To their great surprise and relief, the new commander was young, about thirty years old, spoke fluent English, and, unlike the previous camp commanders, was a captain. Captain Sakai immediately established a positive relationship with Wim. Every morning Wim and Frits had to report to his office, now without their interpreter. Braber's translation skills were no longer needed because the new commander could give them their instructions in English. The captain also required them to report on anything in the camp he should know about.

Shortly after the new commander's arrival, the men received another shipment of Red Cross packages. As before, the result was a marked rise in the men's weight. The increase was even more pronounced this time because daily rations from the Japanese had deteriorated once again. Rice

263

distribution was cut first by ten percent and then, shortly after, by an additional five percent.

Also as before, thefts shot up. This time, however, Wim was able to discuss the problem man-to-man with the commander and received a much better response. The first thieves caught red-handed by their roommates were turned over to the Japanese for punishment. Their sentence consisted of a beating and seven days in the stockade on short rations. By the third incident of theft, with each perpetrator netting the same harsh punishment, the thieves got the message and decided that a can of Spam was not worth the risk of being beaten, being imprisoned for a week, and receiving nothing but a mouthful of rice and a little water for the duration of their confinement.

With the criminal minority's reign of terror now effectively squashed, the rest of the men felt better protected, resulting in a perceptible improvement in the atmosphere in the camp. The new commander's push to have the prisoners really wind down on their day off also raised the men's spirits. He encouraged them to set up sing-alongs or other musical entertainment. Wim had made this exact suggestion to the previous commander, the old lieutenant, a year earlier, but it took a changing of the guard to finally have it be implemented.

The Indonesians in particular embraced this suggestion and threw themselves into the endeavor. Every tenth day the musically talented among them provided a concert for the rest of the camp. And at these events the captain and his staff sat in the front row, swaying in time to the music.

Another change concerned the news. Up to this time the prisoners had received the English language newspaper, the *Nippon Times*, on a more or less regular basis. Although the paper obviously had a pro-Japanese slant, it did give the men a picture of what was happening in the world beyond the fence. The men even read about American advances in the Pacific. Then the *Nippon Times* abruptly disappeared. The Japanese mine workers continued to bring their Japanese newspaper to work with them, probably figuring who could read kanji anyway? Well, Braber could, that's who. So every evening Braber gave Wim and the other officers a summary of what he had learned.

As the war in the Pacific deteriorated for the Japanese, even the Japanese newspapers didn't report much on that front. The papers did, however, continue to faithfully provide maps and reports on what was happening on the European scene. When Braber's knowledge of kanji characters came up short, the Japanese paper often unknowingly helped him by printing European names in hiragana, the Japanese interpretation of the European sounds. Thus Wim and the others followed both the Russian and later the American advances on an almost daily basis.

Soon getting even the Japanese newspapers became increasingly difficult, and the ones Braber did see were largely silent on the war. Although no one knew anything, Wim and the others felt that "something" was happening.

One noticeable aberration was that coal was piling up at the entrance of the coal shaft and was not being shifted. The slowdown allowed one of Wim's men, who was a mining engineer in private life and thus accepted by the Japanese as a *honcho*, or supervisor, to introduce some mining improvements for the men's safety. These changes also resulted in more efficient production. Except for the safety factor, this outcome was, of course, not to the prisoners' advantage, but since the coal wasn't being shifted anyway, it didn't much matter.

Air raid shelter in Fukuoka #7, 1945

Although the dreary daily routine continued as spring turned into summer, something was definitely in the air. And then the something became more concrete. Next to the parade ground in front of the camp, the Japanese ordered the POWs to dig three air raid shelters. Each of the long barrows was meant to shelter about a hundred men.

Wim and the others were both elated and apprehensive. Did this mean that the war was now going to be fought on Japanese soil? And what about the POWs? After having endured three and a half years of captivity, would friendly fire from the sky wipe them out?

Not until much later did they learn that in the middle of March the Americans had firebombed Tokyo and other Japanese cities, including Kobe, Osaka, and Nagoya. Hundreds of B-29s carried out these incendiary raids just before dawn, with the aim of destroying large industrial complexes. Tokyo's raid alone killed an estimated one hundred thousand Japanese people and wounded an equal number. Overall, approximately eight million were made homeless as a result of these raids.

Shortly after the shelters at the camp were dug, the alarm blasted its high-pitched wail into the night. The men on the day shift were roughly roused from their sleep and herded into the shelters. The night shift, already underground, was ostensibly protected. If the mine were to receive a direct hit, the night shift men would likely have been entombed with no hope of rescue.

About three hundred men on the day shift squeezed into the earthen dead-end dugouts. That the ones furthest in weren't suffocated is surprising, given the lack of ventilation. The all clear sounded a short while later.

Not long after, at around eleven in the morning, the alarm screamed its warning again. And again the guards drove the men into the dugouts. Frits, who was detailed to keep order, was at the mouth of the shelter and saw what he described as a magnificent sight: "High up in a cloudless sky, there were hundreds of American bombers, placidly sailing along to whatever was their target. It was just marvelous seeing those big white birds floating so effortlessly in the high sky, nothing to disturb them, not a Japanese fighter in sight. That was the first time we realized the end of our ordeal might be at hand."

266

Beginning of the End

The prisoners, catching a whiff of freedom in the air, became more daring when composing songs for their concerts. Assured that the English-speaking commander didn't understand Dutch, the entertainers changed the words of familiar tunes to subtly herald the approach of the war's end and their liberation.

But a whiff of freedom was all they got. For now the only change in their dreary routine was the reduction in their food rations. In July the new commander decided to shake things up. He instructed Wim and the other Dutch officers to organize the Futase Olympics. The prisoners were to assemble a team of their men to run against two Japanese teams: one composed of Japanese soldiers, the other of Japanese civilian mine workers.

Elaborate preparations followed. Wim and the other officers were handed a bucket of chalk and told to lay out the course. On all fours they meticulously measured out the track for sprints of one hundred and two hundred meters and relay races of four stretches of fifty meters. For two days the Japanese guards hovered over them as the Dutch officers drew white lines on the packed brown dirt.

No spectacular pageant greeted the Olympians on the opening day of the Futase Olympics. Instead cheering members of the local community appeared to root for the Japanese mine workers team. Not surprisingly, whether on purpose (why risk incurring the wrath of a Japanese who has been bested and thus has lost face?) or because of the poor physical condition of the prisoners, the results were disastrous for the POWs. The prisoner team as a whole, as well as every individual POW who raced, lost to the Japanese. The Japanese spectators wildly cheered each racing win as though it were a victorious battle in the larger war.

As the final indignity of the competition, the Japanese ordered the four Dutch officers to race against each other. Clearly, this last race was meant to make the officers, and especially Wim, look foolish. To turn the tables, the four officers faked an enthusiastic start, setting out with a will. Gradually three of the officers began panting in exaggerated fashion and dropped behind to allow Wim to triumph. Raising his arms in the typical runner stance of breaking the tape, Wim crossed the finish line first, beating the others by several lengths. The Japanese spectators applauded loudly, unaware that the officers had rigged the race to make Wim, the POWs' commanding officer, look good. In the end Wim's reward was neither a gold medal nor a crown of laurels, just more of the same old camp life for him and his fellow prisoners.

Perhaps the reason for this Olympics charade was to distract the Japanese and bolster their faith in their own prowess and their invincibility. If not all the Japanese guards, at least the Japanese camp commander must have been aware that the tide of Japanese military supremacy had turned from flood to ebb.

In the early part of August 1945, the prisoners noticed no more American B-29s flying overhead, but they did see an ominous red glow that lit up the night sky. It reminded Wim and Frits of the fiery-colored skies they had seen and helped to fuel with their explosives in the four days in February 1942 when Palembang and the rest of Sumatra fell to the invading Japanese troops.

11
Klara
June 1945

No military bands, no squadrons of airplanes, no battalions marching by, no speeches, no singing, no banners, no national anthem. Nothing. We were expected to keep quiet, suppress our mad joy, and await the Allied troops. A strange liberation.

Surprising End

At the end of June the bread distribution stopped, an event that had happened before. The last time it had occurred, we were given cornmeal instead. Cooked as mush, it tasted sharp and bitter. Maya had tears in her eyes when she ate it and got sick as soon as she swallowed it. Yvonne and Robi were heroic about it.

This time it wasn't even cornmeal. It was clothes starch, a blubbery, gray jellylike mass, with the one advantage of having no taste whatsoever. But we didn't care and didn't mind anything because fantastic news reached us from all sides that the war wouldn't last much longer, that the Allies were winning, that the American Navy would soon be landing in Soerabaya. Or were they only rumors?

We caught and ate snails and frogs, when we were lucky enough to find them. A little boy in the house was the master frog skinner. On occasion, delicious roasting smells floated in the air. Nobody could figure out where they came from. We thought we were hallucinating, until we realized that all the cats, abundant at one time around the camp kitchen, had disappeared. A mangy old tom was left behind to meow of olden days.

Mien went to work in the camp kitchen and occasionally brought home a bowl of soup. How we savored this treat. I continued to dig in the garbage and also fermented the clothes starch to make it somewhat palatable. I was able to add a new recipe to my collection: Exotic Fermented Starch Supreme.

A strange Japanese order required a change in the time of day. At half past nine in the morning, it would be noon. No clocks, however, were to be changed. Nobody understood this order.

On July 13 scores of unspecified pieces of news circulated that the Allies were winning the war. For days we anxiously awaited the details. We heard nothing more. Again we thought they were just rumors. In gloomy silence friends gathered at dusk with their pretend cups of coffee and imaginary cigarettes and tried to encourage each other. As the days went by, we became apathetic, too exhausted and depressed even to think. Apparently all the good news was just air. Almost a month went by.

On August 16 megaphone announcements declaring the deactivation of the knitting center aroused us from this bodily and mental torpor.

"This is unbelievable," we assured one another. "This is the end. The Japanese are surely packing and want to take their last socks with them."

As we were preparing for the evening *tenko*, we received our second great surprise of the day. The megaphone-carrying women announced the cessation of *tenko*. Was it a mistake? What had happened? Was the war over? Nobody knew.

The next day we received a triple rice portion. Raw rice. Cooking was allowed. We hugged each other with excitement. We still had no idea that the war really was over.

Then somebody found a note attached to a stone that had been thrown over the fence from the outside world. "Rejoice, ladies," the note read. "The war is over. When you come out of camp, you will want to furnish again. Don't forget that I make good furniture for low prices. Come to my shop with confidence." The note was signed, "Song Li, Batavia." A good businessman, the entrepreneur Song Li.

In no time the news of the note's contents spread. His note was the first real news about the end of the war. Officially we had still not heard anything.

Each day brought some new surprise. One egg for four people, a little dried fish, some vegetable oil, and meat. As I chopped the springy buffalo muscle, the children snatched the flying pieces and ate them raw. The doctors sent out circulars warning us against overeating. A chart with calories was attached to show us how to increase our diet slowly. Was all this true? Was it going to last? Were we really not going to die from starvation? Was the war really over?

The Japanese who had been supervising the girl gang told them, "We are friends now." Then he gave the girls orange cockades as a symbol of the House of Orange, the Dutch Royal House. He did not, however, say anything about the war's end.

The next morning we awoke to the sound of the Dutch national anthem. A large group of Indonesian natives and Indo-Europeans had lined up on the railway embankment beyond the fence. They waved to us and tossed bananas, bread, and letters over the fence for their friends inside. "The war is over," they shouted.

Tjideng camp's main gate
(credit: Image bank WW2—Netherlands Institute for War Documentation)

At ten o'clock some natives from the outside cut holes in the fence's bamboo matting and began bartering. A blouse out, a bunch of bananas in. One skirt for four eggs. The Japanese guards tried to chase the natives away, but they refused to leave. They weren't afraid of the Japanese anymore. The mob outside was strong and healthy, but in rags. We were hungry and didn't care whether we gave away our last skirt. The next day the fence's bamboo matting looked like a colander.

Yvonne wanted to barter for some eggs, so I gave her my housecoat. "Don't give it for less than seven eggs," I shouted after her. Strange how quickly the prices were established.

Five minutes later poor little Yvonne came back sobbing. The crook of a native had pulled the housecoat out of her hands through the hole in the bamboo fence and had run away without giving her the eggs. I had quite a time consoling her.

On August 24 the street leaders told the house wardens that the Japanese had officially informed them that the war was over. The Allies had won. We should be patient, keep calm, and await the arrival of the Allied troops. We returned to our houses and passed the news on to our housemates.

That was all. No military bands, no squadrons of airplanes, no battalions marching by, no speeches, no singing, no banners, no national anthem. Nothing. We were expected to keep quiet, suppress our mad joy, and await the Allied troops. And we did what we were told to do. A strange liberation.

Back in our room, I hugged and kissed the children and Mien. The five of us said a short prayer of gratitude. After that we sang the Dutch national anthem and sat down, wondering aloud when we would get news from Eug, Mien's husband, and from Wim. I thought about Aracs and wondered how long it would be before we would be back there with Mami, Gabor, and Laci.

Some typewritten bulletins were pinned on the wall of the camp kitchen, informing us of the great events of the war. One line read: "On August 6, an A-bomb was dropped over Hiroshima." Typing error, I thought. It should have read: "A bomb was dropped . . .." We didn't know the difference between "a bomb" and "an A-bomb."

272

The Japanese continued to guard us. I saw a Japanese officer who used to check us at *tenko*, cleaning a septic tank with his bare hands amid a shouting, gesticulating crowd of women. Some were even slapping him on his back. Revenge. It hurt me to see it. I turned away. Must we do the same to them as they had done to us? Will we never learn that two wrongs don't make a right?

Luxury items started pouring in. Soap, toothbrushes, coffee, sugar, cigarettes. Mrs. Wilde and I could hardly cope with the distributions. A true treat was putting sugar in a bowl, pouring sugary syrup over it, and eating it with a spoon. Even that didn't seem sweet enough to us. We concluded that the sugar must be some kind of "war sugar" that was not as sweet as regular sugar. In truth our craving for something sweet was so great that nothing could satisfy it during those first few days.

We visited Altien from time to time. She was extremely weak but on the way to recovery, as was her daughter, Marjolein.

A civilian Dutchman escaped from the men's camp and stole into Tjideng where he found his wife walking in the street. They held each other, tears running down their cheeks, oblivious of the crowd of about three hundred of us watching this miraculous reunion.

A few days later a gang of two hundred Dutchmen came to the camp to take over the daily heavy duties of cooking, water carrying, garbage service, and so on. Questions flew back and forth between the men and the women. We heard from them that the men prisoners would be set free first.

Government employees, oil companies, and other big business firms had already set up their organizations and were providing us with more food. Dutch Shell took us under its wing because Wim had been working for them when the war broke out. We Shell women got eggs, fruit, and baskets of charcoal. Everybody was putting on weight, but we puffed up in a peculiar way, as if we were seven months pregnant.

Native vendors were allowed to come in and sell their products at a market newly opened in the camp. We were given East Indian paper money that the natives accepted as legal tender. The Japanese had been printing this money since the beginning of the occupation.

Mien's husband arrived. While they embraced, the children and I filed out of the room to give them some privacy.

American, British, and Australian women were called to the office and told they would be flown home to America, Great Britain, and Australia.

The first letters began to arrive. Along with them, a lot of Red Cross announcements of deaths. Mrs. Ujlaki had lost her husband. Ada Westra came, card in hand, with the same sad news about her husband. Eva van der Weerd came a day later about hers. Long into the night I talked to them, but what could I say and how could I comfort them?

Every day I went to the office to inquire whether the list of the Dutch prisoners who had been taken to Japan had arrived, and every day I was told to be patient.*

A Dutch plane circled over the camp. We waved like mad, flapping sheets and towels. The pilot dropped no flowers, packages, or messages. He just circled and left. We were disappointed. Somehow we had imagined liberation in a different way, with hundreds of planes in the air.

The Dutchmen who came to work in the camp told us that troubles were brewing outside the camp. A few thousand natives, stirred up by the Japanese against the white race, had organized under the leadership of Sukarno, a pre-war anti-Dutch revolutionary who had been educated in Holland. Although still a relatively small group, their number was growing rapidly.

This nationalist movement had started long before the war and was aimed at breaking the Indies away from the Dutch crown and setting the country up as an independent republic. Because of his revolutionary activities, the Dutch had exiled Sukarno from the Indies. He returned during

---

* Now that more and more of the women were hearing about the fate of their husbands, Klara tried to be patient and stay positive, although she had not heard anything yet from Wim. She knew that the POWs who had been taken to Japan and who had survived were now in Manila, but from or about Wim she had heard not a word. Not knowing where he was (or if he was) she wrote him a letter and addressed it to "Captain W.H. Andrau of the Flying Corps, ex-prisoner of war (Dutch), Manila, Philippines." She felt as though, fueled by her faith and love, the letter would reach him and find him whole and healthy in body and spirit.

Klara also had us children write to Wim. For us it was a little like addressing an "important person" but one we couldn't really remember. We hadn't seen our father for three-and-a-half years, which is an eternity in a young child's life, so our letters to this august person were formal and all pretty much the same. See section 14 for the content of these letters.

the war and was assisted and encouraged by the Japanese in his national-istic endeavor. Having a Japanese wife helped him greatly. He gathered together a small group of extremists, whose number grew by means of propaganda, intimidation, and acts of terrorism.

Now that the Japanese had lost the war and would have to leave the Indies, everyone speculated on what Sukarno's plans would be. Did he hope to gain control with the aid of the British? No one could figure out why the Allies were not allowing the Dutch military personnel, freed from the camps, to return to Java.

The reality of the problem was brought home to us one evening. At about eleven at night, we heard crowds of people shouting. They had gathered on the railway dike on the other side of the fence, across from our house. The voices were unfriendly. Shouts and more shouts, and then stones started flying into the camp. A few of them landed on our little porch. Apparently the angry, hungry crowd was preparing to break into the camp. I woke the children, helped them dress, and warned everybody in the house.

By now the tom-toms were beating and the crowd was yelling, "ooee-oo-ooee, ooee-oo-ooee." Hundred of them were shouting this eerie rallying cry. The clamor grew and became a frenzied, hypnotic, surreal, battle cry.

On our side of the fence, Japanese soldiers ran back and forth, roaring orders at each other. They brought a machine gun and set it up in a corner of the camp, not far from our house. They meant business. As soon as the mob heard the tak-tak-tak-tak of the gun, the war cry died down and the natives scattered. It was two in the morning by the time we went back to bed. The next day we heard that Sukarno's extremists were behind this planned attack on the camp.

12
Wim
July 1945

Hiroshima was "hidden by that awful cloud . . . boiling up,
mushrooming, terrible and incredibly tall."

Bombs Away

In the middle of July, as the Japanese were forcing Wim and his men to spend their diminished energy and strength racing in the Futase Olympics, the top Allied leaders were meeting in Potsdam, Germany. Mint-new President Harry Truman, bushy-mustached Communist Party General Secretary Joseph Stalin, and cigar-chomping Prime Minister Winston Churchill* gathered to plan the administration of Nazi Germany's unconditional surrender. Establishing post-war order in Europe and bringing about Japan's surrender in the Pacific were also on the agenda.

Truman, Churchill, and Chiang Kai-shek, the president of the Republic of China (but not Stalin, because the Soviet Union had not as yet declared war on Japan at the time), met and issued the Potsdam Declaration on July 26, outlining the terms of Japan's surrender. The ultimatum warned that if Japan did not surrender, the full application of the Allied military power, backed by their resolve, would "mean the inevitable and complete destruction of the Japanese armed forces and just as inevitably the utter devastation of the Japanese homeland."

The Japanese rejected the ultimatum. The promised destruction and devastation followed.

---

* Clement Atlee replaced Churchill when Churchill's Conservative Party lost to the Labour Party in the 1945 British election.

Later Wim and the others would learn that on August 6, 1945, at 8:16 a.m. a B-29 airplane called the *Enola Gay*, piloted by Colonel Paul Tibbetts, had dropped an atomic bomb on the city of Hiroshima. The crew put on goggles to protect their eyes from the blinding light caused by the bomb, which detonated a few thousand feet above ground.

After releasing its deadly cargo, the plane swerved sharply to avoid the effects of the blast. The crew looked back at what had been a city of approximately three hundred thousand people, but saw little of their target. Hiroshima was "hidden by that awful cloud . . . boiling up, mushrooming, terrible and incredibly tall," Colonel Tibbets would later recall. Despite the horror of this destruction, the Japanese military continued to hold fast to their resolve not to surrender.

Three days later, on August 9, 1945, the crew of *Bock's Car*, a B-29 plane carrying a second nuclear bomb, this one with a plutonium core, set their sights on Kokura, home to a vast number of war industries. Smoke and haze, however, obscured their target. The plane made two more unsuccessful passes over Kokura, dodging Japanese fighters and salvos of antiaircraft fire. Then, with fuel running low, the bomber headed toward Nagasaki, its secondary target. It dropped its devastating load between two of the city's principal targets, the Mitsubishi Steel and Arms Works and the Mitsubishi-Urakami Torpedo Works, destroying both.

Later Wim and the other POWs passed by this area on the train, on their way from Futase City to the Nagasaki harbor and freedom. The sight of the twisted remains of these two industrial complexes and the acres of dust and rubble that had been the bustling city of Nagasaki would astonish them.

The emperor himself had to overrule the Japanese military and accept Japan's almost unconditional surrender. The "almost" part referred to the status of the emperor. Emperor Hirohito would be exempted from any war trials and would be allowed to remain as Japan's ceremonial head of state.

The Japanese military was confronted with a dilemma. The two principles that ruled the military's every move were absolute loyalty to the emperor and absolute refusal ever to surrender. An irresistible force had met an immovable object. What were they to do? For some, the dilemma was too painful. The minister of war chose suicide as the only honorable way out.

The emperor broke the deadlock by going directly to his subjects. On August 15 his recorded radio message, stating that surrendering was his personal will, aired all over Japan. After working out the details with the United States, Japan formally surrendered on the deck of the USS *Missouri* on September 2, 1945.

Raising the Flags

In mid-August the day crew of miners noticed no *honchos* were around as they sat on the ground during their midday break. At one o'clock no one showed up to yell at them to get back to work.

At two they were still resting when the production shift of miners surfaced at the mouth of the mine. "What's up?" one of them asked. Several responded with shrugged shoulders. "Why are we quitting?" No one knew. If it were a Japanese holiday, the crew would normally be forced to work longer, not quit early. "The war must be over," someone said half-hopefully. "Yeah, right—that's a laugh," another retorted, his words laced with sarcasm. Still, something was up.

Additional ragged, dirty, coal-blackened miners ascended from the mine's depths and joined the others. The men stood around, suppressing their excitement, their hopes, waiting. Serious-faced Japanese guards, offering no explanation, maybe knowing little more themselves, marched the POWs back to camp.

Rumors flew up and down the line of trudging men. Had American planes reduced Tokyo and other Japanese cities to rubble? What did the Japanese murmurs of "B-29" mean? Why were there no air raid sirens, no planes in the air?

Back at camp the night shift was ordered to remain in camp. The next morning the men were told that no one was to go to work because the mine company was planning some changes in operation. The POWs, still in the dark, hung around waiting for further instructions.

Wim was directed to be available on short notice for information regarding the new measures. Early the next morning he and Frits were summoned to the commander's office. The Japanese captain, distraught, told them that Japan had done the unthinkable. It had surrendered to the Allies. American forces would arrive shortly to take over the camp. In the meantime he had been instructed to cooperate fully with Wim and the other POW officers. What, he asked Wim, did Wim want to do now?

Suppressing his joy, Wim plunged into take-charge planning mode. What steps would need to be taken right away? Throwing open the camp gates precipitously could be disastrous. No one could anticipate what the reaction would be, both on the part of the released POWs and on that of the surrounding Japanese people. Hostility, anger, and revenge seeking were distinct possibilities and could lead to bloody encounters and chaos. So the former commander and the new camp leaders huddled and came up with a plan.

Obtaining more food was item number one on their to-do list. The Japanese captain scurried off to organize meat and mounds of vegetables for the prisoners. In the meantime, Wim assembled the men and told them the good news that the war was really over. Down would come the "flying meatball," the Americans' derogatory term for the Japanese rising sun flag. The men would assemble for the formal raising of the three national flags—Dutch, American, and British—over the camp.

Volunteers were sought for the various new jobs. Who could help out in the kitchen to handle the additional supplies? Did anyone know how to cut up meat? The men responded with "roars of delight." Could volunteers be found to sew the flags? They needed to be made impressively large. Who would help to install the flagpoles? Never before had so many jumped up so eagerly to volunteer.

Wim had the Japanese bring in a sewing machine and material. In no time the flag crew was busy cutting up the red, white, and blue material. The Dutch flag was the easiest. One broad strip of each of the three colors—red, white, and blue—sewn together horizontally.

The American flag was labor-intensive, with each of the forty-eight white stars cut out individually and stitched onto the blue background, then the thirteen red and white stripes—seven short, six long—fitted together and married to the white-starred field of blue.*

Frits Wilkens recounted that the British flag, to honor the two British prisoners, was the most difficult to sew. ". . . which cross went over which?

---

* Writing about this flag in 2006, Don Versaw said, "I got to see it again at a Futase camp reunion some years ago in San Francisco, the last such reunion that I know of . . . [The] blue field [had] faded to cerulean and the white stars [had] absorbed much of the blue dye. [But] I thought the stripes still looked pretty good."

The two British medical orderlies didn't really know . . . in the end some kind of flag that looked like a Union Jack was made . . .."

While the flag-sewing crew was busy snipping and stitching, other volunteers had attached pulleys to the poles, dug holes, and erected the flagstaffs. By nightfall all the men had completed their tasks and sat down to a meal of rice and stew with real meat and vegetables. The euphoria was palpable.

That night the oil burned well past midnight while the American and Dutch officers wrangled over whose country's flag should occupy the symbolically important middle flagpole. The Dutch were in the majority and had occupied the camp longer, but the Americans had won the war. The grand compromise was that the Dutch flag would fly in the middle position on the first day, and the Stars and Stripes would be in the prominent position on all the subsequent days until the prisoners finally shipped out of the hell of Fukuoka #7.

On August 31, Queen Juliana's official birthday, the men were called together on the old *tenko* grounds. After a short prayer of thanksgiving, Wim addressed his men once again. Although it had been two weeks since the Japanese surrender, the POWs still had no definitive news about when and how they would be liberated. In this, one of his last speeches as camp commander, Wim appealed to his men to be patient and encouraged them to use the remaining time to put aside their petty grievances with their fellow POWs. He urged them to resurrect their *Menschheit* and become honorable human beings once more, despite having been treated like animals for the last three and a half years. Captain Roscoe Price, the American senior officer, followed with a similar message to the Americans.

Then the Dutch flag was raised. As it flapped in the breeze, the Dutch belted out their national anthem, "Het Wilhelmus." Next the American flag was hoisted. A wavering "Star-Spangled Banner" started and petered out (even the most patriotic of Americans, then and now, have trouble remembering how to fit together the jigsaw puzzle phrases of this difficult anthem). Saving the day, one of the American doctors leaped atop the nearby air raid shelter and began a hearty rendition of "America the Beautiful." All the Americans joined in with gusto. Finally the Union Jack went up and the two Brits sang "God Save the King" to wild applause.

Changing of the Guard

With the end-of-the-war excitement, the freedom from work, and the now-plentiful food, the men did not immediately mind the still-closed gates. They were content for the present to take on all the cleaning jobs and other tasks that needed doing within the confines of the camp. Their contentment would not last. Meanwhile Wim consulted with the Japanese captain on the next steps to take toward an open camp.

The first was a changing of the guard, literally. The former prisoners would now be in charge of guard duty at the gate. The Japanese guards would be housed outside the gate and would patrol the outside perimeter of the camp and protect it from violence, if any, on the part of the surrounding native Japanese.

Next was the formation of a three-pronged military police to patrol the town once the gates were thrown open. The patrols would consist of a Dutch NCO, an American NCO, and a Japanese of equal rank. After consulting maps of the town, Wim and the others established patrol routes. A dry run followed to acquaint the NCOs with the town's areas, especially with the unsavory redlight district that surrounded the camp. At next morning's assembly, Wim spelled out the details of the procedure and issued warnings to all the men.

Then came the setup of a schedule for those taking over guard duty. The official handover ceremony followed. The Japanese captain presented his guards. Wim's men disarmed the guards and locked up their weapons in the guardhouse. With the war over, Wim and the others decided that no one would carry a weapon. Then Wim dismissed the Japanese guards. They trooped out, leaving the guardhouse, the seat of their power, to their former prisoners.

The latter immediately established a recording procedure for tracking the comings and goings of those wanting to taste their new-found freedom outside the sharp-bamboo-spike-topped wooden fence. At exactly twelve o'clock, the gates were flung open. Only a trickle of men ventured out. Finding nothing to do, they were back within a few hours.

Only when the Japanese started paying out back wages and the men thus had a couple of yen in their pocket did trips to town and undoubtedly to the brothels surrounding the camp become more popular.* Many were surprised that the local Japanese civilians showed little hostility toward them, especially in view of the terrible destruction and innumerable deaths resulting from the Allied firestorm air raids on the big cities.

The Last Few Days

Wim and the other officers now shared the Japanese captain's office with him. The Japanese captain's role was that of liaison between Wim and any other Japanese Wim and the other officers were dealing with, as well as the go-to person when the former POWs needed anything.

A short time after the establishment of the new procedures, the captain told Wim that the mine management wanted to invite Wim and the other officers out to dinner as a goodwill gesture. Wim declined, telling him the idea was laughable. The captain kept bringing it up until Wim finally agreed to a brief meeting in the camp office.

The mine management team of four showed up the following morning, bowing and smiling. Then came endless speeches, which Braber dutifully translated, of how much they appreciated the good services rendered by the POWs in the mines. Wim replied that they had obviously not given their services willingly and were more than happy to be done with it. That shut them up. After a cup of tea, the meeting ended and the Japanese withdrew.

A few days later the officers received a message that a supply drop would be made that afternoon and asked the POWs to lay out a large white cross in the field outside the camp as a target for the drops. Excitement filled the camp as the men heard the planes circling low overhead.

The first drop was a disaster. Oil barrels filled with supplies but minus parachutes were shoved out of the low-flying planes. Describing this drop, Frits wrote that ". . . one drum landed through the roof of the main building;

---

* According to George Weller, Pulitzer Prize-winning reporter who visited the camp on September 17, 1945 (as reported in *First into Nagasaki: The Censored Eyewitness Dispatches on Post-Atomic Japan and Its Prisoners of War*, New York, Crown Publishers, 2006), the men were paid 10 sen (7/10 of an American penny) and the non-coms were paid 15 sen (about 1-1/4 pennies) for twelve hours' work. The reason the Japanese paid out wages was perhaps as a way of "proving" that the POWs were being employed and were not slave laborers.

fortunately nobody was inside, but twelve men lost their beds for that night. Another landed on a Japanese house nearby, killing three people. It was almost a bombardment."

After the planes left, the men dashed to the field to gather up the goodies. The haul was disappointing. Many of the drums were filled with wet C-rations that had burst open on impact. One drum had apparently contained cans of cocoa powder, "had" being the operative word. The brown powder was now sprinkled over a wide expanse of the field. What did survive, Frits said, ". . . were cigarettes, chocolate bars, and . . . chewing gum, thousands and thousands of sticks. The cigarettes and the chocolate bars were very popular, the chewing gum less so, until the men discovered it was much better than Japanese yen. Then everyone wanted his share."

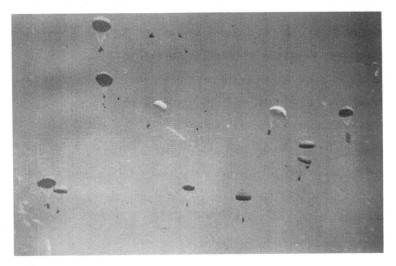

Parachuted food drops over Fukuoka #7, 1945

The second drop was much better organized. This time the supplies were loaded onto wooden pallets equipped with parachutes and dropped down from high in the sky. "Out of the [B29] openings, like giant hippopotamus mouths, wooden palettes as large as bridges crossing the little Nebraska creeks came tumbling out," Don Versaw wrote. "Quickly they blossomed into multicolored parachutes, floating down . . . down. Like flowers tossed at a wedding, red, blue, and white ones."

They landed outside the camp, but even these did some damage, becoming entangled in the haphazardly crisscrossing powerlines and blacking out the redlight district that night.

Entangled food drop parachute outside Fukuoka #7, 1945

Willing arms and backs dragged and carried the heavenly loot back to camp. Included in the haul were stacks and stacks of ten-in-one rations, canned fruit, bacon and other meat, powdered eggs, coffee, sugar, medicine, clothes, and even flea powder. The next morning the cooks, hampered by inadequate equipment—the kitchen had only huge pots for cooking large amounts of rice, soup, or stew—did the best they could to provide scrambled eggs and bacon for breakfast. The bacon was cold, but no one minded. The most enterprising among the prisoners created makeshift hotplates.

Don Versaw and his buddy "ripped open cans of bacon and fried them on a thick, flat piece of aluminum pounded into a sort of a skillet . . . With three-pound cans of cooked, scrambled eggs, which we quickly heated on our sizzling grill, we devoured great gobs with gusto. Then [we] followed the feast with a big can of peach halves each." The finale was a strong

American cigarette that bit their tongues and made their heads swim. Life was definitely looking up for the almost-liberated POWs.

With the immediate needs for food and security met and an orderly transition procedure worked out, Wim and the other officers decided to explore their surroundings and see whether they could find other camps nearby. Some of the men had reported seeing a car at the mine, so Wim asked the cooperative Japanese captain to secure it for them. The next morning a huge old Buick, chauffered by the mine manager's driver, appeared to take them on their journey of exploration.

Before Wim and the other officers stepped into the car, the Japanese captain asked Wim whether they would accept his invitation for dinner in a nearby restaurant. Wim wasn't thrilled with the idea, but the Japanese captain had proved himself to be an upright officer, so Wim accepted. The date was set for a few evenings later.

Not having a clue where to go on their exploratory adventure, they nosed the Buick north toward Moji and ended up in Yawata, the town before Moji, without seeing any camps. Yawata, a former steel-manufacturing center, was a heap of rubble. Making inquiries, they learned there was only one camp between Yawata and Futase, so they backtracked and came to a place with a high fence that looked like it could be a camp.

Inside the gate they shook hands with Luitsz, the Dutch lieutenant in charge, an old friend who had been with them in the camps in Java and Changi. Out came the booze. The camp had a laboratory where the lieutenant had found some alcohol. Luitsz paired it with fruit juice, and there they were, raising their glasses and comparing notes on their experiences since they'd last seen each other. The lieutenant was one up on the Futase crew. He had been told that in two days time an American team would be coming to organize their evacuation.

Once back in Futase Wim learned that they, too, had received a message. The Yankees were coming in three or four days. This news caused a flurry of writing activity. Wim told Frits to retrieve the notes he'd been keeping on the food situation throughout their time in the camp and write them up into a report. Frits had secreted these notes in the boxes of urns containing the cremated ashes of their comrades, a place the Japanese never inspected. Frits also prepared a report on other camp conditions, such as supplies, working conditions, clothing, amenities, and the like.

The American doctor, Barshop, resurrected his meticulously kept medical records, also hidden with the urns. And the mining engineer wrote up his report on conditions in the mines. Meanwhile Wim was preparing an overall report* of events that had taken place since he and his men had first assembled to board the hell ship for Japan in 1943.

VERKLARING.

Betreffende het ongeval overkomen aanVASSEUR, Paulus Ephraim,
Alg Stb.No.44510
Datum: 5 Juli 1944 ten 10.30 ure v.m.
Plaats: Draaierij van het fabrieksemplacement der Honkomijn te
Futase city (Fukuoka) Japan.
Getuigen: J.Knuppel Sgt.Mjr. M.L. No.92435 en
A.A.Schrijn Sgt.Mjr. M.L. No.92882.

Beschrijving van de gebeurtenissen:
Op genoemde datum en tijd was ik werkzaam aan een der draaibanken
in b.g. fabriek. Een der voor mijn werk gebruikte moersleutels
viel door trilling van het support van de draaibank en kwam terecht
onder de draaiende klauwkop, waardoor de kans ontstond dat de
sleutel door deze kop gegrepen zou worden en door de werkplaats
geslingerd zou worden, wat gevaar voor de omgeving zou opleveren.
Ik trachtte den sleutel te grijpen met het gevolg dat een uitstekend deel van de klauwplaat mij zoodanig aan de hand verwondde,
dat ik naar het fabriekshospitaal vervoerd werd, alwaar de middelvinger van mijn linkerhand geamputeerd moest worden terwijl de
ringvinger gebroken bleek te zijn.
Ik werd hierna opgenomen in de ziekenzaal van het krijgsgevangen
kamp 'm aldaar verder behandeld.
De genoemde getuigen Knuppel en Schrijn waren tijdens het ongeval
in de onmiddellijke nabijheid van mijn werkzaam en hebben het
ongeval zien gebeuren.

Aldus naar waarheid opgemaakt:

Vasseur   30 November 1944.

de getuigen:

Gezien: de detachementscommandant,
W.H.Andreu, Res.Kpt. d r M.L.

Compound Fracture 3rd & 4th finger - Proximal Phalinx
Left Hand. Laceration of deep muscle of palm of hand adjacent
to the 3rd, 4th, + 5th fingers - Left Hand :: Amputation of
third finger, reduction of fracture of 4th finger by the Japanese
doctors. Functional result as of the 30th of november, 1944 as yet
poorly functioning left hand.   Capt Barshop, med dept

Sample mine accident report, 1944

---

* Bits and pieces of the first draft of Wim's report have been inserted throughout this account.

287

Sample of Wim's report on treatment of POWs, 1945

On the appointed day, two American lieutenant colonels drove up in an olive green Chevy. They apologized for the delay, a month having transpired since the Japanese surrender. Now all transportation arrangements had been finalized, they said, and the camp would be evacuated in three days. The plan was for the men to be trucked to the train, which would take them to Nagasaki, or what was left of that city. There they

288

would embark for Manila, in the Philippines, where huge refugee camps were being set up to receive the thousands of ex-POWs.

Details needed to be worked out for the transportation of the over five hundred men, including the sick who would be transported by ambulance, as well as the almost sixty urns containing the cremated ashes. According to the colonels, Wim was to hand the urns over to the American Army in Nagasaki, which would incorporate them into a monument eventually to be built somewhere in Japan. Frits noted that the records of the men were stored separately in a large suitcase for safekeeping.*

After clarifying the details of the evacuation, the American colonels left for the next camp, which turned out to be the camp that Wim and the others had discovered on their exploratory trip in the big Buick. Luitsz, the Dutch lieutenant in charge of that camp, had exulted about being evacuated ahead of Fukuoka #7. But the Americans had missed the camp on the way down from Moji, so Frits noted with some satisfaction that their camp would be evacuated before Luitsz's.

While preparing to be evacuated, the camp received an unusual visitor. Pulitzer Prize-winning reporter George Weller, defying MacArthur's blackout orders, slipped into Nagasaki to report on the devastation caused by the bomb.† Then later he visited several of the camps, including Fukuoka #7, to interview some of the POWs. Don Versaw was one of those interviewed by Weller.

The evening after Weller's visit was the evening the Japanese captain had invited Wim and the other officers out to dinner. The captain came toward dusk. The restaurant wasn't far, he told them, there was time for a drink. With a flourish he produced a bottle of Suntory whisky. They had never heard of this brand, but they found it to be quite good.

---

* Some records were found in the suitcase my sister Yvonne and I retrieved from the Dutch Red Cross in Holland in 2005. Could this be the suitcase Frits was referring to?

† As reported in George Weller's *First into Nagasaki: The Censored Eyewitness Dispatches on Post-Atomic Japan and Its Prisoners of War*, New York, Crown Publishers, 2006. Don Versaw remembers Weller's visit but thought that Weller was a member of the Allied Armed Forces because he was dressed in contemporary GI clothing. Don was among those interviewed in the "office" Weller set up in the mess hall. Not until the book came out in 2006 did Don realize that George Weller was "a newspaper reporter on the loose."

Mellowed by the drink, they set off in the moonless dark on a rough road heading only the captain knew where. Ten minutes later, like a splendid apparition, the brilliantly lit restaurant appeared before them. A pile of slippers greeted them inside the entrance. Following Japanese custom, they shed their shoes and donned slippers. Padding single file on the reed floor matting alongside a wall of brightly painted screens, they followed their host around the corner and into "a large room where a long low table had been laid out . . . at one side a long row of grinning, bowing Japanese: the mine management!"

The sight stopped Wim and the others short. They had been tricked. Deciding to make the best of it, they sat down cross-legged opposite the Japanese, who continued smiling and bowing and sucking in their lips. The evening began with a round of sake, served warm, as is customary. Young Japanese women kneeled behind the men, with each attendant/geisha serving two customers. Their principal job seemed to be to keep the men's cups or glasses filled.

Frits's geisha noticed that he didn't seem to like the sake, so a glass appeared and she poured him a beer, an action that was followed by the other geishas on the POW side of the table. Meanwhile several members of the mine management made speeches, translated by the Japanese captain, and raised their cups of sake in toast after toast "to the glory of the POWs who had done so much for their mine." Wim responded with a few words, Braber translating, that that had not been their wish and that they had not done so voluntarily. The speeches stopped and the food was hurriedly brought out.

Wanting to provide what they considered a European meal, the Japanese offered the POWs three dishes: soup, vegetables, and horribly overcooked beef. By the time they finished the soup, the rest of the food was cold.

When little bowls of rice and tea appeared, signaling the end of the meal, Wim and the others heaved a sigh of relief. It wasn't, however, the end of the evening.

At the captain's suggestion, the men stretched out their cramped legs under the low table and readied themselves for the entertainment. Half a dozen additional geishas dressed in traditional costumes and with elaborate hairdos appeared. They entertained the guests with dancing and with music from guitarlike instruments.

After one more nightcap of whisky, the men called it a night and trooped back to camp. Frits's assessment of the evening: the music was too screechy and the food awful, but the dancing and the drinks, except for the sake, were worth a thumbs-up.

Goodbye to Futase

On September 20, 1945, the Dutch prisoners were slated to leave on the 10:57 p.m. train to Nagasaki. That morning some of the men made a final trip into town and came back with surprising news. No more than five or ten minutes from the camp, they had found another POW camp whose inmates seemed to be Chinese.

The Chinese POWs apparently didn't know that the war was over for them too. Wim and Frits brought a few of the Chinese officers who spoke passable English over to Fukuoka #7. Wim showed them the stores of food that Wim's group didn't need anymore and suggested the Chinese organize a Japanese work crew to carry the supplies over to their camp.

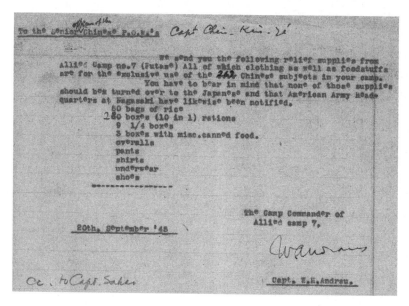

Wim's memo for surplus food to go to Chinese POWs, 1945

The officers were delighted. With the tables now turned, the Japanese ex-guards were made to lug the rice for their ex-prisoners. That evening the Chinese officers paid their respects to Wim and the others by seeing the Dutch ex-POWs off at the train station.

One last surprise was in store for Wim and the other Dutch officers. At midday on September 20, a few of the NCOs suggested mustering the men to go over the evacuation procedure one more time. Wim didn't feel it was necessary, but at the NCOs' insistence, he acquiesced. At 2 p.m. with the men assembled as for *tenko*, the warrant officer stepped forward and gave a little speech, thanking Wim and his fellow officers for all they had done for the men during the last thirty months. Then he unrolled a scroll on which a statement of their appreciation was written up in beautifully styled calligraphy.

The officers were speechless. For once even Wim was taken aback and mute. It became a highly emotional moment for this war-weary group of officers and the men they had led during thirty months of near-starvation, cold, beatings, sickness, fleas and lice, dirt, exhaustion, and fear.

Wim (left, seated), Japanese Captain Sakai, and Allied officers of Fukuoka #7, 1945

After this last *tenko* the men scattered to gather together their pitifully few possessions and prepare themselves for departure. In a diarylike account of these hectic last days, which he entitled, "The Last Days of Japan (i.e., of our stay)," Wim wrote:

20th Sept

<u>9 p.m.:</u> The 336 Dutch of Camp 7 are leaving tonight on the 22:57 special train to Nagasaki. I'm going to stay till tomorrow morning to close up the camp and leave the damn place the last. I have nailed a big board on the front gate:

CAMP CLOSED—STRAGGLERS: BOARD ANY TRAIN FOR NAGASAKI

The boys are making a hell of a racket—crowding in the front yard around our own band, singing; there's beer and illegal sake, some are *"un peu gris."*

<u>9:10:</u> Roll call in the rooms; there are three men missing, damn fools. Probably have gone to Fukuoka trying to leave by plane instead of by train. The trucks have arrived: First company *"Aantreden—compleet. Los!"* [Line up—complete. Go!]

Five trucks fill up in no time, the population is crowding around— singing, shouting of the men—2nd company, 3rd company, 4th company, two hospital ambulances with the sick—twenty-two trucks on their way to the station. One truck is filled with 30 Chinese officers whom we "liberated" in their camp (1 kilometer from ours) today and who are seeing us off at the station. The Packard (my camp staff car) closes the procession. The whole town is in an uproar. Brothel avenue waves goodbye to the Dutch boyfriends.

Before entering the station the departing soldiers had to battle their way through hordes of Japanese women. The men had obviously been successful in fraternizing with the women, "no doubt helped by the large supplies of gum, for all of them were chewing," Frits noted.

It took a while to get everyone on board. The MPs even had to be sent to wrench some of the men away from their new Japanese girlfriends. But, finally, all were on board except for the Chinese officers; the former Japanese commander, Captain Sakai; Wim, who would close the camp and leave the next day; and Père Jerome Bonnet.

Trucks loaded with ex-POWs leaving Futase for train to Nagasaki,
September 1945

Père Bonnet was an old French Roman Catholic priest who had lived
most of his life in Japan. He had wanted to establish contact with the
POWs when they first arrived in 1943 but was forbidden from doing so.
Some of Wim's men had discovered him when one of the palettes had
fallen on his house during the second supply drop. Since then he'd been a
frequent visitor to the camp

At exactly 10:57 p.m. the train pulled out of the station on its way
to Nagasaki, taking the ex-POWs, shepherded by Frits and the other officers, on the first leg of their trip to freedom and home. Meanwhile Wim
returned to the camp for one more night. As he wrote in his account:

I go back to the camp, offer some beer to the former Japanese Camp
Commandant, the Japanese Doctor, and the Chief of the Local Police.
At 1:00 a.m. I chuck them out; clean up the office; have all the rifles,
mortars, machine guns, bayonets, and swords counted; nail the doors
shut; and clean our officers' quarters, leaving all clothing and American
food supplies for the Chinese prisoners to fetch in the early morning. I
sleep for the last time on the Japanese *tatami* from 4:00 a.m. to 5:30 a.m.

Wim with Père Bonnet (in black robe) at railroad station, overseeing departure of ex-POWs for Nagasaki, September 1945

At 8:15 a.m. on September 21, the remaining one hundred Americans, making as much of a racket as had the Dutch the day before, climbed onto the trucks. Someone had mounted the camp bell on the first truck. The clanging bell added to the exuberant turmoil. It sounded like the fire brigade on its way to a three-alarmer.

Wim had a ten-meter large "GONE" sign printed in chalk on the ground outside the front gate of the camp so that any future B29 planes wouldn't drop food supplies on the empty camp. And then, with a final look around at this enclosure that had been his prison for two years and four months, Wim left "this miserable place as the last ex-POW of Futase."

When the train pulled in, Wim uttered his final goodbye to Père Bonnet, to whom Wim had given some of the remaining belongings from the camp for use in the hard and meager years to come in Japan. He also said goodbye to Captain Sakai, who, Wim felt, had behaved in an exceptionally gentlemanly manner during what must have been for the Japanese captain an extremely humiliating time. It would be Captain Sakai's job to guard the camp and the arms and supplies in it until the arrival of the occupation army.

And, finally, Wim said "goodbye to Futase forever."

Leaving the Land of the Rising Sun

The former prisoners, giddy with excitement, laughed, sang, and cheered as the train ate up the miles on its southwesterly trek to Nagasaki. Here was the beautiful part of Japan the prisoners had had no knowledge of during their forced stay in Futase.

Orange and lemon trees heavy with fruit hugged the rail line. Flowering bushes covered the hillsides. Green tea fields and terraces with ripening rice gave way to more mountainous terrain with large stands of evenly spaced small pine trees spread out on either side of the tracks. Only occasionally did signs of destruction from the American bombing raids mar the rural beauty.

But in the afternoon, when the train approached the outskirts of Nagasaki, the devastation was overwhelming. "And then we saw it," Don Versaw wrote. "Nagasaki! Or really what had once been Nagasaki. Across the great valley was a big bare spot where the city had once stood; now, except for around its fringes, it was no more."

Slowly the train crawled past the areas where once the Mitsubishi Steel and Arms Works and the Mitsubishi-Urakami Torpedo Works complexes had churned out Japan's war matériel, only to be forever stopped by the explosion of the second atomic bomb. History had come full circle. The torpedoes used in the attack on Pearl Harbor, which had brought America into the war, had likely been produced at the Mitsubishi-Urakami Torpedo Works. And now America's second atomic bomb, which ended the war, had wiped out this self-same torpedo complex.

Acres and acres of urban wasteland met the eye. No houses, no buildings, just wood ash and rubble, with only an occasional bent concrete chimney, like "a downcast and forlorn sentry watching over the desolation," Don Versaw wrote.

"Miles and miles of former Nagasaki are one big ruin," Wim wrote. "So I have also seen this historical site. It is unbelievable!"

Only when they witnessed the extent of the destruction did some of the former prisoners realize that they probably owed their freedom to this single bomb with its unbelievable power. Later they would learn how tenuous their very lives as POWs had been. On August 1, 1944, Tokyo's War Ministry had issued the "Kill-All Order," It stated:

> When the battle situation becomes urgent, the POWs will be concentrated and confined in their location and kept under heavy guard until preparations for the final disposition will be made . . .. Whether they are destroyed individually or in groups, and whether it is accomplished by means of mass bombing, poisonous smoke, poisons, drowning, or decapitation, dispose of them as the situation dictates. It is the aim not to allow the escape of a single one, to annihilate them all, and not to leave any traces.

About a month after the Americans dropped the bomb on Nagasaki, the cruiser USS *Wichita* sailed into Nagasaki's harbor. Its mission was to recover ten thousand Allied POWs who had been held in the prison camps on the island of Kyushu. Within a matter of days, twenty sailors—carpenters, plumbers, and welders in civilian life— had created an all-purpose center for receiving and processing the freed prisoners. The newly transformed dockside bombed-out railroad station contained a delousing station, hot showers, a mess hall, and a reception area.

At four in the afternoon, Wim's train pulled into the damaged waterfront station. As he and the other Allied ex-prisoners detrained, they were greeted by an American Navy band playing "When the Saints Go Marching In" and by a bevy of Red Cross women offering them ice cream. To Wim it seemed like a dream. When the American rescuers realized that some of the prisoners had been so starved that they threw up the rich ice cream after only a few mouthfuls, they quickly brought the men broth instead.

After a short debriefing and medical exam, Wim entered the delousing station with the others. In the first room the men stripped down to their birthday suits. The discarded clothes and any body lice or lice eggs lurking within the clothing's folds were headed to a fiery end. In the second room the men took hot showers with lots of foamy soap and were dusted with powder. In the third room they were issued new American Army uniforms: one set of green underwear, shirt, and pants to wear, plus another complete spare set, along with long johns, two undershirts, and two drab olive green towels in a duffel bag. In the last room they received toothpaste, toothbrush, razor, shaving soap, as well as chewing gum, cigarettes, and so on.

"There was just no end to it. Had we been Americans," Frits noted, "we could also have picked up purple hearts and whatever other decoration was going."

An hour later, deloused and scrubbed clean, Wim exited the center and found himself quayside, overlooking Nagasaki harbor. Rain pelted down, pockmarking the harbor's water. Sheltered by an overhang, Wim chatted with two other officers as he waited for a launch. Ships of every description and size jostled one another in the harbor. A short time later a landing barge appeared and brought them to the USS *Chenango*, where Wim reconnected with Frits Wilkens, the other Dutch officers from the camp, Pieter Braber, and part of his Dutch troop. The rest of his former campmates had left for Okinawa earlier on another cruiser.

Wim, sharing a large cabin with Braber, luxuriated in the ship's amenities. Real spring mattresses, copious amounts of American food, hot showers at his fingertips, an endless supply of coffee. The next morning Wim was up at daybreak and climbed up to the flight deck with Wilkens, Braber, and Fasse to look out over the water. The last time they had looked at the ocean from the deck of a ship, they had been prisoners on the *Kyokku Maru*, the hell ship that had transported them as slave laborers to Japan a lifetime earlier. The expanse of the flight deck was so great that walking up and down it that first morning tired them out.

Now that he was clean, well-fed, safe, and surrounded by a pleasant crowd of ship's officers and pilots, Wim's only task for the next two days was to rest and enjoy the leisure. He devoured the newspapers on board, trying to catch up on all the events that had occurred during the last months concerning Japan and the war, information the Japanese had tried to withhold from the prisoners.

The *Chenango* sailed out of rainy Nagasaki harbor and arrived in the bay of Okinawa on September 23. The entire 3rd Pacific fleet, consisting of hundreds of American warships and transports, lay at anchor. Like swarming bees, fighter planes and flying fortresses buzzed around purposefully from place to place.

During the meal that evening, the conversation turned to the mysterious A-bomb that had ended the war. The scientifically astute Braber had refined his idea of what it was all about and held a simplified lecture on the atomic bomb, a sort of nuclear physics 101, for the benefit of the American Navy personnel and the former POW officers. What an eye-opener for the assembled men. Arguably, the bomb was responsible for their sitting here, on board the *Chenango*, no longer the slave laborers of the Japanese but free men on their way home. The wonder of it all kept them talking late into the night.

Frits Wilkens, Wim, and John Fasse on flight deck of USS Chenango, 1945

In the afternoon of September 24, the ship's loudspeakers instructed the men to prepare to leave the ship. "Probably on our way to the airfield, from where we will take off in flying fortresses or four-engine transport planes to Manila," Wim conjectured in his diarylike account of the last days in Japan. "Japan, prison camp, and all the dirt seems ages ago." As he sat waiting to disembark, Wim concluded this first letter to Klara (which she never received):

Dearest Klara,

Still waiting, sitting on my suitcase for the barges to bring us ashore. I am writing these last lines on my knees. I'll try to mail this at Okinawa airfield. Everybody is very impatient, but patience is the thing I have learned during these last years, and have taught the men of my troop. I'm going to be very patient at home. And I'm going to be and do a lot of other things, too; you'll be surprised!

I'm still firmly confident that you and the children have also pulled through all right, although I haven't received any news since 1942. Your last words were "Do not worry." I've stuck to that. It would not have helped anyhow if I had worried. So just think that one of these days in the very near future I'll drop in, as if I had been on an inspection trip to Sabang, Ambon, or Bato. This last trip has been 3-1/2 years, but I have not changed, i.e., looks, spirit; for the rest feeling quite fit and youthful. We are going to start life again! Full of beans! You joining? Wonder if will recognize the kids (ladies).

Longing badly.
1000 kisses
Love
Love
Wim

13
Klara
October 1945

No one issued us orders, no one prohibited us from doing this or that,
no one punished us. We couldn't get over the giddy sensation of freedom.

 A Letter

We could leave the camp for a few hours if we had a slip of paper signed by the camp office. I tried it once, just to satisfy my desire to know that I could go out if I wanted to. A few hundred yards from the gate, a lone vendor was selling fruit by the side of the road. I wanted to buy some bananas. The selection and the bargaining took about a minute. As I was getting out my money, the vendor looked around furtively.

"Please walk on," he said. "I will put the bananas in the grass on the side of the road. When you walk back, pick up the bananas and leave the money in the grass. If someone sees me talking to you, I will be treated as a traitor." This was Sukarno's method of intimidation.

We heard that British troops had landed in Batavia. On September 29 the British took over the camp sentry duties from the Japanese. A day later a commission of high-ranking British officers visited the camp.

They were brought to our house, well known for its crowded condition—one hundred twenty-seven people in a small family house. The officers shook their heads at what they saw. They looked at us, still miserably barefoot and shabby, and exclaimed, "Terrible. Horrible." Then they left. We were dismayed by their attitude. Would a few warm words or a smile of encouragement have been too much to expect?*

---

* See http://www.youtube.com/watch?v=c0jA2vHhB4E for footage of Tjideng shortly after liberation.

One Scottish Tommy cheered us up with his bagpipe and announced that a movie would be shown. The soldiers stretched a screen between the trees and we settled on the ground to watch *Snow White and the Seven Dwarves.* Yvonne, Maya, and Robi were enchanted. It was their first movie ever.

Children, including Maya (half-hidden, with hairband) and Robine
(half-hidden in shadow at right) cluster around war artist, Tjideng, 1945
(credit: Image bank WW2—Netherlands Institute for War Documentation)

More news of men who had died reached the camp. Every day I went to the little Red Cross office set up in the camp, holding my heart in my hand. And every day I returned still holding my heart. No news. I cheered myself up each time by reminding myself that no news is good news.

On the twentieth of October 1945, Feetje handed me a letter. A letter from Wim. From Wim! I turned it over and over in my hands. I looked at his strong handwriting for a long time. When my insides had finally calmed down, I opened it.

He was in good health, in Manila, in the Philippines. I should try to get some news to him. He hadn't heard from us since 1942. The letter was addressed to our old home near Bandoeng, our bungalow in the *sawahs* on the Lembang road. He didn't even know we had been in a prison camp all this time and he hadn't received my letter as yet.

I gathered Yvonne, Maya, and Robine together and showed them Daddy's letter and then I read it to them:

14ᵗʰ Oct 1945

Dearest Klara,

Since Sept 26ᵗʰ in Manila camp, hungry for news from you or about you all. Some news has been trickling in from wives of some of us here, which has removed some of the anxiety about the treatment you have received during the past years under Japanese rule. Those women in protected camps—we took it—were also safe from rioters. I am wondering about you, darling, and the children. All these years and particularly this last month I have kept myself from worrying, just because . . . well you know, we had agreed not to—me trusting in your qualities and your good luck to get through these trying years.

In case the Japanese have not given you a direct rough treatment, there remains the question: have you and the kids suffered from any disease, illness, undernourishment, or malnutrition? I must force myself not to think about this possibility; have seen too much about it in Singapore and Japan and heard about all those unfortunates in Siam and Burma.

If you received in the meantime my letter from aboard the aircraft carrier that brought me with my troop from Nagasaki to Okinawa, you will know about my whereabouts up to the 23ʳᵈ Sept. From Okinawa we flew to Manila and plunged in to a lot of work in this large "Recovered Personnel" camp in the neighborhood of Manila.

We all hoped to find news and letters from Java, but instead learned about the complications arisen in Java . . . And there again is the old question, darling: How are you??! How are Yvonne, Maya, and Robi?

While writing this I'm trying to picture you all. Picturing you in my optimistic imagination based on my great faith in Klara Sima and our joint good luck. I won't fill this letter with all the bad news we got about so many that died in Siam and Burma. All those poor wives who pulled through in Java will suffer that loss on top of the suffering they may have gone through themselves . . . .

We will have loads of work in the next week or so, because word has come through at last that preparations for shipments have to be made. I do not think I will belong to the first but rather believe we—that is Frits Wilkens, John Fasse, and some others working at Dutch Headquarters in this camp—will be some of the last to go. But we are coming too, you may be sure—and none the worse after these years as prisoners. I think all these men are going to be very, very good husbands and fathers. And I'm going to be a very good lover too. Would that help you to recover more quickly? Because there is still quite a big stretch of wonderful life ahead of us, believe me!

I cabled Vader and Moeder [Wim's father and mother] on the 1st Oct. asking them to try and contact you as soon as radio communication between Holland and Java is established. So far no cables nor letters to Java could be sent from here.

I am also writing to Stan Wilson so that UOP Co. can reserve a room in the Stephens Hotel in Chicago on our way to Balaton [i.e., Aracs] one of these days. Balaton plans have grown perhaps beyond your recognition. The confinement in the Japanese prisons has driven me to break down a number of walls and add extensions to our mansion—all on paper, so far. You just wait and see.

Cheerio darlings. Kisses of all sizes, shapes, durations, and frequencies in unlimited numbers.

Your
Wim—Daddy

That evening we said a special thanks to God. Do I have to add that I slept with that letter under my pillow and carried it with me in my blouse, next to my heart, during the day?

Free Again

Soon after Wim's letter, which became the great divide in our life—Before The Letter and After The Letter—the evacuation of Tjideng began. We were to move to empty houses in town, from which the Japanese had cleared out. Many women were able to return to their pre-war furnished homes in Batavia. The lucky ones found their belongings almost untouched.

Feetje, whose husband had returned in good health, had already gone. Before she left we said goodbye to each other with grateful hearts for our mutual friendship during the past trying years. Reintje's husband had also come back, but Johtje had lost hers. Mien had left with her husband for Bandoeng to join her sister. Altien's husband had arrived too and had accompanied her and Marjolein to a hospital in Batavia. We had lost track of Mrs. Wonder, who had been moved to another camp shortly before liberation.

Many women who were on their own didn't want to leave the camp because they felt more protected inside the fence. Gruesome stories were circulating about the violent behavior and the racial hatred of the revolutionaries.

White people had been attacked with knives. Some had been hacked to pieces, their body parts thrown into wells. Homes had been raided. With order not reestablished as yet, owing to the insufficient number of occupation troops, nobody felt safe. Despite these problems, the Dutch military was not allowed to return to Java. Some higher political considerations that we didn't understand were behind this decision.

Except for the towns of Batavia and Soerabaya, the Japanese forces still controlled Java and the other islands. The Japanese reportedly helped to incite the population against the Dutch and Europeans in general and placed their weapons at the disposal of Sukarno and his followers.

One morning we received word from the camp office to be ready to be evacuated at noon the next day. I hurried over to Ada Westra and Eva van der Weerd and asked them to come with us. They were both deep in mourning over the loss of their husbands. I thought a change in their surroundings might distract them.

The next morning, while I was packing, a Dutch sergeant brought me a note from one of Wim's friends who had come to Batavia for a day and could see me that morning. I had to see him, of course, and get "live" news about Wim. Leaving the packing to the children under Yvonne's direction, I took a chance standing on the road, waiting for some military vehicle to give me a ride.

I managed to reach the Hotel des Indes, where I met Jaap de Jager who told me that he and Wim were in a military camp in Manila and that Wim was well and would fly over as soon as he had the chance. My visit was short because I had to hurry back in order not to miss the truck that was to move us. The children had packed everything. How reliable they were. The truck driver and two other men with him who were there to help load and unload were all Japanese. What a strange feeling to be served by Japanese. *Tempora mutantur*.

Before climbing into the truck, I stopped a moment at our garden and stroked the parched soil in a goodbye gesture, thanking her for having fed

Dismantling fence around Tjideng, 1945
(credit: Image bank WW2—Netherlands Institute
for War Documentation)

us so faithfully. Gardens, too, have souls. Then we picked up Ada, Eva, and their children and drove out of the Hell that was Tjideng.

Some two or three miles outside of Batavia, the truck deposited us in front of a big house, empty except for a couple of cupboards. The water faucets weren't working and neither was the electricity, but there was a deep well in the backyard and plenty of moonlight at night.

We selected our bedrooms and spread out our mattresses. We had space and privacy. What luxury. In the spacious living room, which echoed in its emptiness, we joined hands and danced around, shouting, "We are free. We are free."

Then we went for a walk. We went wherever our fancy took us. No one issued us orders, no one prohibited us from doing this or that, no one punished us. We couldn't get over the giddy sensation of freedom.

We played some games before the children's bedtime. When all was quiet, we women settled on the pebble floor of the roof terrace with cups of coffee, which we placed on the little wooden box that served as a table, our only piece of furniture. We smoked one good American cigarette after another.

As we looked at the moon, the stars, the bottomless dark-violet sky, we planned our future and remembered our past. At times we fell silent, until one of us would exclaim, "Free again." The words were magical and echoed in the depths of our being. About three in the morning, when the moon, the Lovely Lady, was weary of her long, heavenly promenade and retired, we finally stopped celebrating and retired as well.

We spent the next few days in blissful intoxication. Freedom had the same effect on us as would champagne. We laughed and giggled like children without any apparent reason.

Fruit vendors stopped at the house, and we bought. The egg man came by, and we bought. The meat man and the *toekang sajoer*, vegetable vendor, stopped by, and we bought more. We didn't really need to buy so much because a distribution center for the evacuees had been organized. We could get all the cooked rice we wanted and plenty of canned food, but we craved fresh vegetables and the freedom to buy whatever we wanted.

The Australian Red Cross sent a wonderfully thoughtful package to every woman: yards of cotton material, knitting wool, lipstick, and face cream. These little feminine items completed our metamorphosis from the debased prisoners of war we had been. The lipstick was indeed precious.

A *baboe* turned up, asking for work. She was glad to earn some money again from the *njonja besaars*, grand ladies, as we were called in Malay. We gave her a lot of food and I also gave her some old curtain material that I still had in my suitcase. When she saw the material, she burst into tears. We counted sixty-five patches on her old sarong.

She lived in a nearby *kampong*, village, and came every day for a few hours to wash the floors, carry water, and so on. One morning she didn't turn up but sent a little girl with the message that the extremists had spies in her *kampong*. Any villager found selling to or working for Europeans would be severely punished. Apparently the revolutionaries were everywhere. One of the villages nearby was burned down because the people were selling to Europeans. We saw the flames, like giant orange-red geysers, shooting up to the sky.

Several more days passed as we became used to our freedom. One day Ada and I felt independent enough to undertake an excursion to town. We stood on the street corner and waited for a kind-hearted military jeep driver to pick us up. No other means of transportation was available. An Englishman stopped.

"Get in ladies and keep your heads down," he said. "There's sporadic shooting going on. I don't want to be driving two cadavers into town."

At the Red Cross office and at the temporary post office, we registered our new address. And at the Hotel des Indes, considered the Ritz of Batavia, we had an ice coffee. It was the only thing they served and it was divine.

The streets were a sorry sight, with most shops still boarded up. Earlier the shopkeepers had feared the Japanese. Now they feared Sukarno's revolutionaries. Numerous Scottish soldiers, Gurkhas, and Sukarno's followers walked the streets. The latter didn't economize with their hand grenades. The Hotel des Indes, the headquarters of the British Army, had recently been bombed.

Everywhere huge posters announced in English: "We want liberty." "Out with the Europeans." "We have a right to our own country."

We were lucky to be here. Batavia and Soerabaya were comparatively safe, except for daily individual attacks. The rest of Java was in turmoil. At the hotel we heard that extremists had attacked a truckload of camp evacuees on their way from an inland camp to the port of Soerabaya. They had overpowered the Gurkha guards and had shot and killed a hundred and thirty-five women and children.

The population was confused. The Japanese had left or were in the process of leaving, and the Dutch military hadn't returned to establish a secure and safe environment for those who were exiting the prison camps. Instead, an insufficient number of foreign troops, whose language nobody understood, tried to maintain order. The situation was perfect for the revolutionaries to gain ground.

14
Wim
September 1945

Also along the runway, long lines of intact, fierce American bombers stood rigidly at attention, testament to America's plan to invade the Japanese homeland had Japan not surrendered.

On to Manila

Okinawa, which Don Versaw described as "teeming with troops and airplanes on the ground" and with "vehicles of all kinds going at high rates of speed all over the island," awaited Wim and the others. As the sun was setting, Wim, Frits, the two dozen or so Dutch, and the large American contingent disembarked from the *Chenango* onto the *terra* not so *firma* of Okinawa—that is, onto a series of strung-together flat barges that connected the ship to the pier proper. With the barges heaving up and down on the waves, the men lurched from side to side as they made their way to the pier. The end of the pier was as busy as an airport taxi stand. Every minute or so another truck would pull up, load up with men, and take off. Wim and Frits made sure everyone made it onto one of the trucks before they themselves boarded the last one.

After a long journey into the dark night, they arrived at an army camp made up of rows and rows of wall tents. They dropped their gear on their assigned cots and joined the mess line for yet another hearty American meal. Wim and Frits expected to meet up with the rest of their Dutch group in this tent camp but instead found they were a tiny island of Dutch in a sea of Americans. They later learned that the ship their men were on had had engine trouble and had drifted around for days until a repair ship had come to its rescue. Therefore Wim and Frits and the small group of Dutch from the *Chenango* arrived in Manila three weeks before the rest of their Dutch campmates.

Two days later Wim and his Dutch comrades awoke in the predawn darkness, climbed onto a truck, and were driven to Okinawa's main airfield. Wrecks of suicidal kamikaze planes and the damaged remains of their targets, evidence of Japan's futile last-ditch effort to stop the Americans, littered the huge open flat space. Also along the runway, long lines of intact, fierce American bombers stood rigidly at attention, testament to America's plan to invade the Japanese homeland had Japan not surrendered.

Wim and his group were dropped off underneath a C46 and waited there until the plane's crew awoke. As the lightening sky heralded the start of a new day, a door in the plane was thrown open and a chamber pot was thrust out and emptied. Next several faces appeared, followed by little splashes of water as the crew brushed their teeth. Then the pilot stuck out his head and jokingly asked if they wanted a ride, as though they were teenagers standing on the side of some country road in Kansas with their thumbs out, hitching into town.

On board they found no facilities at all, not even benches, and had to park themselves on their duffle bags or directly on the floor. Three hours later the plane landed at Clark Air Base near Manila in the Philippines. A bus took them from the plane on a long ride through the lush countryside to a huge army tent camp. As they exited the bus, a Dutch reception committee made up of a Dutch navy commander, an air force captain, and a handful of NCOs practically embraced them.

"Andrau," said the captain. "Just the man we need."

A thousand men had already arrived in the camp, the captain explained, but many thousands more were expected and they just couldn't cope, would Wim and Frits please "volunteer" to take over the organization of the camp. With refusal not an option, Wim set up a command structure: at the top, the triumvirate of Wim, Frits, and Jaap de Jager, under them a second-tier command of eighteen other officers and NCOs in charge of groups of approximately four hundred men each. As the number of Dutch evacuees swelled to seven thousand, Wim and his fellow officers had to squeeze them into accommodations initially meant to cater to eighteen hundred Americans. At times it felt as if they were expected to replicate the equivalent of the miracle of the loaves and fish to find cots for them all.

With Sukarno's revolutionary movement in full swing and the political situation in Indonesia tenuous, the Americans realized that the Dutch couldn't be shipped back there, but they also realized they couldn't get their men to cater to the Dutch indefinitely. What, everyone wondered, were they to do with the Dutch? The solution they came up with was to hand the whole operation over to Wim and his fellow officers: the housing, daily operation and maintenance, kitchen, discipline—in short, the lot.

Besides dealing with the daily operations of the camp, Wim was also tapped to be a military courier. His job entailed delivering important documents to various members of the U.S. Armed Forces in the Pacific (AFPAC), among them a bound photostatic copy of the Japanese surrender documents.

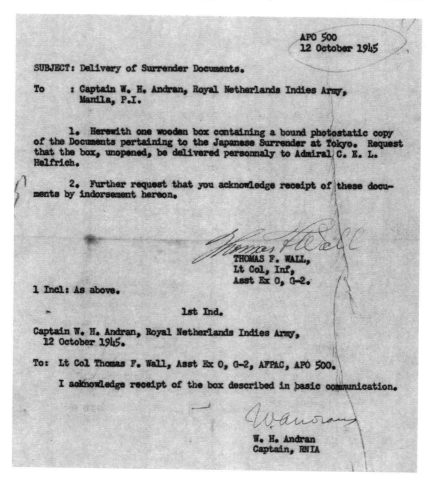

Wim's order to deliver copy of Japanese surrender documents, 1945

Letters

With his hands full dealing with the myriad problems associated with his new responsibilities, Wim tried not to worry about Klara and the children. He had written Klara twice to their address in Bandoeng, but perhaps she was no longer living in their bungalow in the *sawahs*. Surely she was alive and well? He had great faith in her strength to face anything that life threw at her, but, still, why didn't she write? Jaap de Jager was to fly to Batavia the next day, so Wim dashed off another letter for Jaap to deliver to Klara if he could locate her:

Klara darling,

In a hurry. Another few lines, which Jaap de Jager, who is leaving early tomorrow morning, will carry along and will try to deliver to you in person. We are awaiting the arrival of General Bakkers today, who is supposed to bring several bags of mail from Java.

Even here at Dutch H.Q. we do not know for sure when and how the 7000 ex-POWs from Japan will return to Java, but are prepared to ship them in big lots within 2 weeks from today.

As I am reasonably certain that my previous letters have not gone astray, I won't repeat the things I wrote before.

I cabled Vader & Moeder care of Mees & Zoonen Bank, Kneuterdijk, Holland, as my first cable to Victorialaan never yielded a reply, thinking perhaps Wassenaar was wiped out and Vader & Moeder were staying in Epe. But it has now been 4 days and an answer has not yet come in.

I am wondering if Evert [Wim's brother] ever tried or managed to contact you, for if he was released from Army/Air Force duties, he would no doubt, I should think, travel via the Philippines.

There is a lot of wondering I did, do, and will continue doing until I finally hear something, from somebody, somewhere. So far have been living in splendid isolation. I am completely prepared to hear also bad news, if it must be. What about Mami, Gabor, Laci?

Did you ever meet Viola Ankerman, Hungarian girl? Jan Ankerman, her husband, died in Thailand, I learned.

More love, more kisses
Yours, W.

With news finally reaching Manila, not only about the chaotic political situation in Indonesia but also about the horrendous conditions of the camps in which the European women and children had been interned, Wim became increasingly concerned. By all accounts, the worst camp seemed to be Tjideng under the command of Lieutenant Kenichi Sonei, notorious for his cruelty, especially when the moon was full. Was it possible that Klara and the children had been interned in Tjideng? And if so, were she and the children okay? On October 16, he wrote again:

Dearest Klara,

Again a few lines after my letter of 2 days ago. Every few days there is a plane going either to Morotai, Balikpapan, or Batavia, and, although nothing new has happened here, I will send some lines as proof that we are coming closer every day. Gosh, it will be close when we finally meet.

Press News tonight told us that, at long last, the British will soon occupy Bandoeng and give protection to the camps there. I wonder where you have been interned all these years. In Bandoeng? When were you fetched from our bungalow at Isola? Your last note from there I got in our camp in May or June 1942, telling me that you were well settled again, teaching to a little class of some 5 children, if I remember well. In the Trein Kampement at Tjimahi I got, some time around Aug/Sept, the box with toilet articles, cigarettes, soap, etc. and also razor blades, which lasted practically through my years in Japan.

As none of us here has heard anything from Bandoeng, we are all very much looking forward to getting news from there. This week General Bakkers is expected here from Java and is supposed to bring a lot of mail with him. The plane that left on the 15th Oct. is to return to Manila next week bringing along all the information about the camps and the lists of names he can collect.

Tonight we learned from a Canadian officer who belonged to the advanced troops occupying Holland (as a matter of fact this particular major was the first Allied officer to enter Rotterdam) that Scheveningen is practically destroyed. A great part of The Hague, as well. Utrecht and Hilversum have been spared. The famine must have been terrible in the provinces of Zuid Holland and Noord Holland.

Still no news from Vader and Moeder. It is not unlikely that Wassenaar has also been wiped off the map. The Germans had many camps there and used to fire their rocket guns from The Hague and surroundings. Maybe Vader and Moeder stayed in Epe. I will cable to Epe again.

From Evert I have heard nothing either; wonder if he is still in Australia. Helen [Evert's wife] cabled me last May from the States. At that time Vader and Moeder were still quite all right. Have heard no news from Laci in Lisbon or Gabor in Balaton, to whom I wrote also a few times during prison life.

Well, darling, I am looking forward to a picture (if photographers ever made pictures in the Japanese internee camps) of you four. Herewith a repetition of the sort of love and kisses I sent you in my previous letters—hot stuff.

Yours ever,
Biga [Klara's pet name for Wim]

And then, finally, to his immense relief, a letter from her and even brief notes from the children*. They were alive. Klara hadn't received either of his letters as yet when she'd written. Their letters must have crossed each other as contact with Indonesia was being reestablished.

---

* The letters from us children were written in Dutch and are translated here.

15, Oct. 1945
Kamp Tjideng
Batavia

Edes, draga Szivecskam [Hungarian endearments],

Can it be true that this letter will reach you? After how many years of silence? At times I thought this miserable war would never come to an end. Have had two postcards from you in 1944 from Japan, and one in June this year. I must say I got a horrible shock when I realized that you were so terribly far away. How did you stand things? Are you in good health? And how long shall I have to wait for news and for your arrival?

Now about us: In August 1943 we were "concentrated" in Kamp Karees in Bandoeng. Last December we were moved (with 1 koffer [suitcase] and a rugzack [backpack]) to this camp. It was a little bit of hell here. But we stood the hunger well. For months every day I dug in the garbage carts, but all this I can tell you personally later. We were never ill, and now we are looking well and enjoying food, which we get plenty of.

The children always received lessons and I hope they are not too far behind with things. They behaved really charmingly all these years and were a great help to me. Sometimes I think the following ten years won't be long enough to compensate them for all the nice things they have missed. I have been taking Italian lessons and got so far as reading books and talking rather brokenly.

Laci tried everything to get in touch with us. In 1943 got a telegram through Hungarian Legation in Tokyo saying that they are all well. He also had fl. 1500 transferred to me, which was not paid out because you are Dutch. Had the money sent back. In 1944 got a new sending from him, again fl. 1500, which I received on paper. Had to sign a receipt for it, but the Japanese put their hands on it. (Couldn't have used it anyway.) Last April I had a Red Cross letter from Laci, dated last December, saying that everybody was well at home, and Aracs flourishing.

Good gracious, can you imagine that we will go back to Aracs in the near future and try there to forget these rotten years!

And what with plans for the future? How and where shall we begin life again? This waiting now is a bit difficult.

The chaos here is more or less complete. I don't understand anything of the situation. The PTT *[post office],* spoorweg *[railway], etc. are all in hands of the revolutionaries. We are not even in touch with Holland or Europe. The camp is guarded by the British. They are busy thinning the camp and sending hundreds of people to other guarded parts of the town. Women whose husbands are back get* gezinns-interneering *[family accommodations]. Those who can support themselves may go out freely. I made us register as belonging to the BPM, and get extra help and money from them. I think all Bandoengers will be moved back to Bandoeng, but nobody knows anything definite. Heard from Else Schouten (in Bandoeng) that v.d. Vloodt is in Singapore and wrote that you passed through there in 1943 in good health. Know very little about Europe. Heard that Hungary reports under Russia. That will give a nice mess! Poor Mrs. Merz died in camp from dysentery. How many thousands have died!*

My darling, I long terribly for you. If only some news reaches us soon. The children are also so impatient. Why does Daddy not come to us?

My fondest love,
Klara

16 Oct. 1945

Dear Daddy,

We are all healthy. But we are still in camp. We are guarded here by British soldiers. And we hope that you come home quickly and we go to Aracs. Did you receive the postcards from Mami? We have a lot to eat. Goodbye, dear Daddy.

Many kisses from
Yvonne

Dear Daddy,

We are healthy. Are we going to Aracs with the boat or with the airplane? We are hoping that you are coming soon. See you soon, Daddy.

Many kisses from
Maya

Dear Daddy,

We are all healthy. When are you coming back? We wish you were already here. We were very hungry but we have a lot to eat now. Come back soon.

With many kisses
Robine

Overjoyed, Wim replied as soon as he got Klara's letter of October 15.

> *23 Oct. 1945*
> *Manila*
> *A.P.O. 711*
> *Inter-Island*

Dearest Klara,

Just imagine, today the long expected (more or less over-vice) general arrived from Batavia and, like a good Santa Claus, brought your letter of the 15th — the first news that actually reached me after all these years! Gosh I'm relieved and happy that all is well now; we will talk about the hard times later or perhaps better try and forget them if they have left no marks that would remind us of them.

Rolf Naber, another BPM-ML officer of my group yesterday happened to see and even read the cable Vader & Moeder sent in answer to my 2 cables. The whole trouble with all cables and letters has been, and to a certain extent still is, the delivery. This cable that I had not yet received contained Vader & Moeder's news: "Both well, Klara and children OK, Batavia Tjideng." That is what Naber at Manila telegraph office very accidentally saw through the guichet *[ticket window] of the one cable on top of a pile, which was mine. Well I was born on a Sunday and have been very lucky all along, and intend to continue to be!*

. . . I will now almost certainly stay here with Dutch HQ until all ex-POWs have been shipped. Jaap de Jager will, in the meanwhile, have told you this, I suppose. However, there is a good chance we will get air transportation with the HQ staff and might, therefore, not arrive any later than the troops. Don't figure on demobilization at once; conditions in Java most likely will require our continued military duties. The infantry and another corps will be policing and keeping order and occupying outposts, etc.

I have a feeling that the ML will have to occupy airfields and take care of all the services connected with them and that will bring me perhaps back to working for an oil company. . . We will see what UOP Co. has to say about my eventual reemployment.

So Aracs home has not been used as HQ by the 5th Russian tank division or something like it, but instead is flourishing! Can you beat that!

Yvonne, Maya, Robine

Hello, darlings. Daddy is writing in a hurry in English so that this letter can go on the plane to Batavia. Coming home really soon—2 weeks perhaps. So long all of you.

Love, kisses
Biga

Practically on the heels of her first letter, Wim received another one from Klara. Finally one that was a reply to his letter. Now they were in actual in contact:

21 Oct. 1945
Kamp Tjideng, Batavia
Laan Trivelli 127

Darling, Darling, Darling,

Your first letter—just imagine—your first letter has arrived! It was at 10 p.m. last night. I woke the children (Robi was unwakeable) and I had to translate the whole epistle to Maya and Yvonne. We were so terribly happy. Today I keep on rereading it from time to time, and I am entirely with you all day long. What the children liked the best was the last sentence about the different sorts of kisses. Typical, eh?

This letter of yours is dated 14 Oct. Manila. I didn't receive the other one, written on the aircraft carrier.

Gosh, what a lot of things we will have to tell each other. You didn't even know that we were also war prisoners. For 2 years. Protected camps is a nice name, a nice camouflage, I should say. In the Bandoeng camp (Karees) it was really not so bad. But from December 1944, when they transferred us to here, leaving all behind except a koffer *[suitcase] and a* rugzack *[backpack], the* danse macabre *started.*

There were two horrible camps in Java: Ambarawa and Tjideng, because of the beasts of Japanese camp commanders who headed them. Ours was Sonei, a real saddist. His plan was to starve us to death. Good thing the war came to an end, because in another 6 months, half of us would have been gone.

Even I started to show the first signs of starvation, but was never ill. Neither were the children. We belonged to the very, very few, who had no kamp-buik *[camp stomach—i.e., swollen belly]. Digging in the garbage carts and digging in my little garden saved us, I think.*

They found Sonei's files, with future plans for Tjideng—to shave all women (I don't mean under the arm!) and send them to Borneo (leaving all children behind), to work in some kind of mines.

What a lot of horrible things have happened to war prisoners in this war, in Europe as well.

But you know what is remarkable in your letter? Never a word about yourself. Don't you think I would also like to know whether you were starved, etc.? And are you quite well now? When you left the quinine factory—you remember?—we didn't know it would be for 3-1/2 years. And a good thing too that we didn't know, darling, isn't it!

Soon after I lost touch with you, I started earning some money. I set up—don't laugh—a Dutch school for the first, second, and later third grades. Not only taal *[language] and* rekenen *[arithmetic], as all other teachers in the neighborhood did, but I included geography, Bible stories, and gymnastics. Had great success. Friday afternoons I gave free gymnastics lessons and games for children in the neighborhood. Had 15-20 kids on those afternoons.*

I also gave private English and French lessons. Gave altogether 27 lessons a week, and earned between 30-45 guilders per month and free milk. Since expenses were reduced to 50 fl. per month, I was almost self-supporting. When my jam-making business started flourishing, I made even more. But then this rotten camp business came. With the result that I went to camp with about 1400 fl., of which I spent nearly all on smuggled eatables of all kinds. Was also glad to help some people who had nothing. I still have some 250 fl. left in Dutch money, which Sonei did not get out of me in spite of house and body searches.

Now about camp life I will tell you everything when you are here. The last situation was: 127 people in a house of 6 rooms. No bathroom or WC. We are still making the wandelingetjes *[little walks] with the chamber pot, but lots of people have moved out. We are 53 now. Water supply is better now. Can carry the water by day from a distance of 70-80 steps with buckets.*

We were living in a room with Mevr. Hommes and daughter (from Pladjoe) and Mien Morra, a distant relative of yours, wife of the Bandoeng dentist. Hommes and child broke down completely and had to be taken to the hospital last July. They are still recovering. Husband has turned up and just called on me some days ago. Mien has left for Bandoeng, husband has also turned up. Now we are alone in the room.

. . . The camp is being guarded by Scottish troops. Some days you may go out freely, some days you must have a pass for it. I am sure I am the only one who has not been out as yet. I don't know, it doesn't attract me. It's not real as yet. They are thinning the camp by moving people into good houses, partly or wholly furnished, in protected areas. They're being fed from here.

Everyday we get rice, a soup at noon, and a sort of stamppot *[vegetable and potato stew] with meat in the evening. In addition we get distributions of coffee, tea, sugar, soap, milk powder (once), little bit of cocoa (once), some cookies, a few lovely chocolate bars (American) (once), and plenty of cigarettes. Pity the latter are not English or American, but a homemade brand. Nearly everybody exchanges them for eggs, bananas, etc. at the* passar *[market]. We've had this* passar *for the last 3 weeks. Only Chinese may come in and sell. The extremists don't allow the natives to sell anything to us. But you ought to see how they try to do it anyway through holes cut in the fence that surrounds the camp.*

During distributions we are given lots of mangos, but almost no other fruit. We buy these at the passar. *We have been given 60 fl. per person and I received 500 from BPM, with which I buy lots of fruit, tempeh, potatoes, cookies, and every day a few balloons for the children, their first real toy for ages.*

The general organization of things is rotten. You always get to know things par hasard *[by chance]. For instance I heard from someone that we could write to Europe. I went to the Red Cross post office (the PTT is still in hands of the extremists) to inquire and found out that it is so. Why didn't they let us know via a* circulaire, *I asked.* "Dat weet ik niet, mevrouw" *[I don't know, ma'am] was the answer. And so it is with everything. Someone just came to tell me that all wives of war prisoners must move out. Whether within a day or a week is not said. Anyway we have a chance to be in a better house when you come, my Bigatje.*

It's a lovely plan to go home through America and arrive in the spring in Aracs. So you have been enlarging our house! And I've been doing the same! I also want space, space, and no people. Rest. Am extremely curious to hear what the UOP thinks.

And how are we going to enjoy life? It's funny, I am longing to have really nice clothes, and—don't laugh!—some good jewelry. And I want to see the whole world. I don't care how. And what about good schools for the children? Where? I would love to keep them a whole year in Aracs to let them enjoy trees, plants, fruit, pets, and all other animals. We'll buy a little pony for them, and lambs, and rabbits, and doves, and cats, and dogs, and bees, and chickens, and ducks, and pigs, and— anything else?

And what else are we going to do? I am going to love Biga. Continue doing it with all my heart. And the rest doesn't really matter, does it?

Yours (rather possessively!),
Klara

p.s. I wish I would hear from Europe. Please try to send cable to Laci, Lisbon, Hungarian Legation. I can't do it from here.

Wim was distressed with the news that they had been interned in the hellhole of Tjideng and were still being held there. What horrors she and the children must have had to endure, but at least they were alive and well now. How resourceful Klara had been. He knew he'd been right not to worry and to trust in his strong little Hungarian wife. He couldn't wait to see her and the children again.

26 Oct. 1945

Klara darling,

We have now reached the stage of answering each other's letters. "Communication has been established!" This time in a terrible hurry because Rolf Naber just got orders to leave and will take this letter along. Yours of 21ˢᵗ Oct was just dropped in my tent.

*I will not speak anymore about treatment and living conditions
we had under the Japanese after having heard from others and
read now in your letter how the bastards treated the women in
Java and elsewhere. I have written so many times from Japan,
always telling others that I am and always have been perfectly
all right, fit, optimistic, and, although practically all the boys lost
weight at a terrible rate, I have found that my digestive organs are
apparently unusually efficient, because my weight has always
remained about the same—65 kilos—as usual in peacetime.*

*Let's forget for the moment a further exchange of memories of
the past* misères. *My plans about keeping the children for about
a year at Aracs with cats, dogs, chickens (I ran a chicken yard in
my camp!), pigeons (you wrote me in 1933 you did not like those
quarrelsome things), and ponies, etc. are so much in line with
yours that I must ask you, "Whose idea was this first anyhow?!"
Of course, mine! Just ask my officer friends, Frits Wilkens, John
Fasse, and the others, and they will confirm that "de ouwe" [the
old one] (the usual nickname for the captain of a ship as well as
the commanding officer of a company or camp) was just a bit
crazy about Balatonfüred [town near Aracs].*

*Besides space, comfort, peace, I want to see beautiful things
around me from now on. #1 Miga [Klara] with lots of pretty
things and clothes—I had figured that out already—to be
accomplished in San Francisco and Los Angeles. I have also
planned, with the help of the American officers in my camp
(one having a ranch near Denver) how to travel on our way to
the East Coast.*

*Darling, there are so many things, that I cannot write about all of
them now and perhaps better wait until we can talk them over. I
am perfectly all right and full of naughty beans, but, in a way
fortunately, too busy (shipping people) to grow impatient myself.*

*I am so very glad that you quietly stay where you are instead of
running about with the chance of running into trouble. Trust
that you will decide for yourself when the time has come to
safely move to a better place (perhaps even to Bandoeng), but
not until BPM or ML chiefs advise you to do so.*

I will cable Laci (wrote him and Gabor a few times) knowing now that he is still in Lisbon, as you are telling me. By the way I studied some Russian, but forgot most of it again because of the busy life the camp in Japan gave me. It's a pity Hungary had to bet on the wrong horse in 1940. Wonder if the Russian influence is going to be a nuisance or a disaster.

Anyhow, Hungary was spared the lot most other countries suffered with respect to famine and destruction of cities. Wonder if you saw the pictures of the German cities. You know now that we drove through Nagasaki. A Canadian staff officer who arranged the surrender of the Germans in Holland is here in our camp in Manila and told us in detail about all the fighting and suffering in Holland.

All in all we may consider ourselves lucky to have pulled through. If the last year has not actually left any physical or mental scars, well, then, nothing more than time is lost, and we are going to make up for that. You bet!

All love
Wim

Yvonne, Maya, Robi

You have to be patient for another few weeks before Daddy and his harem are back together. . . We will perhaps be going partly with a big seaplane and partly with a boat first to America and then to Aracs. If Uncle Laci is still in Lisbon, he'll come and pick us up. Study your geography well. Do you still speak English and Hungarian? Look up Manila on the map and then you'll see that it's close by and that Daddy, as soon as he can get a plane, will come back soon. Bye, dear children.

A big kiss
Daddy

Although a trip to Java to reunite with his family was not yet possible, Wim took advantage of every opportunity to slip another letter into the hands of whoever was flying there. Now that he was assured that his family was alive and well, the anticipation of their reunion would make the actuality of it even sweeter when it finally did take place, or so Wim assured himself at any rate. In the meantime he just kept on writing and spinning out detailed plans in rich Technicolor for their future.

His letters were also full of questions. Had she heard what had happened to this one? Did that one survive? Was Klara in the camp with so-and-so's wife? And what had happened to all of their belongings when she moved into the camp? Was there anything left of their bungalow in the *sawahs*? He'd heard that the Japanese, at the time of their surrender in 1945, had blown up their munitions and explosives in Lembang, the town not far from their bungalow.

In addition Wim tried to explain why the remaining 6,500 ex-POWs (himself included) were not being allowed to return to the waiting arms of their wives. It was a question of politics. The talks between the Netherlands East Indies government (i.e., the prewar colonial government) and the new, self-anointed Indonesian Nationalist government had not as yet been held. Thus with nothing decided, the arrival in the Indies of twenty thousand or more Dutch ex-POWs from Manila, Singapore, and Bangkok was considered undesirable.

If the Dutch troops returned to the Indies armed, the British, who were responsible for the occupation, would object. The Americans, in their turn, refused to furnish the Dutch with arms in Manila. Arms could be furnished to the men on their arrival in Priok, Batavia's port, from the supplies the Dutch government had purchased from the American base in Hollandia, New Guinea. The catch, however, was who would provide the shipping facilities?

If, on the other hand, the men returned not as regular troops but purely as ex-POWs before the political situation was clarified, the result would undoubtedly be chaos and would cause many bloody incidents. In short, Wim concluded in his October 29th letter to Klara, the RAPWI (the Released Allied Prisoners of War group) had to make well-planned preparations to receive and process this huge number of restless and no doubt randy group of men before shipping them back to Indonesia.

After describing to Klara this chess game the Allied powers were playing out over the fate of Indonesia and of the Dutch ex-POWs, Wim returned to personal matters close to his heart:

. . . Do write me about yourself. Any clothing left? And apart from the clothing, what about . . . well, others may read this letter; but just tell me . . . or better not, others may read your letter here.

What do the children look like? Is Yvonne handy and clever? Is Maya still the promising faithful future farmer's wife? In as much as Maya was always a mystery to Mami [Klara's mother] before we went to Europe in 1938, Robi is still a mystery to me. Has she grown out? She was still the fat baby.

Can't you give me some description of my children . . . your children? I am quite glad to have three daughters. They must bring their boyfriends (eventually their husbands) to Balaton. Balaton extension designs provide for special quarters in my (i.e., the men's) wing of the building.

This letter is rambling, but I can't give any news from here, just ask questions. Do the children still sketch? How far did Yvonne get on the piano? And then a lot of rather very intimate questions about yourself. It may be several weeks still, but in the meantime, give me some "chats" by letter.

So long, darling. Love,
your Wim

Then again, on October 31, another letter to Klara and one to the children:

Dearest Klara,

Today is Robi Juliet day, and I am again wondering what you have made of this child. I feel—don't laugh—that I have not done more to it than the "soldier"* side, Robi having first been (as a result of circumstances) Mami's [Klara's mother's] child and thereafter yours, but I will try and catch up, you wait and see. Please give a description of soul, character, and appearance, so that I can prepare my tactics of approach . . .

Well, darling, it continues here very much the same. Although the American food is, of course, excellent and plentiful, and

---

* "Soldier" and *soldaatjes* (pg. 329) [little soldiers] can be assumed to refer to the activity of a certain part of the male anatomy that stands at attention.

the Red Cross canteen is generous in giving out drinks, candy, cigarettes, etc., the 6500 men are getting restless (soldaatjes among other factors)— "We want to go home!"—no wonder. The political situation in Java, the preparatory work of the RAPWI, and the ships are the three factors that will decide our future move into the arms of our likewise impatient wives.

Just this moment I heard that Jaap de Jager stopped at Hotel des Indes and talked to you. Also, the radio just announced that a British general was murdered in Soerabaya and that the British are putting down their foot, at last.

Write me any gossip at any time. The B25 planes are going almost regularly back and forth to Manila; if you can find a letterbox (Red Cross or BPM or ML), news will be here in 2 to 3 days.

Love, love, Wim

Dear Robi, Maya, Yvonne

Happy birthday, Robi—today you are eight years old. All of you will receive, for all the missed birthdays in the last few years, a whole lot of presents once I come back and we go to America, because I'm afraid there's not much to buy in Java. And in Manila not either. Here the whole city is wrecked. I think we'll first go to San Francisco, and after that to Balaton. What would you rather have, a little horse or a donkey?

Bye. A kiss for all of you from
Daddy

And then a letter from Klara to Wim on November 3, after she and the children were moved out of Tjideng into a house outside of town:

Tjandjoer weg 10
Batavia
3 Nov. 1945

Darling,

I was so glad to meet Captain de Jager and to hear the few things he told me about you. The same morning at 8 we were told that we had to be out of the house by 2. And at 10 I got the message that I could see him at des Indes, and, by Jove, if you knew how horribly difficult transportation is you would know what it meant to leave the packing to the children. Yvonne helped like a grown-up, and I was back at 12 and packed in 2 hours.

They moved us outside the camp to town, quite outside, in a big house (3 bedrooms, 3 other rooms) with 2 war widows, whom I know well, and 6 children. There is no water, no light, no furniture, but lots of cupboards. The surroundings are very nice, and food distribution comes from Tjideng.

But now, what about future plans? Are you coming to talk it over? Shall I go to Australia? Can't I come to Manila? Can't we go to America? Are you coming to BPM and where to? Write me please what you think. If you are going to stay there long, and I here long, it seems such a waste of time, and I'm beginning to feel terribly lonely in this mess. Have you heard from Laci as yet? Gosh, it's getting dark, and I have only a tiny piece of a candle.

The children are enjoying the space. Running up and down the stairs, through the empty rooms. They can't be stopped. We can buy everything at the door, that's very nice.

4th Nov.

It got so dark yesterday, I couldn't finish. Now I am going to "town" and, following Capt. de Jager's advice, I'll sign up for New Zealand or Australia, if at all possible. (Can always be canceled if not suitable.) I think I've reached the state of being restless. Now I must hurry. I am so longing for you.

Love, my Darling.
Miga

The letters back and forth between Wim and Klara, discussing their plans for the future and the political/military situation that kept them apart, continued in this manner until, finally, in the middle of November . . . .

15
Klara
November 1945

Without finishing my sentence, I ran off the porch, jumped over the front gate, and landed in Wim's arms . . . My heart was singing.

The Reunion

Toward the middle of November, about two weeks after our evacuation from Tjideng, Ada and I went to town again. On the way home, a Dutch captain gave us a ride in a beautiful new Buick. He was driving pretty fast on the wide, deserted avenues, as was another car coming from a side street. The collision was inevitable. Our car whirled around, brakes screeching, breaking glass tinkling, and a damaged horn tooting nonstop. Ada, half fainting, bent backwards with a bleeding head. A jeep stopped, picked us up, and drove us to the British Military Hospital. I held Ada's head as the blood ran between my fingers down to my elbows and, in heavy drops, landed on my knees.

While I held her hand, a humorous, kind Scottish doctor stitched up Ada's surface head wound. After the operation, an assistant doctor gave me a cigarette, a glass of whisky, and an ice bag.

"I don't get the meaning of the ice bag," I said.

He held up a mirror. I couldn't believe it. Above my left eye was a lump the size of a small orange. I hadn't even felt it.

Ada had to stay in the hospital because she had received a concussion. The doctor took me home on his motorbike. What memories sitting on the back of a motorbike had for me.

After having comforted Ada's children, Eva and I settled on the front porch, sipping a cool drink. As I was telling her about the accident, a car stopped some two hundred yards from the house. Two men in military uniform got out and started pulling out some duffle bags.

"Look, Eva," I said. "That smaller one looks very much like Wim."

"You must have bumped your head pretty hard," she said, jokingly. "You're seeing things."

"I'm telling you, he looks exactly like Wim."

"Why don't you have another sip of lemonade?"

"But it *is* . . ."

Without finishing my sentence, I ran off the porch, jumped over the front gate, and landed in Wim's arms. The children, too, were running by then

He has come back.

He has come back!

My heart was singing.

We hugged him, crying and laughing. For a few minutes nobody could say anything. We settled on the mattress in our room and let him tell his story in brief. In between we kept pinching our arms and his to make sure this wasn't a dream. While talking, he unpacked handfuls of American candy bars.

Having come as a military courier, he could stay only two days but promised to come back soon and make arrangements for our evacuation. He told us he would have to stay in the military service in Manila for an indefinite period of time yet, however.

Two weeks later he appeared again, remained three days, and told us that we needed to be ready to leave at a moment's notice. Friends of his would fly us to Manila, he said.

When the children were asleep, he took my hand, looked straight into my eyes, and said, "Please be strong, I have bad news for you. Mami and Gabor are dead and the Russians have looted Aracs."

I couldn't believe it. I just could not believe it. Gabor gone? And Mami? Mami *couldn't* have left me.

I still saw her standing at the edge of our property, erect, sad but smiling, waving goodbye. I had promised to come back. I was a bit late—true—but couldn't she have waited for us? Never before had I felt such pain in my heart.

Although I had confronted my fear and imagined losing everything and everyone during those first few months after being interned in Karees, losing Mami and Gabor and losing our home in Hungary were the only sacrifices I apparently hadn't truly made in my heart. These were the ones asked of me.

16
The Family
November 1945

They had no home and no friends in America—as yet—but freedom beckoned. Together, she, Wim, and the children would start life over again in this new land where all things were possible.

To Balikpapan, Borneo

In late November, on one of Wim's trips to Batavia as a military courier, he learned that something was finally moving. Although conditions in Java were still utterly confusing, arrangements had been made to bring the freed Dutch military men back, at least as far as Balikpapan, Borneo, where a reception camp was being set up and was still expanding.

A British aircraft carrier brought the first batch of two thousand soldiers to Borneo. Next, a small batch of sailors was sent off to Holland by airplane. (Nominally, the navy was a Dutch force and not a Netherlands East Indies one, thus Holland, not Indonesia, was the navy's home base.) Then another batch of two thousand army personnel, also heading for Borneo, followed.

When the final ship that was to ferry the remaining group of men to Borneo was announced, Wim, Frits, and the others charged with shipping the men were told to make sure to account for everyone. After numerous head counts, some sixty men appeared to be missing. Agreeing with the Americans that this last shipment should not be held up and that a search for the missing men would be made later, Frits and the reception committee staff began loading the last batch.

As the men boarded the aircraft carrier, MPs noticed that some of the men were struggling with suspiciously bulky, heavy backpacks. The MPs pulled them out of line to investigate and discovered some surprising contraband: women! Despite loud protests on the part of the men and pleading and wailing on that of the stowed-away women, the Filipinas were led back to the dock, and the ship was sent on its way.

The next few days were spent looking for the missing men. Because of the chaotic situation on the roads, accidents were occurring with alarming frequency. Thus the first thing the searchers did was to check out the hospitals around Manila. There they found many of the missing men, lying prostrate, with broken bones, lacerations, head wounds, and other injuries. The sleuths learned that others of the missing had died. Still others had disappeared into the surrounding villages, probably shacking up with their native girlfriends.

The most bizarre find was that of four men dressed in Japanese uniforms. These four Indonesian ex-POWs were working for an American movie outfit. They had been hired as extras to impersonate Japanese guards in a film the Americans were shooting about the Bataan Death March.

Despite the best efforts of the MPs, Frits, and the reception committee staff, eighteen men remained unaccounted for. Perhaps they had melted into the local populace and had become honorary Filipinos. Perhaps irate fathers had locked them up until shotgun marriages could be arranged, as was the case with one hapless soldier. Or perhaps they were dead. Frits and the others had no way of finding out.

When the first batches of men arrived in Balikpapan, they were set to work to arrange additional accommodations for the shipments that were to follow. Although conditions were barebones and primitive, morale was good, at least at the beginning. The men were happy to be doing something constructive. As time passed, however, the men grew increasingly restless. Similar to the American camp in Manila, the camp in Balikpapan was a tent city. Endless rows of neatly aligned tents housed the thousands of Dutch while the Allied higher-ups wrangled over what was to be done with them.

When the former POWs were finally released, they didn't return to the Dutch East Indies they had known. In their absence, the Indonesian nationalist movement, with Sukarno at its head and with the support of the Japanese, had successfully established its dominion over the islands. The Dutch attempted unsuccessfully to reassert control over their erstwhile colony, but it was a little like trying to stop the incoming tide. The era of colonialism was passing. After several years of bloody clashes, the Dutch finally bowed to the inevitable and relinquished their authority. On December 27, 1949, the Dutch East Indies ceased to exist and the sovereign Federal Republic of Indonesia was born.

Leaving Java Forever

In the evening of December 13, 1945, two Dutch officer friends of Wim's called on Klara. Get ready to evacuate, they told her. They would pick her and the children up at seven the next morning and bring them to the plane. The first leg of their trip was to Balikpapan, Borneo.

Since Ada was still in the hospital with a concussion from the accident, Eva helped Klara to pack their few miserable belongings. Klara left their food supplies and mattresses to Eva. Late into the night the two women sat with coffee and cigarettes, as they had on their first night in freedom, saying goodbye under the canopy of glimmering stars set in the midnight blue sky.

The next morning, after waiting for hours at the airport, Klara and the girls climbed into the bomb bay of a B25 bomber and sat down pretty much on top of one another. As a precaution, Klara had taken along an empty can, which Maya, who was not a good air traveler, filled up bit by bit. In the belly of this metal beast, the roar of the engine swallowed up their every word.

After two hours the pilot handed Klara a slip of paper. On it he had scribbled, "We are returning to Batavia. Cannot land in Balikpapan. Airfield flooded."

Eva was overjoyed to see them back. More coffees and more goodbyes. The take-off was repeated the next day, this time with a successful landing in Balikpapan.

A good half hour's drive through the steamy jungle brought them to a strange shantytown, formerly the Dutch Shell oil settlement. The mess hall was a bamboo structure with a corrugated metal roof. All around it hundreds of men were gathered, the freed Dutch military forces who had been shipped here from Manila. When Klara and the children alighted from the Jeep, the men showered her with questions. "Do you know Mrs. So-and-So?" "Were you together with Mrs. Such-and-Such?" "Did you run into Mrs. So-and-So?" All of them were starved for news of their wives.

In the distance Klara and the children saw the remains of the blown-up refinery. The jagged metal scrap heap, with its twisted steel bars like corkscrews pointing to the sky, was a vivid reminder of the fighting.

Along with other transient passengers, Klara and the children slept on hard bunks in another corrugated metal-roofed building. Early the next morning they were driven back through the jungle to the airport for the second leg of their trip to Manila. By the time they were all loaded in, a murky dawn had broken. They sat in the tail of the plane with soldiers and sailors who took the kids on their laps. Klara passed the empty can to Maya from time to time as the rain dripped onto their necks from badly fitting mica windows.

When the B25 bomber arrived in Manila, the door in its belly opened and a head peered out. Seeing Frits and Wim waiting on the ground below, the man instructed them to "come under the door and catch." He dropped three little human bundles, one by one, into the men's arms. As Klara exited the bomber, Wim reached for her. She sank gratefully into his arms. All through the last almost four years, she had used her wits to keep the children alive and healthy in both body and mind. Now she could let Wim, her life's partner, her love, share the burden and the pleasure of deciding on their future as a united family. Goodbye to Java forever.

"They're Coming to America"

Frits drove the Andrau family to an old monastery just outside Manila, where Klara and the girls would be staying. Wim was billeted in the military camp located some distance outside Manila. He would not be with them during the night and only part of the time during the day. Surrounded by a beautiful garden, the monastery, which had been transformed into a camp for civilians, provided austere accommodations. Compared to what they were used to, it seemed grand indeed. Here they became acquainted with American efficiency and kindness and with the enormous portions of the delicious American Army food.

The next few days were dedicated to getting all papers, passports, visas, and tickets ready for the passage of Wim's "harem" to America. In their first letters to each other, Wim and Klara had been making plans of going to America for a short while and then returning to Aracs, their beloved home near Lake Balaton in Hungary, but now the future was unclear. Aracs had been looted, Klara's mother and her brother Gabor had died, and the political situation, with the Russians in control, was dicey. Friends of theirs in Hungary advised them not to return. In fact several of these friends were themselves trying to leave Hungary.

Laci, Klara's other brother, also counseled a wait-and-see approach. When Hungary had sided with the Axis powers, Laci had found refuge in neutral Portugal. Now he too was country-less.

In addition, as Wim had warned Klara, he would not be demobilized for several months yet. Once the Americans here in Manila were satisfied that all the loose ends at the Manila camp had been tied up, Frits Wilkins and Jaap de Jager would report back to Batavia and be reassigned. And Wim would remain in the Pacific for another seven months of work as a purchasing agent for the Dutch government in the so-called Oil Battalion. His job would be to buy material and equipment from U.S. Army, Navy, and Air Force surplus stock in the Philippines and in Australia in order to rehabilitate and rebuild the destroyed refineries in the East Indies.

First he'd helped to build these refineries. In 1942 he'd helped to destroy them. And now he would be instrumental in rebuilding them. Not to mention the human cost, what a stupid waste of time, money, and effort war was.

During the next week Wim was busy establishing his credentials for his new job with various authorities, as well as booking a cabin for his womenfolk on the *Charles Lykes*, one of the Liberty ships originally built to carry freight. Klara, meanwhile, was filling out forms, applying for a visitor's visa, and getting her other documents in order.

Foreign Service Form No. 257
(Revised August 1942)

Application No. 147

AMERICAN FOREIGN SERVICE

At Manila, Philippine Islands   Date   December 14, 1945

APPLICATION FOR NONIMMIGRANT VISA

I declare that the following statements are true and correct:

Name   Klara Sima ANDRAU

Place of birth Nagybocsko, Maramaros, Hungary   Date of birth May 6, 1898

Nationality   Netherlands
Travel document   Netherlands passport no.A36970, issued by the Netherlands Consulate at Manila, P. I., December 14, 1945, valid until December 15, 1947

Accompanied by   my three (3) daughters, Yvonne Judit, Marianne Hetja and Bobbie Juliet Andrau

Present legal residence   San Carlos Camp, Mandaluyong, Rizal, P. I.
(Street, city, and country)

Address (if any) in the United States   Route 12, Box 585, Houston, Texas.

Purpose of entry   Visiting family.

Length of stay   Six (6) months

I have not previously been refused a visa, deported, or excluded from admission into the United States.
The statements included in my application for registration under the Alien Registration Act, 1940, are hereby incorporated in and made a part of this application.
I understand that I shall be required to depart from the United States at the end of my temporary sojourn.
I hereby agree that if I am permitted to proceed to the United States I shall do so at my own risk and assume all responsibility for losses, or damage which may result in the event I should not be permitted to depart from the United States, or in the event my departure should be delayed.

K. Andrau-Sima
(Signature of applicant)

Subscribed and sworn to before me this 14th

day of   December   , 1945.

Paul J. Haldeman
Paul J. Haldeman

Vice Consul
of the United States of America.

Nonimmigration visa No. 147   issued   December 14, 1945   under Section 3(2) of the
Immigration Act of 1924.   Service numbers 2926.
Visa fee UU$10.00=P20.00

U. S. GOVERNMENT PRINTING OFFICE   10—17329-2

Klara and the children's six-month visitors' visa to the U.S., December 1945

And Frits, Wim's ever-ready-to-help second-in-command and friend, took on the job of chauffeuring Klara from the monastery to the various offices where she would duck in "for just a minute" while he kept the girls occupied. Luckily, and to the delight of the children, ice cream parlors had sprung up like mushrooms all over the city, if the piles of rubble that made up the bulk of Manila could be called a city.

One evening during their short stay in Manila, Wim and five of his officer friends took Klara out to a newly born nightclub. As she had done so very long ago in Holland at the farewell party Wim threw before their departure to the East Indies in 1939, she danced with all the officers. How lovely to be light-hearted again, to listen to music, to dance, and to for-get—at least for a brief moment—the horrors and the heartaches of the intervening years.

On December 22, 1945, Klara, Yvonne, Maya, and Robine, along with eight other passengers, boarded the SS *Charles Lykes* for the thirty-two-day voyage that would take them across the Pacific and through the Panama Canal to Galveston, Texas. For the first week on board, Klara lay seasick green in her bunk as the ship rode the mountainous swells and everything that wasn't nailed down slid from wall to wall and back again on the tilting cabin floor.

Yvonne, Maya, Klara, Robine, and Barbara (cousin) at Evert Andrau's ranch in Houston, Texas, 1946

Meanwhile the girls took their meals in the mess by themselves, made friends with some of the other passengers, and learned how to shuffle cards and play simple card games under the friendly instruction of the sailors.

The captain befriended them and brought them a cake every afternoon at teatime. He even invited them to the bridge, where he let them blow the horn and hold the wheel as they pretended to steer the ship, shivering from excitement and from the cold in their thin cotton dresses.

The children seemed to adapt well to this new adventure. Klara, however, had to will herself to accept it. After only a brief reunion, Wim and she had once again been torn from each other's arms. But what other solution was there for them except America?

For most of 1946 they would be separated. While Wim flew from place to place in the Pacific as part of the Oil Battalion, Klara and the children lived first with Wim's brother, Evert, and his family in Texas, next with Dutch friends of Wim's parents in California, and then as guests of a colleague of Wim's in Riverside, Illinois.

Maya, Robine, and Yvonne in Piedmont, California, July 1946

On November 13 the family would finally celebrate their long-awaited reunion in a hotel in Windsor, Canada. And, on November 19, 1946, tightly clutching their new U.S. immigration visas, they would step over the Canada-U.S. line at the Detroit crossing and enter the United States as legal immigrants on the road to American citizenship.

But all that still lay in the future on New Year's Day 1946 as Klara, having gotten her sea legs, looked out over the endless, empty watery horizon from the deck of the *Charles Lykes*. They had no home and no friends in America— as yet—but freedom beckoned. Together, she, Wim, and the children would start life over again in this new land where all things were possible.

Carrying the hopes of its passengers along with its cargo, the SS *Charles Lykes* sailed on to America.

Epilogue

After the Suitcase

My sisters and I had each received two versions of our mother Klara's memoir. In the first version, she translated into English the penciled notes she had written in Hungarian during the camp years. And in 1959 she re-arranged these diary entries into topics, typed three copies on her vintage Smith-Corona typewriter, and had each copy bound with an original batik cover. In 1988 she reworked and rearranged some of the topics, added material on how she and Wim had met, self-published it as a hardcover, and had enough copies printed to distribute to us and to her far-flung friends.

Thanks to Klara's account, therefore, we knew "our," that is, the female, side of the story well. But what of our father's story? As our uncle, Laci, put it, Wim lived in the future. He was an architect manqué, forever designing and redesigning the various houses he lived in or hoped to live in. When he died, at the age of seventy-six, he was living in Spain in a house he had designed, but he was already planning his next house, which was to be built in South Carolina.

We all knew Wim as a friendly well-liked man, somewhat of a dreamer. What we didn't know is that he was also a put-your-foot-down person, a take-charge person, a risk taker.

We didn't know that he had received the Order of the British Empire medal for "rendering outstanding services in organizing and constructing new air bases in the Netherlands East Indies which contributed greatly to the successful operations of the Allied Air Forces." Or that he had evacuated hundreds of RAF personnel and civilians through his quick thinking, had blown up refineries, and had dodged bullets. Or that he had taken command of a shipload of a fifteen hundred men on a hell ship heading to Japan. Or that, at personal risk to himself, he had objected to untenable living conditions and cruelty by the Japanese in the camp where he was the senior officer in charge of five hundred and fifty Dutch, American, and British POWs. Or that he had pulled many of his fellow camp-mates through the years of starvation and brutality by cajoling them over and over again to continue living, not to give up, to be optimistic. In short, that he was a courageous and admirably strong leader of hundreds of men. That he got things done. That he had dealt with the deaths of over fifty of his men and had emerged seemingly unscarred, optimistic, and ready to start life over.

Awarded British Citations

British Consul Arthur Marlow (left), presenting citations to Capt. W. H. Andrau, Brig. Gen. George H. Olmsted, 1st. Sgt. P. G. Hennes, and Lt. Col. R. W. Keyes (left to right).　(TRIBUNE Photo)

For War Aid

Arthur H. Marlow, British consul general in Chicago, yesterday presented decorations, in behalf of King George VI., to four men in recognition of their war services. Ceremonies were held in the consulate at 39 S. La Salle st.

Those receiving the decorations were: Brig. Gen. George Hamden Olmsted, of the United States army, of Des Moines, Ia., made an honorary commander of the military division of the order of the British empire; Lt. Col. Richard W. Keyes, United States army, Chicago, distinguished service order; Capt. W. H. Andrau, of the Netherlands East Indies air force, of 259 Scottswood rd., Riverside, honorary officer of the military division of the British empire; and Sgt. Paul G. Hennes, United States army, 3349 N. Lamon av., military medal.

Wim receiving Order of the British Empire medal, reported in the Chicago Daily Tribune, November 6, 1948

Those things we didn't know about our father, Wim. And those are some of the things I discovered while writing *Bowing to the Emperor*.

Picking up Wim's suitcase from the Dutch Red Cross in The Hague turned into the start of an eye-opening journey of discovery. As I was flying back from Holland with the old suitcase in the plane's belly, my mind was bubbling with ideas of what to do with this windfall of information.

A series of serendipitous events followed. First the Internet handed me an excerpt of Don Versaw's self-published diary of his experience as a POW, a little more than a year of which he spent in the self-same camp as Wim's. The Internet even coughed up Don's email address. I couldn't believe my luck. Was it possible that Don was still alive? He was.

I had already decided to visit my sisters—Maya in Asheville, North Carolina, and Yvonne near Myrtle Beach, South Carolina—in April 2006 to "interview" them so that we could pool our war memories. I asked Don Versaw whether I could loop around to California to interview him after seeing my sisters at the end of April. Sorry, he said. He wasn't going to be home in California at that time because he was joining his buddies for a Marine Band reunion in North Carolina, a couple of hours' drive from Yvonne's home.

After several excited emails back and forth, I arranged to rendez-vous with him at his reunion hotel in Havelock, North Carolina. Yvonne and I got to talk to him there. I'm grateful to him for giving me a copy of his book, *Mikado no Kyaku (Guest of the Emperor)*, which is an account of Don's POW experience. He was most helpful in allowing me to quote from it and to pick his brain when I needed help in describing certain events to make them more vivid.

The second bit of luck was finding in my paper piles (sometimes it's good to be a packrat) a carbon copy of Frits Wilkens's manuscript, *The Missing Years: 1940-1947*, which Frits had sent to my mother, and she in turn had sent to me in 1984. Frits had been at Wim's side throughout the war, thus the diary was rich with references to Wim and with what the two of them had done and had experienced during the war.

On the off-chance that Frits was still alive (he would have been ninety-five), I asked my Dutch second cousin, Henry, the relative who had identified Wim's suitcase, to check for me. Henry called the three J. F. Wilkenses in the Dutch telephone book. Two replied in the negative. The third didn't answer. Henry followed up with a letter. And, totally by chance, Frits's daughter, Louisette was at her deceased parents' apartment, having come over from her home in Austria. She was in Holland for only a two-week period to pack up the last odds and ends before handing the keys over to the apartment's new owner. She received Henry's letter a day or two before she was to return to Austria. Not only did Louisette kindly give me permission to use information from her father's diary, she sent me photos that Frits had made post-liberation, a few of which are reproduced here.

The third coup was finding original letters, photos, and other documents from the war years in boxes belonging to our parents, which Yvonne had been storing after our mother's death.

Armed with this information and with a prepared list of interview questions, I drove with Yvonne to Maya's home in Asheville for a meeting of the three sisters. The object was to give us a chance to talk about our memories of the camp years.

Pre-Camp and Camp Memories

My first questions—*As a child what did you think war was? What was your concept of war?*—took Yvonne and Maya by surprise. After thinking for a moment, bits and pieces of memory emerged. As children neither of my sisters had had a total concept of war.

Maya said she remembered Wim flying over the house in his plane before the invasion and all of us running outside with sheets, waving them at him. During the invasion Yvonne remembered watching the dogfight of the Dutch and the Japanese planes in the sky above our heads. And Maya added that she felt secure when Daddy was there. The pak-pak-pak shooting noises were far away, she recalled. She couldn't connect them with people and death.

Both of them recounted seeing the silver plane, one of ours, that had crashed relatively near our home in the *sawahs*. Later, during the invasion, when we had temporarily moved to town, they recalled our sleeping huddled together on the floor, saying our prayers and listening to the explosions of the bombs. Still later, when we had returned to our bungalow in the *sawahs*, the concept of war became more tangible when we saw Japanese soldiers all around us in their uniforms and carrying rifles with bayonets attached.

In contrast, my four-year-old mind couldn't wrap itself around the concept of war or of armies at all. I don't have any recollection of the pre-capitulation battles. I knew what a Dutch soldier in uniform looked like and, after the capitulation, what a Japanese soldier looked like. To try to understand what war meant, my young brain placed these two individuals in uniform in an aggressive stance facing each other, with their bayoneted rifles drawn. But then what? I couldn't picture them stabbing each other or shooting each other. There was no blood in the picture in my head. And certainly no armies of soldiers. Just two aggressive frozen figures facing each other in a two-dimensional war poster.

During the occupation, while we were still living in relative freedom, our bungalow, the garden, and the *sawahs* surrounding them constituted our whole world. Wim had been taken away and memories of him began to fade as the months went by. We had few toys, but who needed toys when a bush with an opening could serve as the counter of a take-out eatery, with customers (i.e., our mother) paying a penny for a lunch of chopped-up flowers wrapped in a leaf cone. Banana stalks, minus the bananas, served as horses or as umbrellas in our elaborate games.

When we were tired of playing in the garden, we went exploring in the *sawahs*. Walking along the mud walls that separated one rice field from the next, we would visit the boy in the hut with the high stilts whose job it was to protect the rice fields from the rapacious birds. He taught us how to attach mud balls to rice plant leaves, letting the mud dry, and then snapping the leaf in a whiplike motion, sending the mud ball with its leaf tail hurtling like a bullet over the heads of the ripening rice to scare off the thieving birds.

Back home we played with our dachshund, Pinkie, and the stray mutt, Bobby, who had adopted us and then produced four puppies. And we loved eating *rijsttafel*, especially when we were allowed to eat the rice and the many spicy vegetable dishes with our fingers, as the Indonesians did. The proper way was to use only your right hand to mound a mouthful of rice, then scoop the mound up, and, cradling it in the hollow formed by the bent pinky, ring, and middle fingers, push it into your mouth with your thumb.

In the evenings, after we were in bed, our mother Klara would play piano. Falling asleep to the notes of the *Moonlight Sonata* or some other Beethoven or Mozart piece was like being covered with a musical security blanket. Our mother was there. We were protected and safe. All was well. This perfect life, however, was not to last. Soon we would be expelled from our Javanese Garden of Eden.

During our confinement in Karees camp, which lasted over a year, we three sisters were each other's constant companions and playmates. We were busy all the time and were for the most part unaware of the hardships, the concern for food, and the beatings that occurred and that the grown-ups had to deal with.

Besides our lessons in writing, reading, arithmetic, and geography, we had embroidery classes and Girl Scout activities and even ballet classes for a while. Yvonne remembered roller-skating. And we all recalled watching and helping our mother with the food distribution, collecting fireflies, and playing endlessly with our tiny yarn dolls and empty matchboxes. The matchboxes, when stacked, were perfect modular building units and, when used individually, morphed into beds, armchairs, or bureaus for our little yarn people.

We also spent a lot of time drawing and coloring. Our subject matter was usually a re-creation of a pivotal scene in some fairy tale Klara had recounted to us. It was never war-related or violent, which attests to how successful our mother was in shielding us from the dismal circumstances of our lives as prisoners.

It's surprising how quickly children adapt to what is. Placing a pot on an upside-down iron was the way to boil water for tea. Licking your plate to chase down every last grain of rice was no longer considered bad manners. Your poop was an important commodity for fertilizing the garden. There was nothing strange about naming your tomato plants Mrs. Tomatea and Signora Pomadora or about guarding them to prevent a thief from stealing the ripening tomatoes. You could scrape and eat the inside white layer of the banana peel, although it didn't taste as good as the banana itself. These are some of the things we learned in Karees.

In November 1944, just as we were getting used to life in Karees, came the news that we were being moved to Tjideng, a traumatic experience in the lives of each of the four of us. Moving in itself would have been upsetting enough, but in our family's case it was doubly so because Klara and Maya were suffering from high fevers and would be traveling in the railroad car with the other sick women and children, whereas Yvonne and I would be riding into the unknown separated from them and in the care of a friend.

Maya remembered Klara holding an umbrella over her to protect her from the unbearable heat of the scorching sun as they waited to board the truck that would take them to the train. On the train Maya recalled having to go to the potty and, there being no other place to do it, being mortified as she sat on the pot in the area between the train cars, with Klara holding a piece of clothing around her for privacy. In the various moves from truck to train and, on arrival in Batavia, from the train to another truck, each time hauling their mattress from one form of transportation to the next, Maya remembered thinking, *Now I understand how difficult it must have been for Jesus to carry the cross.*

When arriving in Tjideng camp, after a good deal of lining up and bowing, Klara took Maya to the children's hospital. And left her there. Totally alone. Bereft of family. Overcome with fear and feelings of abandonment, Maya remembered thinking, *Will Mami ever come back for me?*

Yvonne's recollection of the move included being herded into a moving van-type truck with doors that shut completely. For a long time the truck rumbled along. Yvonne tried not to be afraid in the pitch black as she gripped the kettle with water.

She and I, along with our two caretakers, Feetje and Altien, and Altien's daughter, Marjolein, were dumped inside the gate on the main street of Tjideng and forced to endure hours of standing, waiting, bowing, and listening to Sonei's thunderous warnings. When finally released, Feetje and Altien left Marjolein and me with Yvonne, instructing Yvonne to look after us while they checked out where we were supposed to go. *What if they never come back?* Yvonne thought. *What is my job? My role? What should I do if they don't return?* Yvonne's ten-year-old shoulders sagged under the weight of her responsibility.

As for me, my most vivid memory of the journey was descending from the train and waiting in the railroad yard, shivering in the dawn coolness as the first blush of pink tinged the sky and the rails glinted in the early light. I stood there, utterly alone in the world. Everyone around me had vanished. I was overcome with a devastating feeling of having been totally abandoned. The one person, my mother, who had always protected me was not there, and might never be there again. Even now, so many years later, I can still feel a little of what I felt then, so sharp and raw was the emotion.

Much of what Klara wrote about life in Tjideng, one or another of us recalled quite well. All of us remembered our roles in fire making and cooking: Yvonne as the fire starter, Maya and I as the gatherers of sticks and straws, and all of us as pickers as we occasionally burned our bare feet or our fingers hunting for lumps of usable charcoal in the camp kitchen ash heap.

In Tjideng, activities like ballet and embroidery were no more, but Klara still gave us lessons, allowed us to order our imaginary meals, and fed our imaginations with endless fairy tales and stories. Not until much later when I read some of these stories for myself did I realize that Klara had changed all the endings to happy ones.

In the "Pied Piper of Hamelin," for example, after the townspeople refuse to pay the Piper for having rid the town of the rats, the Piper exacts his revenge by piping another tune and leading all the children of the town to a magic mountain that opens and swallows up the children forever. In Klara's version the townspeople learn their lesson, pay up belatedly, and express their sincere regret for their initial refusal to pay the Piper. The magic mountain reopens. The children, their pockets stuffed with lollipops, chocolates, and other sweets that grow on every tree in the land of the magic mountain, return happily to their parents.

Life was harder for all of us in Tjideng and food was minimal, but despite what Klara said about our being heroic, I remember one "food"—clothes starch—that I just couldn't get down. The thought alone of that blubbery blue-gray mass made me gag.

Liberation brought so many changes that events and impressions tripped over each other in their haste, as they clamored for our attention. Patriotism, with orange ribbons for our hair to honor the Dutch Royal House of Orange. Mounds of food. A large white sheet strung between trees on the main street as a screen for the showing of Walt Disney's *Snow White*. (Wonder upon wonders, was there anything so magical? We were transfixed.) The empty house outside the camp where we could run to our heart's delight. The arrival of Daddy, his bags stuffed with candy bars. (Who was this man? I was so nervous I addressed him as "U," the formal "you.") Flying to Manila. Leaving for America on the Liberty ship the *Charles Lykes,* where all sorts of new adventures would await us.

Our real family reunion didn't take place until many months later, after Wim had finished his post-war job in the Pacific and had been rehired by his American company, Universal Oil Products (UOP), in Chicago. Because Klara and we kids had entered the United States on a visitor's visa, we had to leave when it expired and reenter with proper immigration documents. So our reunion with Wim took place in a hotel in Windsor, Canada, just on the other side of the border from Detroit. We lounged around on the hotel's beds, ate red grapes, and listened to Wim's imaginative stories as we waited for our documents to be finalized. And then on November 19, 1946, we crossed the border into the United States of America as legal immigrants and started the five-year journey to becoming American citizens.

Klara and Wim happily together in later years, undated photo

In writing *Bowing to the Emperor,* I feel that I've gotten to know Wim and have been given the chance to appreciate my father for the optimistic, strong leader he was. I hope you too have gotten to know him, as well as Klara, Yvonne, Maya, and me, and that you have also gotten a glimpse of what life was like for us as a family and for thousands of other women, children, and men as captives of the Japanese in World War II, bowing to the emperor.

Thank you for accompanying us on this journey.

Made in the USA
Middletown, DE
20 September 2015